HOW TO CHOOSE WORDS
THAT PERFORM MARKETING MAGIC YOU NEED

No matter what your writing skill, this comprehensive, start-to-finish guide shows you how to write copy that increases business and profits. In the witty, vivid style that is her trademark, Marcia Yudkin reveals everything you'll need to know to use the written word to convert strangers to prospects to paying customers including: choosing just the right format to get your message across; designing your copy to attract the attention of your audience; editing and proofreading your brochure, letter, or ad to make it clear, concise, and correct; collecting testimonials that boost your credibility; finding that creative twist that urges people to buy; and much, much more. Filled with the author's own stories as well as the advice of other successful entrepreneurs, *Persuading on Paper* is a must-read for any small businessperson who wants to pull in more business.

MARCIA YUDKIN is a Boston-based writing consultant who coaches small-business owners and professionals on improving their marketing materials. Her own articles have appeared in hundreds of magazines, from the *New York Times Magazine* to *Computer Update*, and she has achieved publicity for her business in the *Wall Street Journal*, *Entrepreneur Magazine*, and dozens of newspapers coast to coast.

D0110083

"I wish I'd seen this book before I spent thousands of dollars on a marketing seminar. Marcia Yudkin leaves no stone unturned. *Persuading on Paper* says it all."
—Hannelore Hahn, Founder and Executive Director, International Women's Writing Guild

"Offering a wealth of information about writing and designing everything from a simple sales letter to an entire corporate brochure, *Persuading on Paper* is beautifully presented in the easy-to-read style that is Marcia Yudkin's trademark. Additionally, she has gathered insider tips and strategies from the top names in the communications business. A book you will want to keep close by, this is truly a 'must read.'"
—Jim Donovan, author of *Handbook to a Happier Life* and Publisher, *The Small Business Gazette*

"Once again Marcia Yudkin has contributed a friendly and readable book, chock-full of ideas that are fresh and, most important, timely. This book can help anyone create promotional materials that showcase their uniqueness truthfully and with integrity. No hype here!"
—Ilise Benun, Editor of *The Art of Self-Promotion*

"In *Persuading on Paper* you'll learn fresh ideas for promotional tools that every small business, nonprofit organization, or corporation should be using. Marcia Yudkin's book will help you generate ideas and improve the content and the look of your marketing materials."
—Marcia Layton, author of *Successful Fine Art Marketing* and co-author of *The Complete Idiot's Guide to Starting Your Own Business*

PERSUADING
ON PAPER

◇

THE COMPLETE GUIDE TO WRITING
COPY THAT PULLS IN BUSINESS

◇

Marcia Yudkin

A PLUME BOOK

PLUME

Published by the Penguin Group
Penguin Books USA Inc., 375 Hudson Street, New York, New York 10014, U.S.A.
Penguin Books Ltd, 27 Wrights Lane, London W8 5TZ, England
Penguin Books Australia Ltd, Ringwood, Victoria, Australia
Penguin Books Canada Ltd, 10 Alcorn Avenue, Toronto, Ontario, Canada M4V 3B2
Penguin Books (N.Z.) Ltd, 182-190 Wairau Road, Auckland 10, New Zealand

Penguin Books Ltd, Registered Offices:
Harmondsworth, Middlesex, England

First Published by Plume, an imprint of Dutton Signet,
a division of Penguin Books USA Inc.

First Printing, March, 1996
3   5   7   9   10   8   6   4   2

Copyright © Marcia Yudkin, 1996
All rights reserved

 REGISTERED TRADEMARK—MARCA REGISTRADA

Yudkin, Marcia.
Persuading on paper : the complete guide to writing copy that pulls in business /
Marcia Yudkin.
p.   cm.
ISBN 0-452-27313-7
1. Advertising copy.   2. Advertising.   3. Sales promotion.   4. Small business.   I. Title.
HF5825.Y84   1996
659.13'2—dc20   95–34894
                                                                                                              CIP

Printed in the United States of America
Set in Times New Roman

Designed by Jesse Cohen

to Nancy Hopkin,
my best writing coach, ever

ACKNOWLEDGMENTS

Top thanks go to Deb Brody, who proposed my doing this book, and Diana Finch, who clinched the deal. Thanks also to Fawn Fitter and Barb Tomlin, who helped me settle in online; Barbara Tomlin for inviting me to become a special contributor on Prodigy; Jennifer Starr and Nancy Michaels for helpful background conversations; my sister Gila, whose detailed feedback lets me know how I'm doing; my sister JJ, whose legal acumen helps me stay out of trouble; and Mom, one of the best I know at spreading the word. Much gratitude as well to all the people who sent me their marketing materials and answered my questions by mail, E-mail or phone.

CONTENTS

PREFACE

One highly paid copywriter I called for an interview tried to dissuade me from writing this book. "Would you try to teach people to perform brain surgery from a book—brain surgery on themselves? They should leave writing to the experts," he argued.

I disagree. Master writers do have uncommon skill with words, based on a special knack and years of observation and experience. But many of their secrets can be communicated through guiding principles, explanation and examples. My experience as a consultant and coach shows that the average businessperson, if motivated to learn what persuades and what doesn't, can quickly grasp and apply ideas that make his or her written materials at least 75 percent more effective. Some clients, once I pointed the way, have immediately shot through to spectacular results. Brain surgery it's not.

Whether you already have some ability to make your phone ring with business or have always considered yourself a klutz at marketing, this book is for you. You have something to sell—products, services, events—and your materials on paper—brochures, letters, newsletters, advertisements—serve as basic tools to attract and keep clients and customers. So long as you're willing to invest some time, money and effort, the information in this complete start-to-finish guide increases the ease with which your mailbox fills up with orders, your cash register with greenbacks or your datebook with appointments.

Originally I planned to call Chapter 12 "Tricks of the Trade." But I decided to eliminate the word "tricks" and the attitude it implies from the book. Persuading on paper does not require deception. You won't find the smoke-and-mirrors model of hucksterism here, or the assumption that marketing means deep-sixing your integrity. Though words can indeed cast a spell, that doesn't mean you're duping your public. When I do advocate showmanship, it's as a means to a transaction that satisfies both parties. Persuading on paper can also involve plain phrases and no grandstanding at all.

As you'll see, more than anything else communicating effectively about your business requires focus. You're halfway to copy that sells when you know whose attention you want to attract and what benefit, in their minds, they would get out of buying from you. Because most marketing falls short here, I've assembled the best examples, checklists and explanations I could find to help you perform this analysis for your unique selling situation on your own. I've provided plenty of guidelines for a clear, polished execution of your marketing piece as well.

Focus also means keeping both eyes on your goal. It's nice to receive phone calls and notes saying "I loved your mailing" or "Saw your ad in *NTN News*," but if you don't also notice a blip in sales, a bulge of appointments, your printed materials definitely have room for improvement. You'll find tips here for testing what's working and what's not, and for getting the best results at the lowest cost.

Since you won't master the art of marketing and the skill of writing in one quick read, keep the book handy for reference and problem solving. Reread it whenever you get an inkling that your copy can still use tinkering and especially before you send off a new batch of stuff to the printer. When haste, laziness and other human weaknesses tempt you, allow me to remind you of the importance of this challenge. The stakes aren't quite as high as the brain surgeon's life or death. But persuading effectively on paper *can* help transform a struggling business into a thriving one that makes full use of your talents and enables you to live the life you're most capable of.

PART I

◇

GETTING
STARTED

CHAPTER 1

What Do You Need on Paper and Why?

Looking back on the twenty years she has spent working with law firms, Brookline, Massachusetts, consultant Deborah Addis recalls numerous instances of lawyers calling to say, "We just need a simple brochure." She always suspected, however, that what they really needed was far from simple. "They thought it would just be a matter of writing up the practice areas of the firm. But unless that becomes a vehicle for figuring out who you are, what you stand for, what are your competitive advantages, who your market is and so on, you're wasting your time and money. You end up with a showpiece that might look nice on a coffee table but doesn't *market* for you. Some firms take a whole year of wrangling just to decide which areas to emphasize in a brochure, and at others, the partners never manage to come to agreement. Sometimes the whole thing is a case of 'Monkey see, monkey do'—other firms are doing brochures and they believe it's the perfect quick fix. In fact, I've never seen a case where a brochure on its own brought law clients in the door, unless it was part of an overall marketing strategy."

If you picked up this book with a fixed idea about what

you need, please loosen your thinking a little and create room for flexibility. Many of the rules you may have absorbed need to be set free. For example, "If you're going into business, the essentials include professionally designed stationery and business cards." Actually, that depends. Of the fourteen years I've worked as a writer, I've used business cards only sporadically, and had none at all for the first four years or the latest three. Or, "Advertising is the only way to get those customers in your door." Not so. Some businesses build their customer base instead through personal contacts, direct mail or publicity. Open your mind, at least for the time it takes to read this chapter. By taking a thoughtful step back and first analyzing your marketing situation, you'll have the best chance of creating the persuasive tools on paper that achieve your desired results.

Here's a checklist to help you pinpoint the circumstances and purposes your printed materials must suit.

Why Do You Need Anything on Paper at All?

People ask me for my stuff.

Good. Then you do need something. But don't assume that because they ask for, say, your card, the only proper response is to hand over a card. You might be smarter to get their card and put them on your list for regular mailings of a newsletter or special offers. "Someone who says 'Send me a brochure' just wants information. A letter or a press clipping might do," says Ilise Benun, president of The Art of Self-Promotion in Hoboken, New Jersey. "I've seen people miss out on a lot of business because they didn't have what the prospect asked for, so they put it off. When someone asks for my brochure, I send them a copy of my newsletter. People hang on to it more than they would the brochure they asked for."

People need something that explains all the details of my product or service.

Another good reason. When people are ready to buy, many need something that sets forth the specifications of your product or service, terms of the sale, procedure for ordering and so on. But before you compose an ad, information sheet, press release or direct-mail package providing this information, consider whether you should market in one step or two. In two-step marketing, the initial item sparks a motivated reply from a potential customer, who then receives more information by mail, fax or phone. Most experts say that one-step marketing works mostly for small purchases in the $10-and-under range.

Giving too much information early in the marketing process can overwhelm the customer and sabotage the sale. "Most people throw away the first thing you send them," says Ilise Benun. "Forget about fantasies that a brochure will force people to make a decision. Save your ammunition for after a prospect has expressed interest in whatever you're offering."

Printed materials show I'm credible.

True, you're obviously a genuine player in the game of business if you have nicely designed documents that weigh down an envelope. In one study, 92 percent of executives cited letterheads, envelopes and business cards as a major factor in how they rated the quality of other businesses. You can spend a bundle and lose credibility, though, if your stuff includes careless mistakes or you leave out the reassuring details your audience expects. And remember that if you market to, for example, low-income homeowners rather than executives, simple may get you further in the door than slick. Credibility isn't absolute, but relative to your intended audience.

I'm trying to find new clients or customers.

Ads, catalogs, direct mail, publicity and letters particularly help here. Keep reading—other items in this checklist indicate which communication tools fit your circumstances.

I'd like past buyers to buy again and recommend me to others.

Often people who already know you require a different approach from those who have never heard of you or met you. Previous clients deserve the personal contact of a letter, or—second best—a newsletter, if you have a substantial client list. A newspaper or magazine clipping with a handwritten note, "Thought you might be interested in this," also does a good job of reminding people who've done business with you before that you're still there ready to serve them.

I'm looking for a different kind of buyer than I've generally had.

Once you've been in business for a while, you may find yourself wishing for more challenging consulting problems, clients who need you more often or customers less protective of their nickels and dimes. Since whatever you've been doing hasn't lassoed those people, spend some time researching your new target market and figuring out how to hook into their needs and interests. You may have to upgrade the visual impact of your materials, switch formats and craft a new pitch from scratch. Chapter 3 contains additional food for thought on knowing your audience.

People need something tangible to remember me by.

Yes! But you have to decide whether the tangible something should be an imprinted coffee cup, a postcard, a fact-filled tip sheet or an ad every Sunday in the sports section of the newspaper. Through networking, find out what's worked for similar businesses, use trial and error and track how business comes in to discover methods that work for you.

I need people to buy right now.

Only advertising and direct mail can dependably persuade people to part with their money right now. Think up an attractive offer, add a deadline and then write your most motivating copy to put out in an ad or send through the mail.

I'm trying to build a reputation.

Then publicity and publishing are the marketing routes for you to pursue. If your advertising or direct mail reached every member of your target group in the United States, it couldn't have anywhere the impact of being cited in a respected magazine or newspaper, or being recommended on the air. People know that when you advertise or send strangers letters, anything laudatory in your message is just your say-so. But when word about you reaches the public through a reporter, the implied third-party approval does wonders. Read Chapters 8 and 9 if you have this goal, and remember that reputation building takes time.

Everyone else uses a whatever-it-is.

Does that mean you can't find a more effective way to reach your audience? According to New York City artists' advocate Caroll Michels, artists customarily have sent out packets of slides to sell their work to galleries and collectors. "Years ago, people took the time to project the slides, but now most people simply hold that tiny image up to unnatural light," she says. Given that each slide package costs about $15 and that artists depend on the courtesy of recipients to return them, most artists don't send out anywhere near enough packages to make an impact. Those who buck tradition and send out a printed brochure with a cover letter can send out more and get a higher response rate than with slides. "Artists flip out at the words 'direct mail,' though," Michels says, "and they're afraid to try this approach." Dare to try something new, and you could see your budget yield greater results too.

Mark Barnard, president of Bos'n, Inc. in Wellesley, Massachusetts, says he made a conscious decision not to invest in brochures when he started his sales-coaching organization. "During our first nine months we were constantly running workshops without any description of them on paper. People did say, 'Send us your mail piece, and we'll be in touch,' but we knew not to fall for that. Never, never let a mail piece sell for you! Instead we said we'd be glad to come in and show them what we could do—and we turned 'Where's your literature?' into $10,000 worth of business. If we sales trainers can't overcome stall objections like that and sell without literature, then we don't deserve to be in business."

When, Where or How Do You and Prospects Make Contact?

Prospects look for me when they need me.

If you checked this statement, you might be a bail bondsman, a plumbing contractor, a home nursing provider or a computer repairer. Since someone seeking your service probably needs you urgently, you must have a compelling ad that stands out from the competition in the directory or publication that people would logically consult to find you. Primarily that means the Yellow Pages, where most lookers already know they need someone and you want them to choose you. Direct mail or a newsletter to those in a position to recommend you makes sense in this situation too.

I go looking for them.

When prospects can live and thrive without buying what you sell, you need an opener that grabs their attention, keeps it while you explain your offer and then motivates them to act before other matters lure them away. Sales letters, direct mail and text-heavy advertising fit this goal. When your market hasn't encountered your type of service or product before, you need enough space (and time) to educate prospects as well. The first acupuncturist in town isn't going to get busy until he explains at length in an informative brochure, sales letters, columns or advertorials (see Chapter 10) which ailments the Eastern treatment helps and the fact that it's hygienic and painless. Try targeted publicity also, which can help convince your market that they have a need which isn't obvious.

We meet in person first.

Then the size and substantiality of what you give your prospect has great bearing on whether or not the prospect saves it. Winthrop, Massachusetts, marketing consultant Susan Bradshaw didn't have a brochure, since her business focus was still evolving. When she gave out information sheets on regular paper, she noticed recipients becoming confused and embarrassed. "They seemed to feel they'd be insulting me by folding it, and it looked like a lot to read." For networking, she probably would have done better with a folded business card, with room for a concise marketing message. If you find prospects at trade shows, consider whether they really want to lug your heavy catalog or free remember-me paperweight home on the plane.

My stuff is out somewhere for people to pick up.

On a recent drive to Maine, I stopped at a roadside information center to check out the tourist-oriented brochures. Overload came quickly as I scanned the dozens of patiently waiting rows of paper. I found I gravitated toward the pamphlets in a color other than the overused beige or a size besides the ubiquitous 8½ by 4 inches. For example, a calligraphied message about a bed-and-breakfast place, photocopied onto half a sheet of ordinary paper, caught my eye. If possible, observe what happens in the setting where your materials will be sitting. Do people rush by or linger? Do flyers quickly get covered over or removed by other advertisers? Are stacks of catalogs blocking the way for baby strollers or pamphlets turning into litter because of the wind? You don't want to create a nuisance but a resource for people who might need your offerings.

Other Important Questions

Do you offer lots of services or products?

Perhaps you need a catalog. Or you might be better off crafting a separate selling effort for different offerings. New York City businesswoman of the 1890s Dolly Gallagher Levi did just that. In the opening scene of *Hello, Dolly!* she exuberantly hands out separate calling cards for more than a handful of disparate business lines: matchmaker, financial consultant, guitar instructor, short-distance hauler, poodle clipper and more.

How many people do you need to reach?

Some businesses rake in large profits by selling to just a few dozen customers a year. Others equal that take through small sales to tens of thousands of people. In the latter case, you need standard forms of mass communication. While computers can personalize letters or certificates by inserting names and places, complete customization might be possible and desirable when you're approaching key prospects one by one.

Did you check off more than six items earlier in this chapter?

You have many purposes at once, then. Don't assume that one marketing piece can meet all those purposes. You might do better with one piece that reaches out to attract new customers, another with an offer for people who've expressed interest, yet another for longtime buyers of yours and another approach still to spread your reputation among experts who could pass on business to you.

Do you have personal quirks that make it likely you'll use some formats well and not others?

My friend Szifra Birke, a mental health counselor, admits that while she'll shamelessly pursue media coverage, she feels uncomfortable sending pieces asking for business to people she knows. Marketing consultants who work with doctors and attorneys tell tales about professionals who commission ads and then pull them at the first whisper of criticism from their peers. Try to sort through and respect any ambivalence about a medium before you commit to it, or you may see a sizable investment go to waste.

How often do you change direction, location or personnel?

Terri Lonier, author of *Working Solo*, says her friends joke that whenever Terri spends $2,000 on letterheads she then decides it's time to move. Many businesses, though, can't afford to laugh about thousands of dollars' worth of printed materials that need to be stickered, altered or junked. Similarly, outdated ads in directories likely to stay on shelves for years do little for your outreach or image. If basic facts about your business change often, work this into your strategy and format from the beginning. For instance, you could design letterheads to print out one by one along with your letters or invest in a post office box that remains stable throughout several street moves.

Part II of this book contains detailed pros and cons for each written format you might use to communicate with clients and customers. But hang on—deciding you need a newsletter rather than, say, direct mail is only the first of several basic issues you need to settle before you're ready to work magic with every marketing piece you make.

CHAPTER 2

Who Are You Really, and What Are You Selling?

Years ago, Herman Holtz thought he'd found a lucrative business niche. To win any kind of government contract, one had to write a proposal, a chore few people relished. All he had to do, he thought, was put the word out that he was a crackerjack proposal writer and he'd be flooded with work. It didn't work. Puzzled by the poor response, he thought through his prospects' situation and had an insight that made him a much busier man: People didn't want help writing proposals, they wanted help winning government contracts. When he said, "I can help you write better proposals," prospective clients didn't perceive the need. Only if they knew enough to translate that in their heads to "I can help you win government contracts" did they realize that they needed Holtz's services. Once Holtz gave them the translation right up front, business boomed. He had found the benefit that made sense to his market.

As Holtz learned, getting your hands on the words that communicate what you do can be slippery and difficult. "Are you offering what you want to sell or what the client wants to buy?" he asks. "Whether you have a can of beans or an automobile to sell, in the end every business is a service business.

Put yourself in the client's shoes, find out the client's problems, the critical point that will strike a nerve. When you can solve a problem, no one will throw you down the stairs."

The Clout of Benefits

Beginning marketers tend to think of communication with potential buyers as akin to shooting arrows into the air. If one lands in front of a prospect when he's thinking, "I need some arrows," whoosh! There's a sale. This way of thinking assumes everyone knows why an arrow is valuable and can perceive why this model of arrow, 1.1 meters long and tipped with marconium, deserves to be bought. People who buy arrows probably do know why they want them, but the more you make sellers figure out for themselves what a particular set of arrows will do for them, the farther away remains the sale. Sales become more frequent when you offer explicit answers to a prospective buyer's paramount question: What's in this product or service for me?

In my files is a typical example of hiding the benefits: an $8^1/_2$ by 14-inch two-sided conference brochure that simply lists the sponsors, the title of the conference, the location and time, the condensed and expanded lists of the day's workshops and the credentials of the presenters. The reader gets a thorough understanding of the "what" about the conference, but the "why," the "what's in it for me" constitutes pure guesswork. The reader must mentally analyze the benefits of those features to become motivated to attend. In contrast, I have a brochure from Grand Entrance Gates in Mount Kisco, New York, that opens with:

That old saying, "You can only make a first impression once," could not be more appropriate as it relates to the entrance of a magnificent home.

Elegant wrought iron entrance gates, handcrafted by our Eu-

ropean masters, will complete that all-important focal point, by
adding an old world touch or contemporary flair.

If I had a magnificent home and hadn't thought I needed an
iron entrance gate, this copy might change my mind. If I had
already been shopping for iron gates, this does a terrific job of
reinforcing my vague notion of what it would add to my property. Note that the benefit of Grand Entrance Gates—they provide an elegant focal point for the entrance to a home—even
shows up in the company name.

Explicitly stating a benefit cuts right through the torpor of
late-twentieth-century customers barraged with more than two
thousand marketing messages each day. To maintain our san-
ity, we develop thick defenses that subliminally counter,
"Bull!" "Heard that one before" or "So what?" to most of the
solicitations. But some get through. I'll never forget how a financial planner introduced himself in one of my seminars. Instead of using that job title, he said, "I'm _____. I help people
create wealth and pass it on intact to their children." A stunned
silence fell on the group. None of us had ever heard that benefit stated so clearly and unmistakably.

Part of the impact of benefits derives from the fact that few
marketers, amateur or professional, bother to make them clear.
According to Bob Bly, author of *The Copywriter's Handbook*,
90 percent of all marketing copy concentrates on the product
or the service, not its benefits. A statement like "I provide financial planning services to people with middle and upper-
level incomes" passes through the intellectual part of our
brains, while "I help people create wealth and pass it on intact
to their children" hits home in the part of us that worries, fears
and hopes. When you put the advantages of an offering in
terms buyers care about, money changes hands—in your direction. Copywriter Louise Gordon of Cambridge, Massachusetts,
created a vast improvement in a sales piece for a product that
conditions power for high-end audio systems when she
changed "so-what" lines like "reduces total harmonic current

contents" to "reduces total harmonic current contents for freedom from hum and other distortions." Benefits motivate, while features merely inform.

Why, when practically every book ever written on marketing stresses the importance of benefits, do so few business communicators follow the advice? I've come up with three reasons. First, we get so wrapped up in the minutiae that are most salient to us that we forget to step back and take the customer's point of view. Self-centeredness, while natural, makes our copy less effective. Second, we shy away from the necessary effort. "It takes thought to define the benefit of a product," says Alice Crane Kovler, a freelance copywriter in Cambridge, Massachusetts. "Let's say you're trying to market the fact that a hotel has big picture windows. That's a feature. The benefits may be that you're overlooking the Seine and seeing all of Paris walk by." And third, sometimes the reasons people buy seem so odd to us that we'd rather not believe or act on the evidence.

Once a publisher wanted to unload an overstock of coffee-table picture books on American history. After trying to emphasize the beauty of the photography and the fascinating storytelling of the text, the postcard that finally emptied the warehouse read something like "Do you have a BIG BOOKCASE? If so, we have a BIG BOOK for you." When I tell that story to authors and publishers, I hear nervous laughter. Because most of us in the book business don't want to believe people buy to fill up bookcases, I think it took courage even to try pitching that benefit.

Thinking back on my own experience, I remember being surprised to learn that more than half of those who came to a weeklong writing workshop in New Mexico mentioned my photograph as the deciding factor. They said I looked sympathetic and nonthreatening. In other words, I would teach how to write without devastating their fragile egos. Now was I smart enough to incorporate a photo and the benefit of compassionate instruction into further marketing? Not really.

When I made up a flyer to promote my editing-by-fax service, I forgot completely about including a photo and almost rejected a testimonial from a client that ended with, "After a 'Marcia edit,' I feel confident enough to submit my work." I called the client and said, "Could we change the 'confident' part to talk about how my editing helped you get published? I think that would influence people more." She replied, "Marcia, that's the honest-to-God reason I go to you, and I'm sure I'm not the only person like me." I kept her statement as it was.

By the way, those stories illustrate another big temptation when it comes to defining benefits: assuming that people in your target market resemble you. In the following chapter you'll learn how to understand your audience, but in the meanwhile, please don't skip the exercise about benefits coming up. Even if you think you're already focusing on benefits, you may find you've overlooked some relevant motivators. Like me, you may have the marketing scuttlebutt you need and not be taking it seriously.

From Descriptive Features to Motivating Benefits in Five Easy Steps

1. Place a sheet of paper crosswise in front of you and divide it into three columns. Head the left-hand column "features" and list the details about a service or product you provide. Let's say, for instance, that you're an attorney who handles divorces, among other things. The features of your divorce service might include the following:

   - Free initial consultation
   - Credit cards accepted
   - Evening hours
   - Sensitive to women's issues
   - 15 years of experience

2. In the middle column, write in all the benefits you can think of for each feature. Do this by asking questions like these: What's good, from the client's point of view, about a free initial consultation? What does the customer get when we accept credit cards? What need do evening hours satisfy? What advantage do our clients get from our sensitivity to women's issues? Fifteen years of experience—so what? Benefits for the divorce service might look like this:

   • Free initial consultation: No-risk chance to find out what we can do for you

   • Credit cards accepted: Can spread payments out— helps ease financial pressures

   • Evening hours: Convenient—don't need to take off from work

   • Sensitive to women's issues: Because we understand how courts treat women and children, we can help you achieve the custody and financial arrangements that are best for you and the children

   • 15 years of experience: Reputation and know-how that enables you to get a better settlement

3. In the right-hand column, list the evidence you have that people care about each benefit. Kinds of evidence include: clients say so (good); our caseload rose after we introduced credit card payments (good); intuition (often reliable, sometimes not); no evidence (uh-oh); and everyone does it this way so it must be beneficial (watch out for this one!).

4. Now look over your chart. What did you leave out? Can you think of features you missed that satisfy the benefits you mentioned? For instance, we also keep financial pressure down by offering flat fees for uncontested

divorces. Do you have evidence (like in your file of thank-you letters) for benefits you forgot to include? If you see a benefit with no evidence, is there another proven benefit for that feature that you overlooked? Perhaps clients don't care about your reputation and know-how but do care that with fifteen years of experience, you're able to get it all over with quickly and less acrimoniously. Can you probe any of the benefits one level deeper? Direct mail pro Herschell Gordon Lewis calls this talking about "the benefits of the benefits." For example, with the benefit of a no-risk chance to find out what we can do for you, you avoid the frustration and expense of trying to switch lawyers in the middle of a case.

5. Last, reread what you have written and ask yourself, What's most important? Which one or two benefits could you stress to pull in the most business? Your answer may lead directly to a powerful headline for an advertisement or brochure. For the case at hand, it might be: We help women hold on to their assets and their children during a divorce.

Don't worry if you feel overwhelmed with new perspective on your business. If you simply added relevant benefits to a list of features in your brochure, you'd already be on the road to more effective marketing. For example, doesn't "Evening hours for your convenience" sound more alluring than simply "Evening hours"?

Your Problem Is Our Business

Sometimes you want to answer the question, "Who am I and what am I selling?" by talking about the customer rather than yourself. As Herman Holtz said, if you can solve someone's problem, you'll be welcomed rather than kicked down the stairs. If your prospective customer already realizes he has a problem, you have the opportunity to make an immediate, powerful connection by offering a way to solve the difficulty. Feature the problem and remedy in your marketing and you come off as a savior, not a salesperson. Then either the question "What's in it for me?" won't come up at all, or it will settle back down the moment it arises. Just be sure to use your prospect's frame of reference and language, not yours.

For example, B. F. Boudreau, a computer consultant in Waltham, Massachusetts, has just three words on the front cover of her brochure: "Puzzled by computers?" For someone who needs a computer expert on call, Boudreau's message cuts right to the quick. "Advice on spreadsheets, databases, systems management" would work nowhere as well as an opening line, since it states the solution in the very terms that make her prospect's eyes glaze over. Similarly, the second week of April, a firm called Watkins and Company, in Woburn, Massachusetts, ran an ad in the local paper that read, in part, "Tax-time troubles? Procrastinators call today—extensions available." Compare the immediate relevance of that problem-oriented appeal to "We prepare 1040s."

When you choose a felt problem as the focus of your marketing materials, you completely bypass the "So what?" barrier. A problem-oriented pitch works for the same reason you were probably taught as a teenager to ask questions on a date: People come alive when communication focuses on them rather than you. You woo business contacts more easily when your message echoes their worries and hopes than when it booms, "I, I, I." Remember, though, that if you guess at their problems without asking or work backward from what you want to sell to what their problem might be, you could come off like the date from hell who tells everyone, "I'm just the guy (or girl) you've been looking for." Chapter 3 contains additional guidance for ferreting out the problems of your target audience.

It's trickier when potential clients don't realize that they have a problem or don't appreciate the extent of the problem. Classically, marketers use fear, guilt or greed to prime the un-wary prospect to leap for their product or service. If you'd never given a thought to termites, for example, a pitch that be-gan "Is your house free lunch for termites?" might make you ready to sign with a termite inspection service. One of the longest-running ads of all time used the headline "Do you make these mistakes in English?" to get people who might not have thought of themselves as inadequate to start thinking they needed a booklet that would help them fix their deficiency.

You can successfully educate prospects about their prob-lem without laying fear, guilt or greed on thick. At a network-ing event, I picked up a brochure from Precision Lease Analysis of Leominster, Massachusetts, that did an excellent job of this. Under the headline "To Err Is Common" the brochure cover said:

> Most commercial tenants are routinely overcharged by their landlords due to errors. But if you—a tenant in a mall, strip shopping center, professional building or office building—are being overcharged, how could you know? You'd call the lease professionals at Precision Lease Analysis. We find lease errors and recover your losses or we receive nothing.
>
> No Recovery—No Fee

The rest of the brochure describes, in a factual tone, the tact and professionalism with which Precision Lease Analysis in-vestigates a lease, the national standards used for reference and the extent of apparently unintentional errors. If I had had a commercial lease when I picked up the brochure, I would have called them immediately. Interestingly, this piece does not even name the owner of the business, much less spend a panel detail-ing the professional background of its lease analysts. The infor-mation that is included comes across so credibly that I don't care whether they have twenty years of experience at this or two. For their service, a "you, not I" focus works beautifully.

Another successful approach to educating the audience about a problem comes from the brochure of Wordmasters, a firm in Pittsfield, Massachusetts. Their service, writing seminars, falls under the heading of something that companies either find important but not urgent or neither important nor urgent. Hence Wordmasters had to find a way to increase the urgency with which a company perceives their writing problem. Under the heading "Poor writing has cost some companies big money" they provided these examples, along with two others:

- A previously successful manufacturing company lost $35 million in a single quarter, when, according to the company's own annual report, customers flocked to return a newly introduced computer because the "manuals did not offer the first-time user adequate assistance." The loss started a decline that ended with the company filing for bankruptcy.

- A memo from a supervisor at a government-operated nuclear installation ordered rods of radioactive material cut into "10 foot long lengths." Instead of cutting the rods into the ten-foot lengths intended by the supervisor, workers cut ten rods, each a foot long. The cost of the error was so great that it was classified.

The four examples set up Wordmasters as the white knights who charge in to rescue the brochure reader from similar as-yet-undetected disasters.

The problem-solution approach succeeds especially well when you are one of many individuals or firms in a position to solve a problem. Nevertheless, *you* capture the business when you state the problem in terms that connect with customers' concerns and motivate them to act right away.

Making Hay of Your Uniqueness

A third method of answering the question, Who are you really, and what are you selling? involves articulating what sets you apart from the competition. Fred Berns of Dare to Be Different Promotions in Washington, D.C., calls this "tuning into radio station WMYD—What Makes You Different." Berns learned the power of distinctiveness when he came up with the idea of starting a Washington-based radio news service for local radio stations across the country. "When their folks came to Washington to testify at hearings, I would be the correspondent to cover the story," he explains. Berns signed up just two stations initially, one in Nebraska and one in Wisconsin. When his phone went for a long time without ringing, a friend suggested he promote himself as the only firm of its kind with clients around the country. Berns did just that in a news release that got printed in *Broadcast Magazine*. "Within three months I had seventy-five clients who really were all around the country," he recalls. Then a station in Nova Scotia signed on, and in a new round of releases he promoted his firm as the only bureau of its kind with clients around the world. "People called from Australia, New Zealand, Japan and Guam," he says— helping his client roster fatten to a very healthy five thousand stations. (See Chapter 8 on the role of news releases in bringing in business.)

To put your finger on your uniqueness, Berns suggests completing this sentence: "I'm the only _____ who . . ." It may take some digging to arrive at the answer. Berns worked with a kitchen-and-bath designer in Pennsylvania who claimed he didn't have an "only." "We kept going around and around, and I finally got him to say that he's a certified kitchen dealer—and then we had it. In fact, he's the only certified kitchen dealer in central Pennsylvania." In searching for the uniqueness of your service or product, think about education and training (the only judo teacher who's also a physical therapist), price (the only balance-your-budget program for less than $50), specialization (the only desk organizer for telemarketers) and convenience (the cardiologist who makes house calls), along with other factors.

Note that with the cardiologist, I dropped the "only" in favor of just naming the unusual service. Distinctiveness can do as much for you as uniqueness, particularly when other businesses that also do what you do aren't making a big deal out of it. For example, I know that most people who edit for individuals and companies have fax machines and at least occasionally send work back by fax. But I don't know of anyone besides me and my former business partner who have talked about having an "edit-by-fax service." When I gained the capability to accept credit card payments and thus felt more comfortable editing by fax for strangers, I sent out a round of press releases that presented the service as something new. Five or six magazines printed something about me as a result, showing that the *perception* of distinctiveness sufficed to get them to spread the word. Formulations without "only," like "a judo teacher who's also a physical therapist" or "a desktop organizer just for telemarketers," help you become noteworthy and memorable without claiming a uniqueness that you can't prove.

When you come up with what sets you or your product apart, how should you communicate it? If you put it right in your business name, no one will miss it. A company called Historic Research and Analysis in Silver Spring, Maryland, for instance, says what they do at the same time that they say who they are. If your company name does not explicitly reveal your focus, you can do that through a tag line—a clarifying phrase that follows your company name around like a shadow. Below are four effective examples of tag lines.

Peacock Hills Business Services
Helping small firms use PCs for a competitive edge
(Doris Goembel, Persia, Iowa)

Wendy M. Traynor
Alternative financial strategist
(Boston, Massachusetts)

Ryan Consulting Inc.
We bring video solutions to business problems
(Rockaway, New Jersey)

The Business Group
Where business owners meet to solve problems creatively
(Mike Van Horn, San Rafael, California)

Note that while each uses a different grammatical format, all of them make a generic-sounding business name much more specifically targeted. Don't waste your tag-line space with a phrase that almost any business might use, like "Experts at your service," or with boasting, like "Where quality is Job One." If you use envelopes with a differentiating business name or tag line for everything, business opportunities can spring up almost out of nowhere. Several businesses ended up in this book because they sent me, for some offer or other I was running, a self-addressed stamped envelope whose tag line made me curious to know more.

While a pictorial logo sometimes conveys a business's uniqueness visually, without words, the combination of specific words and nonverbal reinforcement in color and design carries much more communicative power. When Laura Lee Lemmon of Dayton, Ohio, puts her company name and tag line, "The Composition Company: An advertising agency for the horse industry," together with a sketch with a horse's head, riding whips and horseshoes, horse owners know instantly that she'll serve them better than an ad agency that doesn't know an Appaloosa from the Appalachians. She carries the theme through with ads and brochures featuring a crowd of horses' legs galloping forward beneath the headline "Keeping you in front of the herd!" Marketing consultant Susan Bradshaw showed me a logo that she felt gave her a strong identity but still only took her halfway. "If someone asks about my logo, I explain how the dots and the sweep symbolize my relationship to the companies I consult for, but I'm hoping to find five words that summarize all that. Then I won't need to say more—my card will market by itself."

If your business is just you, consider whether you want to create the illusion of a much bigger operation or come across frankly as yourself. I remember being astounded to learn that a man who consulted for Fortune 500 companies and called his firm The Such & Such Consulting Group actually worked out of his home, with his wife serving as his assistant. The smoke and mirrors of his business name, his ads and the professional way phone calls and faxes were handled convinced me that he had the backup of a large organization. A few brochures for one-person companies that I've seen don't even name the owner. On the other hand, you can turn the personalized service possible from a one-person firm into a competitive advantage. Mail order tycoon Jeffrey Lant does just that by writing in his catalog, "I'm still the only major business source in America who answers my own phone and doesn't put any barriers between you and me."

Whether you decide to fashion a new identity as a result of reading this book, or just to fine-tune your old one, make sure you express that distinctiveness consistently in all the materials on paper you produce. In *Guerrilla Marketing*, Jay Conrad Levinson suggests thinking in terms of a business *identity* rather than a business *image*. " 'Image' implies something artificial, something that is not genuine," he explains. " 'Identity' is more evocative of what your business is all about and comes across as honest because it really is." I agree that if you write and design your marketing materials as if you're putting on some sort of show, they won't bring in the customers who keep coming back and adding money to your cash flow. Not only do others feel uncomfortable when a business image conflicts with the realities that come across through continued contact, you may recoil consciously or unconsciously from an image that doesn't match your beliefs and feelings about yourself or the business.

This lesson came through dramatically when I had lunch for the first time with Sydney Rice, a personal effectiveness coach in West Newbury, Massachusetts. After spending an animated half hour describing how she helps entrepreneurs and professionals overcome self-imposed and external obstacles to success, she handed me a one-page marketing piece that included her photo, testimonial quotes and three bland paragraphs that made her sound like a mainstream organizational consultant. I read it and looked up at her. "This doesn't sound like you or the work you've just been telling me about," I said. She smiled ruefully. "A marketing expert told me I needed to do it that way. But I don't like it, so I don't send it out much, and it hasn't brought me any business."

Six months later Rice sent me a new brochure with an evocative opening paragraph and clear, forthright questions and answers about her coaching. A different marketing expert had tried to convince her to scrap this piece in favor of a more cut-and-dried approach that had worked well for another consultant. This time Rice stuck to her sense of who she was. "From writing this brochure, I have a better grasp of the uniqueness of my practice," she told me. "Now I can and do speak more enthusiastically about the service I provide. My clients love the brochure and appreciate having something to pass on to friends they feel might want to use me. They also say it helps them explain to others why they're working with me. Best of all, in the two months since I began using the brochure my business has tripled!"

Such is the power of honest communication.

CHAPTER 3

Knowing Your Audience— and Your Competition

"The biggest blunder I see in marketing pieces," says Frank Grazian, executive editor of *Communication Briefings* and a former college instructor in advertising, "is not knowing enough about your target audience. Some copywriters say you should begin with brainstorming, but you've got to do your homework first, and then use your research as the basis for your copy." By "research" Grazian means simply seeking out past or potential buyers and talking with them to discover their hopes, dreams, needs, dislikes and gratifiers. Less than one day of such conversations can give you enough to guide your messages right to the spot that motivates your prospect to ask, "How do I sign on the dotted line?"

In one case, Grazian was asked to write ad copy for a school that trained medical receptionists and technicians. He went there and spoke with students to find out why they had enrolled. These high school graduates, primarily women, he learned, were not going on to college but wanted to be important—and they didn't want to wait long for that to happen. The six-month duration of the school's programs had particularly appealed to them. Grazian led the ad with the headline "Be

Somebody in Just Six Months," and more leads poured in than the school knew what to do with. In another case, a company that had built condominium town houses had sold out the first section but couldn't sell the rest of the properties. Plenty of people came to have a look, but they left without buying, saying either that the condos were too expensive or not expensive enough. Grazian dropped by to chat with the people who had already bought and learned that they were professionals with young children. For them, the lure of the place lay in the ambience and the chance to live among people like themselves. Grazian wrote a new ad that began "Lifestyle for Young Professionals," and five units in the second section sold that weekend.

In-depth understanding of your audience comprises half of the formula for communication that persuades. Add that to clarity about who you are and what you're offering that audience, and you have laid the groundwork for a profitable business relationship.

Knowing Your Audience

According to Sue Viders, a Denver-based art marketing consultant, artists shouldn't get started on creating marketing materials until they know whether they're selling finished originals to a sophisticated audience through galleries, commissioned pieces to individuals or organizations or multiple-copy works to, say, a Kmart crowd. "If you're selling through a gallery, the buyer wants to touch your creativity," Viders says. "So any marketing piece for gallery buyers has to reach out on that creative level. Buyers of commissioned work want to know that you're easy to work with and can take a conception and execute it. You need testimonials for them. And the Kmart type of buyers are often interested in quite different benefits of art: that it reminds them of a place, a mood or a time, that it blends with a color scheme or makes a wonderful gift." Her general point applies to anyone selling a product or service: first identify the group that you're aiming to turn into customers.

In some situations, the user of the product or service is not the one who makes the decision to buy. Carol Batten, marketing manager of Laurel Eye Associates in Charlotte, North Carolina, says that while women over fifty make up the majority of their cataract patients, it's usually the daughter or daughter-in-law of the patient who settles the operation and selects the surgeon. Hence they ran an ad in media reaching the younger age group in which a woman talked about how glad she was that she took her mother to Laurel Eye Associates. Similarly, if you're selling college textbooks you need to keep in mind that although college students plunk down the money for the texts, it's the professors you must market to since they select the required books for their courses. As with all the other factors you should know about your audience, don't assume the users decide what to buy—find out.

Find out too what matters most to your target audience. What are their problems, concerns, needs and triggering motivations? Besides Frank Grazian's strategy of talking with previous buyers, you can learn what you need to know by studying the publications your target group reads and contributes to. When Alice Crane Kovler received the assignment of writing a piece designed to sell an association credit card to real estate agents, she pored over magazines for the real estate trade, searching for clues to their psychology. "I discovered that people who sell houses are always in business wherever they go because anyone they encounter might be a potential buyer," Kovler says. "Since the credit card would use the word *Realtor*, it represented an opportunity to announce their line of business to anyone handling their credit card. So for the cover of the brochure, I came up with the headline, 'Because you're a Realtor and it shows.' "

An informal survey of current and potential clients can tell you what they expect and want from businesses like yours. Mike Bayer, a public relations consultant in Laguna Beach,

California, used CompuServe to survey seventy-one business owners about how they chose a law firm. Eighty-three percent said the law firm's brochures and ads made no difference to them whatsoever; less than half said that the attorney's formal credentials influenced them. What mattered most by a long shot to those surveyed were the attorney's reputation as vouched for by a trusted third party and how well the attorney understood their problem. "Lawyers who tried to wow these people with their credentials turned them off," Bayer says. "The ones who got hired were those who asked questions and gave comfort." Smart readers of Bayer's survey, published in *Law Firm Marketing & Profit Report* and ten other magazines, took note of this surprising information in planning new marketing. Interestingly, Bayer estimates that about half of his own public relations clients derive from his surveys and interviews of lawyers on CompuServe. By establishing himself as a credible information-gatherer in a nonselling context, he earned familiarity and appeal that that audience valued.

Note that audience motivators change frequently and sometimes drastically along with economic conditions, lifestyle trends, technological developments and even the weather. In 1994 Bayer was finding more and more attorneys willing to spend their own money for self-promotion rather than depend on the firm to pay for it. "They've discovered that successful promotion can help them get the attention of the managing partner, position them for switching fields or put them in a good bargaining position for a bigger partnership cut," he says. With this knowledge, not only does Bayer stress different benefits in his communications, he increasingly approaches lawyers as individuals rather than firms as potential organizational clients.

Effective research about your audience often involves sensitive listening and intuitive reading between the lines as much as hard-and-fast number gathering. Here are some open-ended questions you might want to cast into the conversation when you schmooze at lunch or over the phone with members of your target market.

1. *How urgently do you typically need our service or product? What triggers you to find out more information, or to buy?* Frank Grazian suggests the importance of knowing whether your prospects are active or passive seekers of your product or service. That is, do they know they need left-handed garden tools or does the idea occur to them for the first time when they encounter your ad? In the latter case, you'll have a harder sell and must emphasize the benefits of specially designed, special-order tools. But to someone already looking for left-handed garden tools, Grazian says, you have to stress the features that make yours the best on the market.

2. *What made you pick up the phone and call me? Why do you keep coming back instead of going to so-and-so?* As I indicated in Chapter 1, steel yourself for surprises here.

3. *What's the biggest problem you have that most people outside your profession or situation don't know about yet? What's a common problem many people like you have but don't yet realize they have? What problems do you see lurking on the horizon?* A consultant friend told me recently that because of the popularity of checkbook and tax preparation programs, accountants are finding much of their formerly dependable routine business slipping away. If you designed custom databases for professional firms, you could use that knowledge to explain why accountants needed your database more than ever.

4. *How important is price to you? Do you need to know price right away?* Some audiences won't want to know anything else about your offering until they satisfy themselves that it's within their price range. Hiding the price or leaving it off your materials altogether will antagonize this group, or perhaps just as unfortunately, waste your time courting people who will duck out of the running just as a sale appears close.

5. *What's a good time and a bad time for us to approach you?* Direct mail marketers in particular study whether people respond more to mail received on Wednesdays or Thursdays, in summer or winter. But your audience may have idiosyncratic quirks in this regard. Innkeepers might be most receptive to your message on Mondays, the most bothersome day of the week for office workers.

6. *How much information do you need before you buy?* "For the sorts of individuals who hire professional organizers, the last thing in the world they need is another piece of paper," says Ilise Benun, who avoids sending those sorts of prospective clients anything too official-looking. For mid-level managers who have to justify purchases to bosses and committees, on the other hand, the more technical details and testimonial letters you pile into their files, the better.

7. *What are some turnoffs in the materials you see? What telltale slips signal that a particular company or product isn't for you?* Your audience might point to anything from outdated terminology to a vague discomfort with a too stodgy-looking or too politically liberal-sounding style. Ann Miller, president of a speakers bureau in Chassell, Michigan, says she won't give a second glance to any materials that can't be faxed, list too many specialties or splatter the presenter's (rather than the bureau's) own address all over the place.

Regardless of the extent of your research, use testing and feedback as described in Chapter 14 to make sure that your persuasive creations really do elicit the reaction "Wow! This was tailor-made for me!" Feedback and patterns of response and nonresponse can also help you figure out which selling points to emphasize and how, and which to leave out.

Credibility for Your Audience

Since whatever kind of selling piece you produce is not itself the item that people buy, you must take pains to win the audience's trust in your claims. You need to focus on believability here, not truth. Marcia Layton, a Boston-based business plan writer, furnishes new business owners with her best justifications for the necessity of formal business plans but finds that some don't believe her until they hear the same points from an accountant, a lawyer, a banker or an adviser at the Small Business Administration. "Funny, they don't really believe all the information I give, but when it comes from an unbiased person, it's reliable," she muses. Yes, people are that way! Another important principle of believability: People more readily accept specifics than generalities. Some tax advisers tell you to write down $1,997 rather than $2,000 for your annual utility bill, even if it happened to add up to exactly $2,000. In contrast to the IRS, which can pay you unwanted attention when doubts arise, potential customers fade into oblivion when doubts about your offering, your firm or you bother them.

To check your own credibility, begin by rereading your marketing piece and asking skeptically after every claim, "Says who?" If the answer comes back, "Says me" or "Says no one" or "Says someone who isn't trusted by my audience," you have more work to do on that piece. It simply won't take enough readers as far toward action as you want it to. For instance, after returning home from a business conference, I received a letter from another attendee who got my attention by recapping the marketing advice of one of the speakers we'd heard, then saying, "Perhaps I can help!" I read on: "I have a creative and innovative marketing firm that specializes in helping people and companies effectively communicate their message to the end user." The letter then detailed some of the help she could provide. Although she included her hourly fee, nowhere in the one-and-a-half page letter did I find any answers to these questions: *In what way* is your firm creative and innovative? Why should I believe you've helped anyone, much less "effectively" so? What makes you worth your high fee? And most devastatingly, if you can't overcome my skepticism, why should I believe you can help anyone market anything? When asking people to part with money, you must ruthlessly anticipate and meet such objections.

By using the "Says who?" test, this woman would have prevented my doubts. She could have included quotes from clients she'd helped. She could have described specific creative, innovative projects she'd carried out, and their results. At the very least, she could have offered some sort of free initial consultation, giving clients more of a basis to judge whether her services would be worth the investment. The chasm she created while coaxing "Leap! Leap!" was simply too broad. Turn to these credibility boosters to close such a chasm to the width of a crack:

- Named clients or customers describing the results and value achieved

- Enough detail about the product or service so it comes across as distinctive and remarkable

- Endorsements from trusted authorities/experts/leaders in the field

- Awards, degrees, licenses, number of sales, years of experience

- Guarantees, free samples, offers to corroborate reliability

Avoid these credibility diminishers, which keep that chasm forbiddingly wide:

- Reliance on boasts and promises rather than evidence

- A price that strikes the audience as either too high or low for the value described

- Mistakes in terminology, spelling, facts; lapses perceived as sexist, racist, ignorant or amateur

- Any evidence in aesthetics or execution of the marketing piece that the company may not practice what it preaches

Keep in mind that to win credibility, you don't simply pile on credentials. I've observed audiences riled to the point of fury because they thought someone offering help was setting himself or herself up too high over them. Similarly, it is possible to make your materials too gorgeous. If nationally famous penny-pincher Amy Dacyczyn sent out expensive-looking solicitations for her newsletter, *The Tightwad Gazette*, she'd lose points with potential subscribers—even if she somehow got the paper and printing for free. Perception and alignment with your market count. Credibility means convincing a particular audience that they won't be sorry afterward for stepping forward to do business with you.

Multiple Audiences

Dale Conway of Beverly, Massachusetts, keeps her credibility with two divergent audiences by using two entirely different sets of marketing materials. For high-tech corporations like Hewlett-Packard, she gives out professional presentation folders containing her company description, client lists, bio, major project descriptions and a business card headed, "CMA/Conway Marketing Associates/Marketing Communications and Consulting." For spiritually minded individuals and New Age entrepreneurs, she calls her operation "The Star-Spirit Network" and distributes a simple two-sided brochure on ordinary copyshop blue paper. "If I gave those client something slick, they'd think they couldn't afford me," she says. "I want to encourage these folks to take a chance and work with me." For her StarSpirit ads, brochure and business card, Conway adds her middle name, Andrea, so that strangers know she's a woman. That isn't necessary for the high-tech audience, which mainly learns about her through word of mouth. Conway also leaves her street address off the StarSpirit ads and cards. "For the general public, I like to make a personal connection with someone before I give out my address," she explains.

George Berman, a communications consultant in Yonkers, New York, agrees that you must analyze your need for separate materials when you have divergent audiences. "Let's say you're a real estate broker. We'd ask you who you want to get a message to. You'd say sellers, to begin with. 'I want to tell them I'll manage their property, I won't bring people who aren't serious trooping through their house. I'll get them the best price.' But you also want to get a message to buyers. 'I want to tell buyers I can get them the best house their money can buy with no hidden problems.' Then we'd point out that those two sets of messages conflict. You cannot speak to those two audiences in the same brochure or ad." For a less cut-and-dried example, Berman cites a mortgage broker who mostly targets the uniformed services, such as police officers, as well as attorneys. "He needs to tell attorneys the ways in which he'll help them through the mortgage process. His message for the cops is that he'll get them a low-cost mortgage that they can't get anywhere else. Each message is of absolutely no interest to the other group. We've found that if half of a brochure is of no interest to people, they won't read the part that is. Generally you don't dilute your impact by speaking to two different audiences at once, you lose it."

Perhaps you're marketing different services to different groups, as Laurel Eye Associates does with radial keratotomy, elective surgery that enables people aged twenty-five to forty-five to dispense with glasses, and cataract treatments, for a significantly older crowd. You'd be foolish to try to lure both groups with one cast of your marketing reel. Or perhaps you're selling the same service to two groups with wildly differing attitudes. Paul Homoly, a dentist in Charlotte, North Carolina, who advises other dentists on developing a practice, finds diametrically opposed attitudes toward marketing in practitioners from different generations. "Dentists who've been out of school five to eight years see marketing as a natural extension of the doctor-patient relationship, in tune with consumer needs," Homoly says. "For those twenty or more years out, though, it's a highly charged issue. They see marketing as selling things to people that they don't need. Hence to them someone who markets their practice must not be a good dentist. Yet with their ever-increasing overhead, they know they've got to do something." Homoly would probably do well with a separate pitch to the more conflicted group.

Or you may be planning to reach out to a new audience, hoping to add a new customer group for your product while keeping the old. Don't assume that a few superficial changes in your existing materials allow them to perform the same magic for the new audience. Rethink their purpose and plan persuasion for that audience from scratch. Brokers and financial planners, for instance, have traditionally served a mostly male clientele. Now that more women make higher salaries and have decided to charge into the world of investments, companies marketing financial products and services to women are finding that they can't simply change a few photos in their brochures and sprinkle some "she's" among the male examples. Wisely, the brokerage firm Dean Witter produced a planning guide specifically for women that starts off, "Did you know that nine out of ten women will have to handle their own finances at some point in their lives?" and continues with other relevant statistics and well-targeted advice.

Barbara Brabec, a home business expert since the 1970s, dealt with a shifting social landscape in the 1990s by repositioning her business to pull in high-tech folks who did not identify with the term "home business." "They consider themselves *self-employed*," she says. When she renamed her subscription newsletter, formerly *The National Home Business Report, Barbara Brabec's Self-Employment Survival Letter*, she remained alert for signs of losing the group that did think of themselves as "working at home." Similarly, when she sent out flyers for the fifth edition of her book, *Homemade Money*, she noticed that having emphasized its comprehensive application to selling any product or service from home, she wasn't getting as many orders as she expected from the crafts market, which had bought big when Brabec stressed retailing and wholesaling products. "Because I didn't use the words 'retailing' or 'wholesaling' anywhere in the table of contents, craftspeople seemed to think the new edition didn't relate to them," she reflects. To keep the crafts audience along with her while she reached out, she prepared a supplement to her book flyer that explained what specifically sat waiting in the book for people selling crafts products, retail or wholesale.

The same warnings apply if you are expanding your market internationally. For U.S. companies, even doing business with Canada requires adjustment in your marketing communications. If you don't specify "payment in U.S. funds" or list Canadian prices, you could receive checks that translate to lower profit margins when your bank finishes processing them. Similarly, if you list only your 800 number or a number keyed by letters (such as 555-ANI-MALS), European or Asian customers won't be able to telephone you, since 800 numbers only work within North America and foreign telephones don't bear letters. Cultural disparities can run much deeper. According to Robyn Gold, director of Gold Chip Communications in Belmont, Massachusetts, Dutch consumers don't respond well to some typical American advertisements. "We take it for granted that products and people should toot their own horn," observes Gold, who spent three years working in the Netherlands. "To the Dutch that kind of marketing comes across as loud and crass. They grow up learning about the boy who saved his village by plugging a hole in the dike, and they value the self-sacrificing community man, the faithful citizen and the loyal watch guard. So how do they sell products without self-serving talk? Through humor—even political humor, which might be treacherous for American companies."

American software manufacturers have been scrambling to internationalize their products and marketing, but they face obstacles more formidable than foreign alphabets and the necessity for accurate translation. The same message in another language may take up twice as much space as in English—a headache that prevents simple conversion of on-screen layouts or text-heavy ads and brochures. Describing a product's features in inches or degrees Fahrenheit would be incomprehensible outside the United States. You might think that numbers at least are culturally neutral, but what we denote as "4,075.92" becomes "4.075,92" in some countries. In the United States, a "billion" corresponds to "1" followed by nine zeros, while in Europe it refers to a "1" followed by twelve zeros. According to Kumiyo Nakakoji, author of an article on cultural differences in *Byte* magazine, the very concept of "groupware," a product that facilitates the sharing of ideas at meetings, may make no sense in Japan, where people don't customarily challenge each other's ideas in public. Nakakoji also points out that embedded in the American embrace of word processors is the fact that we understand concepts like cursors, tabs and margins because of our familiarity with typewriters—this is not the case in Japan. All in all you'd be smart to get internationally sensitive help before sending American marketing materials out across the oceans.

Even if your audience analysis shows that two audiences share the same motivators, consider making microchanges in wording to make people feel you are specifically speaking to them. When approaching clients in the health care industry, Joel Berger of JHB Communications in Montrose, New York, uses a bio that says he "currently provides communications services and consulting for health care and other professional clients." When approaching engineering clients, he uses a different version that reads, "consulting for engineering, health care and other professional clients." Further down in his bio, he shuffles the order of four items in a list of specific achievements at his previous job, putting the one most relevant to a prospect at the top of the list. Earlier in my career it drove me crazy when a firm said they'd turned down my business partner and me as seminar leaders because our materials didn't say we'd worked with, say, nurse practitioners. "But we had 'doctors' down there!" we'd wail to each other, exasperated. Older and perhaps wiser, I've concluded that it's easier to respect the degree to which every audience feels it's special than to fight the attitude.

Knowing Your Competition

Figuring out the best way to approach your audience should take into account what your competitors are doing to attract their business. When you have easily identifiable rivals, it's usually fairly simple to collect a file of their ads, brochures, newsletters and press coverage. Sometimes you'll need to play spy and enlist the aid of a friend to pose as a potential client and receive their marketing materials and prices. Once you have their stuff, analyze both the content of their message and the ways in which they deliver it. Then you face some decisions: Do you want to parallel what they are doing in their marketing, but do it better? Do you want to deflect their course in a slightly different direction? Or do you want to offer a clear and unmistakable alternative?

To facilitate your analysis, make a list of your rivals' selling points. For each one, ask:

Can I match it?

Sometimes your answer here is no, regardless of your imagination or intentions. When you're up against Harvard-trained practitioners with twenty-five years of experience, and you're one year out of the state training college, you'd better concentrate on creative positioning, through questions #2 and 3. At other times it's easy and important to catch up. If you're a plumber and several counterparts in the local paper's service directory sport Visa and MasterCard symbols, perhaps you should arrange to add them to your ad.

Can I substitute another selling point to bypass their advantage?

As the inexperienced practitioner, you might pitch your fresh approaches or the fact that you handle nothing but, say, leveraged buyouts. In *Positioning: The Battle for Your Mind*, Al Ries and Jack Trout explain that since you can never out-IBM IBM, you're better off staking out a defensible niche that no one occupies. For instance, you can take the high road: We're the premium, high-priced ice cream. Or you can take the low road: Get more for your money at Jagdaw's. Where competitors blur with each other because everyone offers the same benefits and features, you have a special opportunity to wave a hand at prospects with whatever sets you apart. Judy Madnick of A-1 Office Assistance in Albany, New York, included in her brochure her background as a teacher and the fact that she writes a column on grammar for a national newsletter "to make sure they know I'm more than a secretary," she says.

Can I turn an apparent competitive disadvantage into an advantage?

Suppose that the main competitors of your pizza restaurant stress speedy service. Rather than initiate hand-to-hand combat on their field, you might decide to turn your slowness into a virtue. So you highlight "leisurely" (never, of course, "slow") dining in an Old-World atmosphere. The success of this move depends largely on your target market: Do enough

of them really want to linger over pizza and beer? Or suppose
you're a consultant and some rivals underscore their accessi-
bility. Here's how Dan Kennedy of Phoenix attempts to turn
his deficit in that area into a benefit for clients:

> Kennedy is *not* easy to do business with. He maintains a
> grueling schedule of speaking, consulting, writing, managing
> his own business and producing infomercials, so he's rarely
> in his office, almost never takes incoming calls—new client-
> candidates are usually asked to submit information by fax before
> getting a telephone appointment with him, he's militantly resis-
> tant to having his time wasted and has "fired clients" on occa-
> sion for doing so. He is blunt, straightforward and almost totally
> lacking in diplomacy. *He's also expensive* . . . Still, he has a
> number of clients who have been with him for as long as ten
> years, including some who simply will not make a marketing-
> related move without his guidance.

His premise—that he's too busy and too good at showing
his clients how to make money to be pleasant and reachable—
falls apart when you think about it, but emotionally it probably
persuades some prospects to feel honored when they do get his
high-priced ear.

In addition to what competitors say, pay attention to the
formats in which they say it. Where customer expectations of
certain forms of marketing are ingrained, flout them at your
peril. For instance, for decades so many dentists have sent six-
month reminder postcards that patients who do not receive
them might assume a dentist who doesn't send them out
doesn't care about their health or doesn't want them back in
his or her chair. And don't forget the possibility that competitors all do a certain something because it works! Deciding not
to create a Christmas catalog or advertise in the Yellow Pages
might be suicidal for your business rather than original.

When you think about competitors, include players who
might be horning in on your business from other turf (or vice

versa). *USA Today* founder Al Neuharth designed the first national American newspaper with colorful, easily read news snapshots in part because he thought of his competition as television in addition to other newspapers. Similarly, a rock band trying to sell concert tickets competes not only with other rock concerts, but also with stay-at-home entertainment and the more intimate musical experience available in clubs. According to high-tech marketing expert Regis McKenna, any thriving business needs to keep an eye out for what he calls "intangible competitors" too, especially *change*. Industries, products, distribution channels, issues and consumers all change, he points out, and failure to keep up means doom.

But don't let concern with competition become such an obsession that you lose your identity. And for many service businesses, even moderate concern may be unnecessary. "The notion of competition assumes a scarcity of clients and a sparseness of money available to be spent on services," says Dale Conway. "But psychotherapists and consultants don't need a huge number of clients—they're simply aiming for a full calendar, with clients who appreciate them and will say good things about them. I have a good relationship with clients who come to me, so I have no need to feel competitive with other marketing consultants. I'm me and they are them." Try to become like the competition, she warns, and you could end up attracting—and losing—people who aren't happy with you. But if you get clear on who you are and communicate that to those you can best serve, you're on the way to fulfilling your goal.

CHAPTER 4

Choosing an Appropriate Voice

Whenever you write, your style says as much about you as does your content. Key word choices, sentence structures, even favorite punctuation make as much of an impact as the ostensible content of each piece. One person comes across as a stuffy fussbudget, another as a perky cheerleader and yet another as a finger-pointing, thundering autocrat. Compare these three openers from business letters, for instance:

1. I don't get it. I sent you a letter recently on the deal of the century and you didn't call!
2. Like all business owners, you are undoubtedly concerned about maintaining a competitive position in a problematical economy. Would you appreciate a complimentary opportunity to review a program that will keep you apprised of important economic developments?
3. At least seven new ideas about how to run your business: that's my promise if you attend next month's advanced entrepreneurship seminar at the Colonial Heights Hotel.

From the vocabulary and exclamatory sentence as much as the content of the message, writer #1 strikes me as a huckster who probably thinks he'd be the next Donald Trump except for the stupidity of the people he's trying to sell to. The long-winded, wandering style of writer #2, on the other hand, gives me the impression of a windbag who doesn't know how to get to the point. Since neither is a kind of person I enjoy spending time with, I doubt I would read either letter any further. Writer #3, though, by using a slightly unusual sentence structure and packing a lot of specific information into a compact space, suggests someone with professional attitudes and experience and a dash of promotional flair. So long as nothing else in the letter conflicted with this image, I'd feel comfortable that this writer would either deliver on the pledge or honor the money-back guarantee. That's how powerfully writing style can destroy or inspire trust.

Or compare these pitches, taken from ads for therapists:

1. Dr. S. seeks to provide a safe, nurturing environment in which each client may awaken and engage her or his own spiritual resources. Becoming fully ourselves is a life-long journey. Becoming fully present to our unique place on that journey is a continuing challenge.
2. Come discover who you really are, who you really are not, and how to keep them separate. You'll think better, feel better, look better, perform better. Your nervous system will relax. Your immune system will strengthen. Your negative emotions and habits will loosen their grip on you.

From the writing style, I imagine Dr. S's therapy as soothing and slow, and the second therapist's work as a cool, refreshing splash of reality that quickly wakes one up. Note that Dr. S. refers to the client and himself in the third person ("he/she") and uses "our" instead of "your" in a manner that may recall your teachers from grammar school. (It also implies that though you may have spiritual difficulties, you are not alone.) The second therapist addresses the prospect directly and consistently as "you" and uses shorter, snappier sentences. These impressions might be wrong, but the dreamy distance of the first ad would attract very different clients than would the crisp promises of the second.

Writing voices come in as many varieties as human personalities. You need to consciously choose and control your style, since a voice that clashes with the character of your product or service will win you confused, dissatisfied customers, prospects you don't want or none at all. It's easier than you might expect to choose a writing voice that matches your offerings, however. Just decide on the personality you want to convey, follow my tips in your writing and editing, and solicit candid feedback on the extent to which your chosen tone actually does come across. Below are suggestions on voices you might consider for business materials.

Pointers on Personality

Friendly vs. aloof

Business communication experts agree that in the 1990s, friendly makes a much better impression on North Americans than does aloof. As business horizons have expanded, so that we do more and more business with people we've never met, we favor a person-to-person approach in which doing business together involves becoming colleagues, if not friends.

For a friendly stance, address customers as "you" and refer to yourself as "we" or, even better, "I." If you do business on your own, it's stuffy and self-important to use "we," while if you carry on business as a group, an "I" that comes from a named individual helps humanize the company. In contrast, an aloof firm always refers to both itself and its clientele in a descriptive, detached manner. ("Capitol Savings has served discerning investors since 1989. Its investors trust it to keep their money safe.")

Along with direct, personal address, you establish a friendly tone by writing with the words and sentence constructions you would use when you speak one-on-one with someone you know moderately well. Compare, for instance, these two sentences that might come from innkeepers:

1. Caring as we do about all the quandaries that transpire during traveling, we are pleased to be at your service.
2. We're always glad to help you find your way around our island or get through to the baby-sitter back home.

Both sentences use "we" and "you," but can you imagine someone talking about "quandaries" that "transpire" in a normal business conversation? Structurally, sentence #1 isn't conversational, either. Because of the contraction in #2 ("we're" instead of "we are") as well as the subject-then-object structure, it sounds more natural than #1. If you want the cordial, unaffected tone of #2, test your copy by reading it out loud and asking yourself, Might someone say this on the phone or face to face?

Friendly doesn't necessarily mean chummy or intimate, however. In business correspondence with strangers, don't jump immediately to first names or include personal details like "Since I'm still recovering from gall-bladder surgery ..." Someone sent me a letter he'd written as a Canadian business owner to newly elected Prime Minister Jean Chrétien, which included lines of protest like, "Jean, I voted for you!" To me that came across as overly familiar, schoolboyish whining, and destroyed his professional credibility.

Precise vs. general.

The following sentences, from ads in *Entrepreneur*, illustrate contrary possibilities:

1. Earn an *incredible income* by offering parents the highest level of child protection available.
2. Our well-structured, extensively researched commer-

cial cleaning program has proven successful in every area in which we have expanded.

3. You can make $201 profit on a $249 sale, $294 profit on a $447 sale.

4. Bob Carter of Newark, NJ, ran his first small mail order ad in *House Beautiful* magazine—offering an auto clothes rack. *Business Week* reported that his ad brought in $5,000 in orders. By the end of his first year in mail order, he had grossed over $100,000!

Overall, specific numbers and names, as in #3 and #4, produce more credibility than the vagueness of #1 and #2. But whether that translates into more sales depends on your audience, the character of your business and the nature of your service or product. Advertising that your office park has 23.5 percent bigger office suites than the city average may win over bottom-line watchers, while an ad reporting that wearers had 23.5 percent more dates after wearing a certain perfume would have to be taken as a joke. Remember that the abundant statistics and specifications that feed an engineer's appetite will cause a nonspecialist's eyes to glaze over. Similarly, "Save $201.50" might go over big with a middle-income audience while wealthy buyers might find "Once-a-year savings" in better taste.

Colorful vs. matter-of-fact

Here (minus some grammar and punctuation errors) is the beginning of the brochure of Trans World Auto Consultants in Schenectady, New York:

Why, Why, Why?

Why put up with the frenzy of shopping for a new car at a dealership?

Why have some aggressive salesperson try to slam you into a car you don't want?

Why should you have to haggle over a price of a new auto and not know if you got a good deal?

Until now there was no other way to buy a new auto.

With the repetition of "Why?" and the choice of loaded words like "frenzy," "slam" and "haggle" (instead of the plainer "bargain"), Trans World puts its money on an emotional appeal to car buyers. And notice the lively personality that comes across in this brochure opener from Stevenson Industries of Winston-Salem, North Carolina:

> What would we do without family get-togethers? The last time you and your relatives gathered you had a great time . . . right? Well, maybe you had some minor disagreements, but that can always happen, even in the best of families. The main thing is that you knew who was who and your correct relationship with your relatives . . . right? Oh no! You say that you disagreed with Aunt Matilda on whether you and her daughter's child Amy were second cousins once removed?
>
> This relationship guide should answer your questions once and for all.

This effective lead sets an at-home, storytelling tone while conveying vividly the problem that the product solves.

Compared with the colorful style in those two excerpts, this brochure from the Boston Computer Society opens more straightforwardly:

> The fastest way to become a satisfied computer user: Join the BCS today.
>
> Sooner or later, you will have questions about your computer. It doesn't matter what kind of computer you use or whether you're a beginner or advanced programmer—questions will arise.
>
> Fortunately, all you need do to get answers to your questions is become a member of The Boston Computer Society. At the BCS, there's no question that is too easy or too hard.

Appropriately, the BCS style does not call attention to itself. This organization would alienate many potential members if it projected an emotional or overly playful image. The same goes for most business-to-business services or products. Notice, though, that matter-of-fact doesn't have to mean sacrificing the personal touch to become distant or dull.

Timid–assertive–aggressive

See if you can guess which is which in these three pitches for nutritional supplements:

1. I think you might find yourself in better health after trying AZ-EZ supplements.
2. You'll like the way you feel after using AZ-EZ supplements.
3. You're throwing away your health unless you rely on AZ-EZ supplements.

In most situations, the confident assertiveness of #2 gets the best results. Timidity, as in #1, rarely sells. Just as low self-esteem can unintentionally come across in bad posture, I've seen a lot of people unknowingly communicate self-doubt in their writing. Get rid of any apologies ("Although I don't work with Fortune 500 companies . . .") and any qualifiers like "probably" or "it seems" that are not necessary to protect you legally. In proposals and sales letters, the present tense ("This program brings you . . .") conveys more confidence than the future ("This program will brings you . . .") or the conditional ("This program would [or should] bring you . . .") In the three numbered examples above, the verb "using" shows more self-assurance than "trying," and "rely on" shows more confidence still. One writer sent out a flyer inviting people to an event publicizing her newly published book, with this printed along the bottom: "Please come and spare me any further embarrassment."

It made me cringe and imagine an ordeal rather than a cele-
bration, and I didn't go.

At the other extreme lie threats, heavy-handed guilt trip-
ping, insults and bullying. Some marketers believe people
don't act unless you hold a hammer over their heads. Jeffrey
Lant, the author of *No More Cold Calls* and *Money Making
Marketing*, has no patience for pussyfooting. He writes these
sorts of harshly worded admonitions to his readers and
prospective clients: "Stop this stupidity right now!" "It sickens
me just how many marketing communications are on the
wrong track" and "If you're not doing this, you've apparently
decided to slice your wrists and quietly bleed to death." While
in person Lant is amiable and considerate, I find his persona in
print frightening. But as with a lawyer I know who tells people
in trouble that they've been "a horse's ass," such tough talk
seems to gratify or amuse as many people as it appalls. I know
that if I suddenly adopted either Lant's or the lawyer's tone, I
would drive away clients who enjoy my equally honest but
supportive approach. And I would feel uncomfortable with
clients who take verbal abuse in stride.

Serious–light–humorous

In the early spring of 1994, I received an envelope in the
mail bearing this message:

> Q: What are the five most frightening words in American
> politics today?
> A: United States Senator Oliver North.

While I didn't save the contents of the envelope, from the
Democratic National Committee, I'm quite sure that the whole
mailing continued in a tone of foreboding. Anything that
caused the slightest smile would dissolve the solemn spell
intended to induce me to reach for my checkbook. Stick to a
serious tone if you're selling children's bicycle helmets, dis-

ability insurance or bankruptcy prevention counseling. Paint as vivid and terrible a picture as possible of the catastrophe your product or service forestalls. Avoid any words associated with pleasure, and try injecting drama with short, one-sentence paragraphs.

Like this.

If you don't depend on fear to motivate customers, you may be able to afford a lighter tone. For example, I received what looked like a greeting card from an address I didn't recognize. In a flowery script on a purple background, the text read:

> [Front] What we had was so special. When we were together, the world seemed like a wonderful place. Now that you're gone, it just seems cold and lonely.
>
> Sure, things were difficult at times. But our relationship means everything. And even though we're apart, we can still work it out . . . together.
>
> [Inside] Please accept this graphic user interface front-end disk, and $50 worth of free services your first month, as a token of our affection.
>
> We miss you . . . We need you . . . And we want you to come back today.
>
> OK, have we grovelled enough yet?
>
> Love, GEnie

I had abandoned my free trial membership with this on-line service, and this insouciant missive did indeed warm me up to the idea of trying again. But for those businesses that need a rock-solid image, like banks, any levity—much less GEnie's snuggly wit—might be too much. Would you patronize a bank whose advertisements made you smile? I wouldn't.

Humor reaches further for yuks than lightness and represents a risk in marketing—even when laugh production fits your business image. Readers who miss the joke can get annoyed. Others, despite your innocent intentions, can get offended. I remember waiting for some copies in a newly opened private mailing center and picking up a flyer about its business services. Turning it over, I saw what looked like a horoscope and searched for my sign. For Cancer, it said, "You are a very patient person. You can fall asleep waiting for things to happen. You have a keen memory and often recite boring, obscure things to your few friends. Cancers are easily influenced and many have actually drowned when told to go jump in the lake." Confused, I read some of the equally insulting comments about other horoscope signs and left the shop wondering about the business judgment of the owner, who obviously thought this vein of witticism would win him customers.

Chatty vs. all-business

On the outskirts of Bozeman, Montana, sculptors Harvey Rattey and Pamela Harr publish a semiannual newsletter to keep in touch with almost eighteen thousand people who have expressed interest in their bronzes over the years. This excerpt should give you a sense of the chatty tone of the message that accompanies photographs of their new work and an order form:

> We're still chuckling over the recollection of our stay in Brigham City. After making a dash from the motel pool to our room, we found that Grandma had locked us out when she threw the chain latch off its track and couldn't get it unhooked. We stood at the door in our swimsuits reassuring each other that 30 degrees really wasn't all that cold, while Grandma in a tizzy was trying to beat the latch off the door with a plastic bottle of mayonnaise. Fortunately Harvey found a screwdriver in the van and squeezed it through the gap in the door so she could remove the screws and release the latch.

Besides the personal stories that would be out of place in the usual business newsletter, the down-home-on-the-range voice comes across in distinctive word choices like "when the snow flies this winter," "sculptures in the works," "a grand display" and "when you're out our way." Harr adopted this tone thinking of the family Christmas letter as a model, and the newsletter keeps them in touch with a huge extended family likely to recommend their artwork to others even if they don't buy themselves.

At the other extreme, an all-business voice not only shuns amusing anecdotes, it incorporates words and phrases common in the corporate world. This sample comes from the self-description in Boston copywriter Paul Wesel's brochure: "His strategic marketing approach focuses on customer needs-based solutions and he has a proven track record in transforming complex subject matter into powerful and effective marketing communications." Except for "customer needs-based solutions," which verges on jargon (see Chapter 13), this nicely and clearly weaves together phrases that signal to executives and managers that he's part of their world.

Commanding vs. beckoning

Literally, sales literature can't command; the seller lacks authority over the buyer. But an advertisement or sales letter can adopt the attitude of a taskmaster firing out orders: "Buy now! Don't let this opportunity slip away!" Or it can assume the side-by-side demeanor of a polite request, as in a letter I received from an accountant: "I would like to assist you in these ever-changing times . . . If you or your company is in need of an accountant, please feel free to contact me." In another form of beckoning, the copy extends the offer as an opportunity, almost as a favor from the seller to the buyer. For instance, a letter which sold every last place on a 1968 around-the-world expedition began:

As Chairman of the Admiral Richard E. Byrd Polar Center, it is my privilege to invite you to become a member of an expedition which is destined to make both news and history. It will cost you $10,000 and about 26 days of your time. Frankly, you will endure some discomfort and may even face some danger.

On the other hand, you will have the rare privilege of taking part in a mission of great importance for the United States and the entire world. A mission, incidentally, which has never before been attempted by man.

Take special care when using the word "invite," since it invokes a host-guest relationship in which the host—the inviter—pays for the event. The global expedition letter didn't cause any confusion because it stated the price up front, but when I received a letter from a friend "inviting" me to attend her new workshop, I reread and re-reread the letter: Did she mean I should come as her guest? While the brochure mentioned a price, the letter did not. I debated calling her for clarification, but decided it would be too embarrassing if she hadn't meant me to come free. If we hadn't discussed her ideas so often I would have known this was just another way to make the sale, but when she wrote in the letter, "Your insight and contributions will greatly enhance the learning, and I would very much like to share the work with you," she could have meant this as overriding the stated price—or not.

Note that whether you're beckoning or commanding doesn't simply depend on whether you use imperative verbs. The brochure of a Maine ferry company ends, "Come aboard Casco Bay Lines and discover what Maine people have been keeping to themselves all these years!" which comes across as an invitation, despite the direct address of "come" and the exclamation mark. The following envelope copy also has that gentle tone: "Get a free pint of Ben & Jerry's and 60 free minutes from the phone company that speaks for you. Open fast, it's melting." Appealing words like "discover" and "free" override the grammatical format of a command.

Veiled vs. candid

You've undoubtedly read cagey ads that take the attitude. "Here's an opportunity to become a millionaire, like me. I can't tell you everything about it here, but it's not this or that or the other method. Send $49.95 and you'll receive complete money-back-guaranteed details." These only work if they use every trick in the book to win credibility and induce action. Compare that close-to-the-chest approach with the cards-on-the-table attitude in this letter opener, written by Mark A. Small of the U.S. Note & Mortgage Company, Inc. in Saratoga Springs, New York:

> Dr. Referral asked me to contact you regarding our investments. However, we recognize we are not for everybody.
>
> If you are seeking volatile investments with tremendous profit (and loss) potential, we're not for you.
>
> If you favor government guaranteed, 100 percent liquid investments with the associated low rates of return, again we're not for you.
>
> But if you are seeking investments that perform predictably and reliably with moderate yield and relatively small risk, your search may be over. You can expect U.S. Note & Mortgage Company, Inc. investments to have these qualities . . .

"We sell to wealthy individuals and small corporate pension plans," says Small. "Even though our investment is truly superior, no one pays attention if we present it in the typical overinflated 'salesly' manner. The almost standoffish approach we use in both our negotiating and our literature distinguishes us. Does it work for us? You bet."

Recently I read a masterful ad in the veiled genre from a guy named Jeff Paul. He'd managed to crowd about 2,500 words onto one magazine page, and I read every one of them—four times. He divulged very few details about the mail order system he had devised, so what was it that snagged me? I think it was how he managed to be confessional and evasive at the same time. Some excerpts:

> With my book, "How You Can Make $4,000.00 a Day Sitting At Your Kitchen Table in Your Underwear," you are PROTECTED BY MY SIMPLE GUARANTEE. And I would be an idiot to risk ruining my $200,000.00-a-month business to steal pocket change from you. Wouldn't that be incredibly stupid? . . . By the way, Peggy HATES the title I've put on this book. She says that it's bad enough that I do sit around the house in my underwear, why tell anybody about it? I embarrass her. I'm a little "unpolished." Well, I guess I just want you to understand that I'm just a plain, ordinary guy . . . EVERYTHING I've done to go from dead-broke to making over 2 million dollars from home in 3 years, YOU can do too.

This ad parted me from $19.95 plus shipping, even though I already enjoy sitting around the house in my bathrobe whenever I feel like it.

Folksy vs. sophisticated

In contrast to the folksiness of the in-your-underwear and in-a-tizzy voices, some materials appeal to readers with the cosmopolitan composure of a man lounging around in tails. In *The Atlantic Monthly*, a fairly highbrow magazine, I found an ad for a product that included some words and phrases only highly educated, rich people use. "If you've ever had occasion to . . ." "marvelous," "the substantial drawback," "awfully high" and "even after hardest and longest use" all put me in mind of characters in a British drawing-room film. Since the product in question was a $39.95 ceramic pen, such word choices made sense. In marketing to sophisticates you might even get away with using semicolons, which signal abstruse stuffiness in most other contexts.

I haven't exhausted the personalities possible to express in your marketing materials, but the above should give you plenty to think about. Before or while writing, settle into a chosen personality the way an actor would, and as long as the personality fits you, appropriate words should flow. Follow the suggestions for feedback and polishing in Chapters 13 and 14, and take special care to adjust anything that might break the spell.

Promotional Protocol: The Facts-to-Hype Continuum

Besides choosing a personality to express throughout your materials, you need to match how promotional or sales-oriented your voice becomes to the purpose and format of each piece. In a 1992 survey of 139 editors of newspapers ranging from large metropolitan dailies to community business journals, Kay Borden found the greatest complaint about the publicity-seeking mail they received to be "reads like advertising." If you're producing advertising, however, the language that pleases journalists may lack the oomph necessary to get people to act. For each marketing piece you create, decide where the language should fall along the five points of a continuum from an objective, disinterested orientation to a subjective, self-interested sales pitch.

Strictly objective	Slanted	Mildly promotional	Strongly promotional	Hype
1	2	3	4	5
No sell	Soft sell	Medium sell	Hard sell	Oversell

With a goal of sales, you'll find very few situations that call for stance #1—as objective as a highly professional news reporter. Rigorously impersonal and nonjudgmental, this kind of writing sticks to verifiable information and includes no calls to action and no opinions except those attributed to named parties. It's hard to sell when you're this ruthlessly objective, since even the tiniest bit of favoritism toward your own company would send the piece skidding toward the right on the continuum. Still, in some competitive situations you win over skeptics by dispassionately laying out all the facts like any disciplined news gatherer. See Chapter 9 for a discussion of situations that merit "white papers."

Slanted writing, at point #2 of the continuum, uses journalistic style less strictly, for self-interested goals. Remember the last résumé you composed? You probably labored valiantly to put the most positive, grand spin on ordinary achievements, calling yourself a "front-line customer service representative and problem solver." The objective, no-sell label that would appear in the newspaper, though, would be "receptionist." Slanted writing does not address the reader as a buyer and avoids "you" except as a magazine article might use it. Publicity releases to the media—always in third person—and promotional newsletters—in either first or third person—usually contain slanted writing. Only a sharp eye and journalistic questioning can separate soft-sell writing in third person from its no-sell cousin. First-person soft sell, appropriate for some letters and newsletters, contains only facts—presented neutrally but selected for their impact. "Two of my books, *Smart Speaking* and *He and She Talk*, were recently featured on *Oprah*" would count as soft sell.

Certain telltale words and writing techniques automatically kick your marketing piece farther right along the continuum, so for slanted writing, beware of including any of the following:

- Any offer or invitation extended directly to the reader. ("Send $29.00 to . . ."; "Come join us on Thursday evening . . .")

- Superlatives without any specific, mentioned basis or source. You can say, for instance, "Frances Treat, named Best Gymnastics Coach in the East by the Eastern Sports Association" but not simply "Frances Treat, the best gymnastics coach in the East."

- Opinions or judgments, unless set inside quotation marks and attributed to a specific person. For example, "Top-quality services offered range from data entry to database management." Top quality says who? Compare " 'Their top-quality service is sure to satisfy the most finicky office manager,' says Timothy Kuow, president of Top Drawer Furniture Systems."

- Adjectives commonly used in sales situations, like "unique," "fascinating" or "only," as in "only $9.95."

- Any strings of all-capital letters or any exclamation points.

While the soft sell suits materials such as publicity, newsletters and letters designed to sell without appearing to do so, materials that are obviously selling pieces, like brochures, ads and direct mail, belong in the #3-to-#4 range. Unlike the quasi-descriptive writing of the soft sell, medium-sell to hard-sell writing frankly speaks directly to the reader about what he or she will get on buying and urges the reader to act. The difference between levels #3 and #4 consists primarily of how repeatedly and emphatically a piece makes its solicitation. Medium-sell writing gets your attention, develops a point, asks you to do something and then takes a bow and vanishes. Hard-sell writing pounds its points and asks for action again and again and—whoops, one more time, like the nag who just won't quit—again.

Here are medium-sell lines occurring toward the end of three ads, after copy that presents a problem and explains how a company or product solves it:

- If we sound like a firm you'd like to work with, give us a call.

- So make a mental note to do one more thing today. Give us a ring at (800) XXX-XXXX, and we'll send you our Office Info Kit. Then ask around or, better yet, drop by your nearest computer store and check it out. They'll probably let you play with it right there.

- For more information about both domestic and international connections, call your AT&T Account Executive or 1-800-XXX-XXXX.

Instead of gracefully letting you make up your mind, the hard sell takes on the role of a barker, shouting the same message in different words over and over again. In one insistent ad for Yves Rocher face cream, I counted twenty exclamation points. (Three of them were: "Guaranteed to make you look younger . . . feel better . . . or your money back! Don't wait! Try it today!") Another full-page ad for a weight-loss device called Acu-Stop 2000 used only two exclamation points, but came across as a hard sell because it spent most of its words hammering home claims that Acu-Stop works and its guarantee and just two sentences explaining what it is. Similarly, a four-page letter I received selling a guide to saving money on Yellow Pages advertising spent three-quarters of its space urging me to buy it now, and only one-quarter on what the guide contained. The more sophisticated your audience, the more hard-sell tactics backfire. The less you have to say about the benefits of the product, however, the more you'll be tempted to escalate to a hard sell. Interestingly, the $10,000 polar expedition direct-mail letter, excerpted earlier in this chapter, worked its magic without ever exhorting or goading the reader. It concentrated on the trip itself and remained quietly and firmly in the groove of a medium sell even as it asked for the order:

But first of all, you must decide about this trip. If you have a sense of adventure, a certain pioneering spirit, and if the prospect of taking part in a mission of worldwide significance and historical importance appeals to you, perhaps you should consider joining the expedition. It is doubtful that you will ever have another chance like this . . . To reserve your place in the expedition, just drop me a note on your letterhead or personal stationery, with your deposit check for $2,500, made out to the United States Trust Company . . . I hope we may hear from you soon—and that we will welcome you to the expedition.

The hard sell becomes objectionable when it bears the signs of "hype," a word that appears to date back to the early 1900s, when it was used as a verb meaning to trick, deceive or short-change people. Of seven current meanings listed in the 1987 *Random House Dictionary*, most carry the negative connotation of exaggeration, trickery or questionable methods. With hype you're attracting interest with a vivid balloon that upon being pricked deflates to nothing. Hype oversells by going beyond the genuine attractions of a service or product. Since as P. T. Barnum was supposed to have said (but didn't), "There's a sucker born every minute," hype can stimulate impulse buys. But it rarely attracts lasting customers or clients. Use it with great caution, and avoid it entirely for trying to persuade journalists, educated consumers or "I'm from Missouri—show me" folks.

What belongs in slot #5?

- Promises that sound impossible and aren't made credible. "Buy a Vim Van franchise and make a fortune!" "No more bad hair days, ever!" "The three-minute phone call that could save your marriage." As the cliché goes, if you believe these, I have a bridge I'd love to sell you.

- Irrelevant but enticing information. A direct-mail piece for *Writer's Digest*'s novel-writing correspondence course details the multimillion-dollar successes of first novelists John Grisham, Robert James Waller, Donna Tartt and Amy Tan, without any indication that any of the four participated in any novel-writing courses, much less the *Writer's Digest* program. So what are these superstars doing in this sales letter? Someone bet that aspiring writers would ignore the logical gap and jump for the money.

• Unsubstantiated, self-serving boasts. This headline on a full-page ad got my attention: "Women business owners: If you attend only one conference in 1994, this should be the ONE!" All right, I thought, why? Only one-ninth of the page contained any information even tangentially related to that claim, with a generic, uninteresting list of topics. The rest of the space trumpeted the sponsors and how to sign up. This ad definitely flunked the "So what?" test.

• Puffery—exaggerations. Consider this come-on: "Imagine . . . selling a product that everyone wants . . ." Now what could that be? Money? Sex? Nope, *cruises*. Sorry, you lost me there. I can think of plenty of people who wouldn't go near even the *QE II* if you paid them. Similarly, my suspicions always get activated at the label "best-seller" applied to a book I've never seen on any recognized best-seller list. Here's one more ridiculous hoo-ha, accompanying a photo of a sleeping baby: "Believe it or not, there are business people experiencing the same kind of peace"—for a furniture rental place. Hey, come on, who really loses sleep over furniture? When you reach too far to be clever, you mock the genuine need for your product.

To sum up, here's the same service—Mr. Willy's haircuts—presented through each of the five approaches along the facts-to-hype continuum.

1. No sell: Mr. Willy's salon, at 45 Lockerbee St., caters to a young, fashion-conscious crowd.
2. Soft sell: Mr. Willy trained with Sansome Gidale. His clientele has included such TV and film stars as Nora Heller and Debra Langer.
3. Medium sell: For the "Hollywood Look," call 555-6622 for an appointment with Mr. Willy.
4. Hard sell: Call now for your once-in-a-lifetime chance for that glamorous "Hollywood Look." Remember, after June 15 Mr. Willy closes his appointment book to new clients, so call 555-6622 today!
5. Hype: Now you can look like a movie star, too! Only Mr. Willy gives you the look that causes heads to turn and people to whisper, "Didn't I see her on What's-that-show?"

CHAPTER 5

Culling Content
for Your Materials

Let's suppose that you've decided what you need in the way of materials on paper, you've figured out the benefits or solutions that you want to offer to a specific audience and you've chosen a personality to express in your stuff. But ideas are just rattling around in your brain. Nothing exists on paper. How can you get started? Here's a focused series of steps to follow once you've reached that stage.

Six Steps to a Finished Marketing Piece

Collect ideas

Strange as this may sound, the best way to resolve the tension of "I don't know what to write" involves increasing the tension first. Studies of great innovators in science and business show that the inspirations that prove valuable usually arrive after a period of direct attack and conscious thinking that ends in frustration. Giving up, the creator heads outside for a run, does the dishes or goes to sleep. And voilà, seemingly out of nowhere, ze answer comes. That period of direct attack on the problem has as much to do with the breakthrough as the running, dishwashing or sleeping. Keep mulling over the question, "What should I say in my brochure [ad, letter]?" and keep track of everything that arises as a possible answer. Use a notebook, a folder or an electronic file for gathering ideas.

Dump everything you can think of that might inform or entice a client into your collection system: features, benefits, background information, advantages over the competition, analysis of your audience, reasons to buy, objections and doubts to overcome, people to quote on how great your product is, incentives to buy—in short, all of your marketing ammunition. If you've collected sample pieces from your competitors, go back through them now and make notes on what you like and don't like about what they have done.

Set aside enough time for thoughts to gel, collect and develop—at a minimum, one week. Although sometimes a mental bolt of lightning provides a dazzling concept right at the start, as a rule, the more options you can generate before settling on The One, the better. This is especially important if you're planning a whole marketing campaign, rather than a one-shot piece. According to the makers of IdeaFisher software, fresh visions and solutions tend to appear among the final 50 percent of ideas produced during brainstorming, while the most stale, commonplace approaches typically come up earliest.

Have patience. Copywriter Dick Dunn of Providence, Rhode Island, says it took him fifteen hours to come up with the three words that headed an ad for De Laval ship centrifuges and distillers: "Man hours overboard." The ad went on to detail how the company's equipment saves shipping companies money, and won him the prestigious Hatch award. Similarly, Pamela Kristan of Dorchester, Massachusetts, who helps people organize their work lives, spent three hour-long sessions and reverie time in between to come up with her business name and tag line, The Practical Matters: Integrating everyday details with inner vision. "A graphic designer and I generated words and phrases out loud," Kristan remembers. "We looked words up in a thesaurus and came up with more words and phrases. 'The Practical Matters' came in a dream between our first and second session, but the tag line took more work. We chose every word carefully. I wanted something that was distinctive but understandable, and I was so tickled with what we came up with that I showed my card to everyone and doubled my income compared with the year before."

Formulate an attention-getting opener

For an ad, press release or catalog page, this means the headline; for a newsletter, the headline for your lead article; for a brochure, the line on the cover panel; for a direct-mail piece, either the envelope copy or the overline before the salutation; for a personal sales letter, your opening line. Advertising experts say that about five times as many people read headlines as read the rest of an ad. As David Ogilvy puts it, "Unless your headline sells your product, you have wasted 90 percent of your money." The same applies to openings for the other sorts of marketing materials: You must provide the reader with a reason to pay attention to your message. The ideal headline must do more than win attention, however, or we'd be able to sell any product whatsoever with the line, "A Better Sex Life in Three Days Flat." It should also have relevance to what's being sold and, as with "Man Hours Overboard" for shippers, carry resonance for its target audience. Consider these popular options:

Questions.
Ilise Benun suggests opening a letter with a question your audience can relate to, like "Have you ever sent out a thousand brochures and gotten no response—and then concluded that marketing doesn't work?" If she's right that most of her readers will nod their heads knowingly at that, they'll read on to discover what she proposes to do about the problem: "I have some other

ideas about how marketing can work without putting so much money, effort and time into it." Yes-or-no questions can backfire, though, when an otherwise eligible prospect can answer "Actually, no" and quit reading. For this reason, direct-mail pro René Gnam changed a headline for a chiropractic organization from "Does your daughter have scoliosis?" to "What would you say to your daughter if she has scoliosis?" to promote higher, more involved readership. Make sure your question has the power to pull your audience over the "Who cares?" barrier.

News.

A news headline arouses interest by revealing something the reader did not know before. "The value of your company may depend on whether you value diversity," reads the headline on a brochure for a diversity implementation program from Hamlin-Fox of Marblehead, Massachusetts. An ad for Pond's Age Defying Complex announces, "Now there's more to looking younger than fading a few wrinkles." A direct-mail letter from John Naisbitt's *Trend Letter* opens with the news-style prediction, "Huge fortunes will soon be made by far-sighted individuals and companies who cash in on the hot trends of tomorrow." Effective publicity releases often offer news in their headline, such as "The Art of the Deal: Pawnshops Offer Art Dealers and Collectors Loans Based on Fine Art," from Empire Loan of Boston, or "Small Employers Can Prevent Most Personnel Problems," from Easy Street Publishing in San Francisco. These sorts of announcements must be followed by real information, not boasts, or they fall into the snake pit of hype (see Chapter 4).

Promises.

Invitations, claims and suggestions come in many varieties:

- "Live the life you dream." (from *Lotus* magazine)

- "Wake up to big bucks!" (from DemoSource of North-Ridge, California)

- "Discover positive career choices and create a life in harmony with your personal goals . . ." (from Guided Growth of Brookline, Massachusetts)

- "Let [graphic of a personal computer with 'A-1' on the screen] rescue you from [drawing of a desk piled high with papers, from behind which comes a hand waving a flag of surrender]." (from A-1 Office Assistance of Albany, New York)

- "Allow me to trash your home." (from Dennis Does Disposal of Stoneham, Massachusetts)

- "For the perfect smile." (from Dental Associates of New England, Brookline, Massachusetts)

Results.
Unlike promises, a results headline takes the form of a testimonial, usually in quotes. For example, above a snapshot of a smiling young African-American man, Fleet Bank ran this quote: " 'I went to a lot of banks and credit unions for a mortgage but they all wanted too much money for closing. Finally, I went to Fleet. And they really worked with me so I could buy a place. My wife's crazy about it.'—Ron Barber, Homeowner." Someone's own words give this apparently true story more immediacy and human interest than we'd get from a more impersonal headline about the same case, such as "How Fleet Bank Helped Ron Barber Buy a Home." The magnetism of first-person storytelling accounts for much of the allure of one of the most famous and profitable ads of all time, headlined "They laughed when I sat down at the piano, but when I started to play!—" Although that classic ad, for a musical correspondence course, featured a fictional protagonist, today's cynical readers respond better to true stories. A results headline like this one for an NEC microprocessor runs the danger of coming off like hype because the quote was apparently composed by the company: "This new computer RISC chip

technology is really something. It took me one day to complete
an assignment that used to take weeks. Now, if you'll excuse
me, I'm off to have dinner with my family."

Create the offer or the action you'd like your reader to take

When advertising and brochures convey promotional
information without making any request of the reader, they
spread awareness that may in the long run contribute to
a sale. You're usually much better off, though, stepping
right up and frankly asking or telling your audience what
to do. Doing so once or twice keeps you in the inoffensive,
cogent "medium sell" range (see Chapter 4). Ryan Consulting in Rockaway, New Jersey, has half a dozen different
brochures describing its services for different market segments, every one of them closing with a straightforward
action line, such as:

- "Discover what our clients have already learned: It
  doesn't have to be expensive to be good. Call us and find
  out for yourself. (201) 625-5804."

- "If you want to find out how video can help you today,
  call us at (201) 625-5804."

- "When you have a story to tell or a product to show,
  think about using video. Then call Ryan Consulting at
  (201) 625-5804."

Two of the brochures go even further by adding a motivating offer:

- "Call Ryan Consulting today for a free consultation.
  (201) 625-5804."

- "For more information, we invite you to view our information video program, 'We Listen.' This seven minute

video demonstrates how four of our clients increased their sales or reduced operating costs using video. Call us for your complimentary copy."

An offer extends a specific incentive for customers or clients to reach for their checkbook or the telephone—in the previous two instances, a free consultation or a free video. The offer can beckon customers for a low-risk trial, a free sample or a special discount, like a two-for-one dinner or a special introductory price of $25 off. Just saying, in effect, "We're here and we'd like your business" is not an offer and won't have much impact, notes communication consultant Steve Glaser of Champaign, Illinois.

Naturally, your prospects must perceive your overture as at least a reasonably good deal. I was flabbergasted to receive a letter from an author/consultant I had written to that read in part: "For $1,200 (approximately one-fourth of what we charge corporate executives), we will help you find your High Performance Pattern through two one-to-two hour phone consultations as well as independent work done by both you and your High Performance consultant." Nowhere in this mailing did the writer mention a single benefit I would receive in exchange for $1,200. Even if corporate executives might spend $5,000 of their company's money on a whim, I have a hard time imagining a self-employed person who would gratefully snatch up such a poorly sold opportunity even at $100. Remember that what feels like a bargain to you must also seem so to your audience. The polar-expedition letter referred to in Chapter 4 sold out its $10,000-per-person trip by explaining and justifying the offer at great length. When your marketing piece asks a prospect to take a significant leap, spell out the payoff in detail.

To add more enticement power to an offer, provide an expiration date or some other reason to act quickly, along with all the information the reader needs to follow through. Here are some effective hurriers:

- "As a bonus for ordering, you'll receive a free digital stopwatch—but only if you act within the next 30 days."

- "Act fast—special price expires August 1!"

- "Good while supplies last."

Don't be afraid to tinker with your offer. Try specially named packages of services ("The Freedom from Pain Program"), and subtle variations, such as "Buy one, get one free" instead of "50 percent off." Test whether more business comes in when you say "Free initial consultation" or "Free half-hour consultation on your case." According to direct marketer René Gnam, minor to moderate tweaking of your offer can alter response by as much as 300 percent.

Add information that motivates readers to act

While your opener grabs your audience's attention and your offer provides a destination toward which to channel that attention, any marketing piece needs a substantive middle as well. Go back to the stuff you collected in step #1 and select and arrange supporting facts so that you lead the reader smoothly from curiosity to action. The "meat" of your sales pitch—details about your product or service, reasons to buy now or to buy from you, competitive advantages, how or where to make the purchase—gets put together now. While this organizing and writing will probably feel like work, it won't be as painful as facing the proverbial blank page, since you already have a framework for the piece. Read or reread the chapter in Part II that corresponds to the format you're creating to make sure you're including your most persuasive ingredients.

Solicit feedback, polish and check your copy

Never finalize a piece without running it by someone who had no hand in creating it. Chapter 14 describes ways to get the most helpful feedback. Send it through the checklists in Chapter 12 to chop off dead verbiage, check for inclusion of vital information and brighten the colors of your words.

Design and execute the piece

See Part IV on how to plan out and consummate an appropriate appearance for the piece.

PART II

◇

FOCUSING ON FORMATS

CHAPTER 6

Informing and Influencing with Brochures, Flyers and Catalogs

Given all the agony and expense you typically put into a brochure, it comes as a cold splash of reality to contemplate how little time prospects actually spend with them. Most people who don't already know you or your company will not actually *read* your brochure. If it's in their hands and the cover prompts at least mild curiosity, they'll unfold it, scan the interior and glance at the back—perhaps six seconds, total. If they have been seeking your product or service, that six might stretch to thirty seconds. Then comes the moment of truth. Do they reach for the phone? Do they pop it in a file or a pile? Do they stick a note on it and route it to a colleague in more urgent need of your offering? Or do they toss it in the trash?

Even if they do throw your brochure away, it made some impression that might very well influence them the next time a communication from you reaches them or they hear someone speaking about your firm. Your task in creating a brochure, then, becomes how to quicken the reader's interest in doing business with you, and even if it's tossed, leave a positive memory with the recipient. That six-to-thirty-second window of opportunity points toward three key strategies for constructing a successful brochure. In what follows, I'll be talking about brochures in their most common incarnation: a printed piece about a company, person or product that usually, though not necessarily, folds twice so that it slips easily into a #10 business envelope. Then I'll discuss related formats that may do the job equally well for some people.

Plan for Scanners

Since you can't assume your audience will be reading your brochure intently, consecutively or completely, you need to organize your message in immediately clear, distinctive chunks. That starts right on the cover. By filling the brochure cover with the name of the company, a person or a product instead of a motivating message, you put the reader in a "So?" or "Who cares!" mode. For cover copy, use one of the headline strategies listed in Chapter 5 instead of an inert name. "An intelligent question creates tension," says communication consultant George Berman, citing the example of a mortgage broker for whom he placed a game board reminiscent of Monopoly on the brochure cover with the "Chance" corner highlighted. The copy read, "Why take a chance with your mortgage?" Since the broker worked with poor credit risks who feared being turned down for a mortgage, this question motivated such folks to read on much more than would something like "XYZ Mortgage Brokers—Serving Yonkers since 1974." Don't waste the motivational opportunity presented by the cover!

Inside, use subheads to convey other parts of your message at a glance. If you have information in paragraphs, keep them short and indent them to make them more inviting. Even better, organize your important points into lists with bullets (those filled-in circles that take the place of asterisks). Position your most important points at the beginning or end of a list or paragraph rather than bury them in the middle. Place your action line and any offer where they'll be noticed, and make your contact information especially easy to find. I don't mean that you must be brief and superficial, only that the reader should be able to catch the main points during the scan and then read more carefully if he or she wants to.

If you've truly made it scannable, you should be able to give the brochure to people who don't know you and have them accurately answer the question, "What do we do and why should someone hire us?" (or "What's the product and why should someone buy it?") after looking at it for just ten seconds. It sounds brutal, I know, but in our over-informationed age, quick communication is essential.

In Content, Emphasize What, Why and How

Most brochure writers put too much emphasis on "who." Not only do they feature the name of their company, product or themselves as if that's a selling point, they bore the reader with too much "me, me, me" or "us, us, us." Even biographical information can be slanted so that it comes across as a benefit, as I'll illustrate shortly. But a company or individual profile shouldn't be the first thing to hit the prospect upon opening the flaps. If you have aroused their interest on the cover, prospects mainly want to know, in this order:

• What can you/your product do for me?
• Why should I hire you/buy this product from you?
• How can I find you/order the product?

Concentrate on answering these questions.

Either in paragraphs, a bulleted list or a series of questions and answers, lay out the features and benefits of the product or the service(s). Remember not to record these details factually, as if for posterity, but to persuade, to sell. So keeping your particular audience in mind, link features with their advantages, as explained in Chapter 3. Or speak to "What can X do for me?" through the problem-solution angle. Since readers will assume you've placed your most important points first, carefully consider the order of items in a list or in paragraphs.

For services, you probably already know that an individual or company biographical profile is essential to help answer the question, "Why should I hire you?" But too many service providers expect objectively recited facts about their history, training and triumphs to attract clients. To heighten the persuasive power of a bio, list all the facts that you want to include, then for each fact pretend you're a prospective client and ask, "What's in that for me?" For example, a chiropractor might have on her list, "Practicing since 1982," which does not clearly state how that is supposed to matter to patients. An improved version might read, "Dr. Linda Gergen has been freeing patients from chronic pain since 1982." The list of an interior decorator might include: "Certificate from the NAIID." Better: "Martin Rossini received a solid grounding in color, design and psychology from the New American Institute of Interior Decorating, where he completed a rigorous certification program in 1991." As in this example, spell out in words any acronyms (like NAIID), abbreviations or lettered degrees (such as LICSW) that your audience might not understand.

If a biographical statement goes on for more than one sentence, do not lead off with the chronological beginning of the person or company's history. Instead, start with a benefit-oriented summary sentence, and then include the details that support it. Here's an excellent illustration, slightly shortened, from a visionary organizational consultant launching a new seminar program:

> Faxon Green has been called "evolution in action" for producing increased market share and profits while assisting leaders in their efforts toward innovation, risk and change. Her consulting began more than 20 years ago with Arthur D. Little. She later became a Teaching Fellow at the Harvard Graduate School of Education in Adult Development Psychology, then Senior VP/GM of

Circadian Technologies, Inc., where she co-created and managed a service-based consulting firm derived from new scientific knowledge of the human brain. Now, as Founder of the Feeling-Mind Institute, she expands her work as a researcher, writer, speaker and corporate consultant with Fortune 500 senior executives, smaller entrepreneurial firms and non-profit organizations.

I have seen service brochures without any bio, usually when the person in question has no particular qualifications aside from happening to be good at what he or she does. Since the absence of a bio will raise doubts in some prospects' minds, fashion a credible if brief statement about what enables you to get results, mentioning relevant factors like hobbies, predilections, experience and personal qualities. Use these intangible, less universally recognized qualifications just like the more tangible or recognized ones. A psychic, for example, might say he "discovered his talent for divining the future at the age of eleven." Laura Lee Lemmon, who creates advertising for the horse industry, engenders credibility without any formal credentials by calling herself "a lifelong horsewoman who also has years of experience as a writer and graphic artist."

In addition to the bio, service providers should include at least two of the following three elements in the brochure to complete their answer to "Why should I hire you?": a client list, testimonials and a statement of philosophy, approach or mission. If you serve individuals, the client list may not apply, but testimonials greatly dramatize your impact on both individuals and companies. Since I elaborate on how to solicit terrific testimonials in Chapter 21, let me just say here that they should enrich your self-portrayal with specific, nuanced praise and back up your credibility by coming from named individuals. The statement of philosophy, approach or mission requires more explanation. Where a service seems especially intangible, like psychotherapy, or where differences among competitors lie mainly in their methods or personal qualities, as with fitness trainers, you may want to include a paragraph or two outlining the assumptions, beliefs and practices characterizing your work. This also applies to products whose value is largely subjective, like fine art. Here are two examples:

1. Sacrifice and its relationship to birth, decay, death and rebirth are conveyed in my work. In my paintings I create a space where living forms experience their own sacrificial process by changing from one state of being to another. The image of a tree is used as a generator of life forms and a valuable link in the process of decay. Alluding to the Biblical references that fire transforms sacrificed living forms into a state of smoky transparent vapors, I use steel wool and a palette knife to transform and remove forms from the canvas or wood panels, leaving ghostlike subtle images of what used to have a heavy and solid presence.
   —Howard Lerner, Artist, Brooklyn, New York

2. *Change is difficult.* Even though life requires us to change, requires us to make transitions—large and small, now or later—few of us feel perfectly at home with the changes life requires us to make. For many of us change will only be undertaken when forced upon us by external circumstances and events seemingly beyond our control. But some people, knowing that change is inevitable, sensing that growth and learning are natural and healthy responses to life, will attempt to be the directors of their own transitions, authors of their own life stories. And the best directors enlist a cast of competent professional supporting players and put them to good use. The best directors listen to their intuition and attend to their Heart's Desires. The best directors know where they're going and enroll others to help them focus and attain their grandest visions.
   —Mark Brady, Ph.D.,
   Counselor for Change, Menlo Park, California

For products available only from one source, answering the question "Why should I buy this from you?" involves dwelling on the advantages of your product vis-à-vis its competition as well as providing reassurance about doing business with you. Make sure that the distinctiveness—even better, uniqueness—of your offering comes through unmistakably and that you've bolstered your credibility as a supplier by extending guarantees and providing believable testimonials. Although I have seen something like a client list used for products (e.g., "In use at:" followed by a list of large organizations), generally you won't add much selling power for a product with either a list of previous buyers or a philosophical statement. If you sell products available from other sources as well, you need to emphasize your fast service, money-back guarantees, knowledgeable staff and other advantages vis-à-vis competing suppliers. Testimonials covering those issues will help you too.

Last, any brochure must clearly answer the question, "How can I contact you?" or "How can I order the product?" Don't bury your contact information inside long paragraphs and force the reader to hunt for it. Set it off from other copy either on the front panel, the bottom of the inside panel, or on the back. If you have a tourist spot, a retail shop or other place of business you want people to travel to, include directions, a sketch map or both. For customers unfamiliar with your area, relate your location to someplace they will know, as in "three blocks from the White House" or "two hours by car or bus from New Orleans." One of my pet peeves is so-called "prestige" addresses like "1 Exeter Plaza" that don't exist on city maps. If you want customers to come by, why compel them to call for directions? Even worse, why make them feel dumb for not knowing how to get there? A brochure I received from *Inc.* magazine sold me on attending a small business exposition, but all it said about the location was "World Trade Center, Boston." Despite having lived in or around Boston since 1987, I did not know where that was, except somewhere off my beaten path. And when I called to find out, the ordertaker could not tell me either the street address or the closest subway stop. How much kinder to print on the brochure, "164 Northern Ave., less than a mile from Route 93," or "Free shuttle bus from South Station on the Red Line," or even, "Directions upon registration"!

Clear ordering instructions are so essential when you're selling products or events from a brochure or catalog that some pros write and design the order form first, before the rest of the copy. But you can go beyond clarity by making an order form a selling tool as well. Instead of simply presenting blanks for the buyer to fill in about the order, reiterate the benefits of your principal products where customers can check off what they want. For example:

___Yes! I'd like to experience a naturally sweatfree summer. Please send me my sampler kit of Preter Naturally Yours products for the incredibly low price of $9.95.

To reinforce your appeal further, restate your customer service policies—guarantee, quick shipping, etc.—on the order form. Such repetition helps not just for the obvious reason that it reminds readers who have seen the information elsewhere on the brochure, but also because some prospects will notice it *only* on the order form. Remember my first point, plan for scanners?

Reinforce Your Professionalism

In that six to thirty seconds a typical prospect spends with your brochure, it has the capability to coax him or her to think better of you than before, make no dent one way or another or eliminate you from serious contention for a business relationship because of how you have presented your copy. For the best response, make sure the brochure is appropriately designed and printed, neat and absolutely free of errors. This should go without saying, but I have seen numerous smudgy brochures, some misaligned or misfolded and many marred by typos and grammatical goofs. According to artists' advocate Caroll Michels, even some painters and sculptors pay shockingly little attention to the aesthetic impression created by their brochures. Similarly, I was startled to note a dangling modifier (see Chapter 13) on the brochure of the highly paid corporate copywriter I alluded to in the preface. "Yes, they should know better," you may be thinking. "But I'm not an artist or a writer, and people won't hold a smudge or a misspelling against me."

True, some people may be as oblivious to sloppiness as you were, but for others, visual or verbal slips consign you to the underworld of incompetents. Whatever credibility you built up with your client list and testimonials crumbles. Remember that unlike a typed letter for a certain occasion or an ad in the newspaper, people take a brochure as having been produced with care and thought, with its details within the company's control. If you're a contractor, no one wants to think you'll let ninety-two-degree angles stand in the place of square corners. Or that you'll fudge numbers in your billing because, after all, you're not an accountant. Because a significant number of people think this way, a careless brochure can do you definite harm. Refer to Part IV to learn how to safeguard the positive impression other aspects of your work might create.

On the other hand, some small details boost that impression greatly. Business owners who have added the three letters "U.S.A." after their city and state report that it enlarges their image to that of a big international operator. Likewise, people who include electronic-mail addresses say it makes them seem up-to-the-minute, especially if their field falls outside the high-tech realm.

Flexible Formats

Several consultants told me that they had no brochure, but used an alternative that allowed them to select relevant information for every prospective client. "I have a folder," said Steve Miller, who calls his Federal Way, Washington, business The Adventure of Trade Shows. "When someone asks for information, I stick in my Executive Profile [questions and answers about what he does], my updated travel schedule and client list. I then add articles I've written and testimonial letters that would specifically pertain to that prospect. I have a library of over 150 articles and over 100 testimonials to choose from. I also have a book, but don't send it to everybody, only the really strong prospects." Similarly, Bill Birnbaum of Costa Mesa, California, wrote, "When a prospective client contacts me, I send him or her a bio, a 'Scope of Services'—five pages on letterhead, which one might argue is actually a brochure—a copy of my book (yup, expensive investment), a few back issues of my newsletter and an audiocassette copy of my recent interview on strategic planning, my specialization."

Advantages of the customized folder option include being able to target prospects to a bull's eye with its contents and being able to furnish more-to-date and pertinent information than with the typical brochure. And by making up the contents to order, you avoid having to pay for and store thousands of preprinted brochures. The folder itself need not involve anything special beyond a color and texture that matches your stationery and your image. However, each folder costs more to mail, and the standard folder size of $9\frac{1}{2}$ by $11\frac{1}{2}$ inches doesn't quite scrunch comfortably into the ordinary file drawer. For high-end services where each prospect represents thousands of dollars in potential billings, they make a suitably formal impression along with a personalized cover letter. You probably want to take this route if you approach relatively few new organizations a month or if you're just starting out and don't feel ready to commit yourself to a set-in-print description of what you do.

In a hybrid of the brochure and folder approaches, some people use a preprinted brochure with relatively permanent copy and matching inserts just a bit smaller than one of the panels. The inserts include that season's price list or event list, or a list of services chosen from among other lists for a particular set of interests.

Flyers and Other Concise Informers

I remember how the major innovation in flyers spread, seemingly at the speed of light, while I was in college. At one time, flyers consisted just of self-contained one-page notices tacked or stapled to bulletin boards. If one caught your eye when you had no pen and paper handy, you faced the choice of either having to come back or tearing down the whole flyer to take with you. Then some brilliant, anonymous person got the idea of adding small cuts perpendicular to the bottom edge, where the item and relevant phone number to call were written for a handy tear-off-and-take-home reminder. "Wow!" I thought. "How convenient!" Then the tear-off method seemed to turn up everywhere. Flyers tended to be white in those days, so another innovation somewhere along the line was advertising cars, rides and typing services on brightly colored paper. Also, national companies started making up advertising posters with a pad of tear-offs pasted to the front, although local companies and individuals didn't seem to use that method. The only other new thing I've noticed in the world of flyers is that some cities have services where you can pay to have yours posted on a certain number of bulletin boards in some geographical area, placed under the windshield wipers of cars in a given location or handed out on busy sidewalks.

Besides distribution on cars or bulletin boards or hand to hand, flyers might form part of a sales packet sent through the mail, be folded in thirds and sent by themselves or sit stacked up at libraries, apartment house lobbies or health clubs. Just about the only method of distribution you must avoid is placing them in postal mailboxes, which will get you into trouble. Simple to design and execute, flyers can provide an incredibly cheap and sometimes very effective way of bringing in immediate customers. Their only risk: antagonizing environmentally conscious citizens who think you are littering public space.

Since your message may come within the prospect's line of sight for just one second or less, your flyer's headline has to be a grabber. Only someone waiting forlornly at a bus stop will read beyond the headline if they're not stopped by your large initial words. A line drawing or sketched illustration usually comes across better in this medium than a photo, though well-chosen words can do the whole selling job on their own. Include sufficient detail about your offering so you get calls only from serious potential buyers. Vicki Clift, a marketing consultant in Santa Maria, California, once helped a client create a flyer to be inserted into a regional business magazine. The client, a high-end deli, wanted to develop a lucrative office catering and delivery business. Included on the flyer was a die-cut, punch-out phone index card with a tab on the top that screamed, LUNCH DELIVERY! "Not only did the flyer pull immediately," Clift says, "it continued to generate new customers long afterward, because people saved the card."

One-page communications recently received a boost from new technology. When fax ownership reached a critical mass in the early 1990s, faxable one-sheets quickly became de rigueur in the speaking industry. Meeting planners mulling over whom to hire for conferences and conventions didn't want to wait for a slick, heavy kit to reach their office—but wanted a photo and written information about topics, previous clientele and fees immediately. Ironically, this sent speakers who'd been spending a lot of money on their materials back to the basics. According to speaker bureau president Anne Miller, a faxable sheet should be one side of $8\frac{1}{2}$ by 11-inch paper that's either black and white or a very pale solid color. "It's OK if the photo doesn't come across perfectly," says Miller, though some people have a so-called "screen" of their black-and-white photo professionally prepared at a print shop or scan it into their computer. "Make sure there are no designs cluttering the background," she adds. See Chapter 11 for additional tips on designing for the fax.

If you can't imagine a selling piece more concise than a flyer, here's an idea. Business cards, slightly modified, can put more than the usual bare facts into the palm of someone else's hand. A business card that unfolds once gives you an inside panel that you can format like a mini-brochure. Even if you stick to the traditional dimensions for a card, what about printing an advertising message on the back? The front of Allan Cohen's card—he publishes the *Working from Home* newsletter—looks conventional, but on the back he has an additional ten impressive lines:

> WHO SHOULD SUBSCRIBE: Consultants, Writers, Accountants, Photographers, Graphic Designers, Architects, Salespeople, Insurance Agents, Bookkeepers, Public Relations Specialists, College and University Business Educators, Computer Programmers/Analysts, Real Estate Agents, Contractors, Government Agencies, Meeting Planners, Secretarial Services, Interior Designers, Freelancers, Artists, Entertainers, Professional Speakers, Financial Brokers, Property Managers, Translators, Trade Show Organizers, Entrepreneurs, Small Business, Part-Timers *and* retirees interested in extra income and wanting to stay active.

The card of Edward Deevy of Deevy Gilligan International in North Andover, Massachusetts, prints the business's tag line across the bottom of the back: ". . . providing consultation and training to organizations on the move." It could have fit onto the front, but people receiving a card do usually glance at the back, even though very few use that space. In Chapter 11 I discuss a few other untraditional locations for selling messages.

The Challenge of Catalogs

Unlike a brochure, which centers on one product or service, a catalog offers a procession of products or events for sale. Usually catalogs arrive by mail in prospects' homes or offices, and enough people like what they find there to have spent more than $51 billion on catalog sales in 1992. "Catalogs have browsers," says Naomi Segal Deitz, a freelance promotion specialist in Portland, Oregon. "The pictures carry a big burden, but the words are very important, too. The copy has to work well with the pictures and be succinct, informative and complete. Never assume a product sells itself—always explain how it meets a need." In other words, benefits matter as much in catalog writing as in other persuasive formats.

Most catalogs feature a consistent voice (see Chapter 4) that puts forth a certain image of the vendor. Since the typical catalog includes dozens to hundreds of items, each with a short description, you need agility and creativity to avoid a formulaic monotone. It's good to start by expressing some enthusiasm for the product and a sense of what it would do for the buyer. Then toss in everything else a prospect needs to know before making a purchase. Once the copy motivates and informs, then you can pass it through the voice test and tweak it here and there to fit the spirit of the entire catalog. Finally you usually need to snip and splice it to the optimal length.

When more than one writer produces copy for a catalog, just one person needs to be in charge of the once-over for tone, says Deitz. That overseer also must make sure that, say, the quill pen on page 16 and the fireplace grill across the way on page 17 aren't both called "magnificent." Even more difficult sometimes, says catalog creator Ava Weintraub, is making competing products in a specialized arena sound different. Weintraub, who founded The Write Stuff catalog of books, audiotapes, scripts and software for writers, had thought she could depend on publishers and producers to furnish appropriate catalog copy, "but their blurbs all seemed to say the same things. They used certain bland words again and again, like 'essential,' 'best' and 'step by step,' and very few actually said anything about what was in the book or what made it different from other books on the topic." Weintraub had to delve into the books and products herself to improve on the copy suppliers gave her.

Besides item descriptions, most catalogs include elements designed to foster a relationship between the company and readers that helps turn the latter into loyal buyers. Foremost among these devices is a letter to readers, usually on the first inside left page and signed by the company president along with his or her photograph. Done well, this letter makes readers feel that a specific someone stands behind the catalog and cares about their satisfaction. The opening letter also conveniently passes company information on to readers, like the fact that you've just cut prices dramatically or instituted a new quick-ship policy. But watch out! The personal touch raises buyers' expectations too. With two different smallish catalogs, I had a question or complaint about a purchase and sent a fax to the person who had lent their signature and identity to the catalog. I felt doubly cheated at receiving no reply to my message, as if someone purporting to be a friend had let me down.

In addition to that just-about-universal letter, catalogs may contain ingredients designed to involve browsers more deeply in the wares of the company. For example, Mind-Ware, a Minneapolis-based catalog of creativity-related products, offered three puzzles scattered throughout its 28-page catalog; readers calling in the correct answers to all three would receive an unspecified gift. The Sounds True catalog out of Boulder, Colorado, offers original Q & A interviews with audiotaped authors, interspersed in 54 pages featuring audiocassettes centered on psychological and spiritual growth. (Some people call this magazine/catalog hybrid a "magalog.") Lyndhurst, New Jersey–based Paper Direct sprinkled its 144-page catalog of predesigned brochure and letterhead papers with "Ted's Tips"—Ted apparently being the company's head honcho and the tips offering valuable advice on topics like how to make your envelopes print well in your laser printer. The Paper Direct catalog also incorporates customer testimonials brilliantly. Placed along the outer edge of right-hand pages, each testimonial includes the customer's color photo, his or her verbal tribute, the customer's name, company name, city and state, a color photo of the piece the customer crafted with Paper Direct supplies, then a bulleted list of the software and paper used. These personified examples inspire readers to imagine themselves ending up with equally great-looking stuff.

So that electrified readers can easily buy, highlight your telephone ordering number on every spread of pages. So that skimmers can more easily find what they might want to buy, every catalog longer than a dozen pages or so should contain either a table of contents up front or an index in back. Page numbers, of course, then become essential. Since the order form needs to be a masterpiece of clarity, I recommend testing it out on four or five people before you finalize it. Ask them to fill it out for a pretend order, and redo it if they say they were confused or they fill it out erroneously. "I've spent as much as a day and a half sorting out what has to go on the order form and what doesn't," says Naomi Segal Deitz. "One manufacturer had different shipping rules for every product line, which made the information impossible to streamline. The company policy necessitated a nightmare of an order form."

As with any other marketing piece, outstanding catalogs only gather a devoted customer base for you when other aspects of your operation, like quality control and customer service, shine too. Yet sometimes a problem that appears disconnected from the catalog, like product returns, actually stems from an insufficiently clear description of the product. For instance, when Ava Weintraub changed the sales copy for a story development software program, she noticed increased sales but also higher returns. "People thought the program would write the story for them, even though the blurb specified they'd end up with just the main character and the plot. People read into things whatever they want to read, so we'll have to head that off at the pass by saying something in the next catalog like, 'It won't write the story for you, but it does the next best thing . . .' Producing a catalog is a constant refinement process, and even when you manage to get everything right, sales drop off after a time. You have to keep the whole mix fresh."

CHAPTER 7

Sales Letters and Direct Mail That Get Results

In February 1994, as I began collecting sample marketing pieces for this book, I happened to be receiving lots of mail. People who requested a booklet I had publicized usually either typed up a standard business letter or scribbled a note that they sent along with their self-addressed stamped envelope. A few people enclosed their brochure, and some of those you have already met in these pages. One man from Trenton, New Jersey, sent a letter, handwritten with distinctly artistic penmanship, that I read, set aside and eventually called him to speak about.

On the letterhead of a company called "The Idea Factory!" Thom Britschge wrote that he had seen my offer, and described his new company by saying, "At TIF! we specialize in creating cartoons to help you communicate. The cartoon is a tremendous communication tool that can have an incredible impact. We can do anything from corporate comic strips for company publications to special fax transmittals to signature character design." After acknowledging the importance of letting the world know what one does, he ended by offering his help and asking me the favor of passing on his information to anyone in Boston who might need his services. To his letter he had paper-clipped two business cards, a photocopy of two sample cartoons and another photocopy of a witty words-and-graphics explanation of what cartoons could do. Even had I not been writing this book, I suspect I would have reread and somehow acted on his very appealing letter.

When I called Britschge, I most wanted to know why he had taken the trouble to craft such a nice-looking personal letter to a stranger. After all, he knew nothing about me other than that I had written a certain booklet. "I used to work at one of the largest architectural firms in the country," Britschge told me, "where everyone did ten times as much work as was necessary because people didn't know what others in the firm were doing. When I went out on my own I decided, whether I'm approaching potential clients, contacting friends or just writing for information, to take the extra time to communicate what I'm all about. Everyone said I had to do bulk mailings to get work, but I didn't think they'd explain me properly." Britschge said that in the six and a half months he'd been in business, he'd written 150 letters similar to the one I'd received, customized for the recipient's industry, with the photocopied samples enclosed. Of the twenty responses he'd gotten, nine turned into business and two of those had already become repeat customers. "It costs almost nothing to do this," he added.

The sincerity and the humanness that came across in Britschge's letter is very powerful stuff. I don't fully understand why, but it cannot be faked, copied, borrowed or mass-produced. As when you smile into someone's eyes while clasping their hand and know you've made true contact, your clear intention and lucid execution can also reach someone and persuade through the miracle of marks on paper. Formulas and slick techniques don't help a letter come alive. Nor does writing experience in and of itself help create an extraordinary letter. Beginners may even have an advantage when they communicate precisely what they want without any hoops and whistles. Seven years ago, I lined up more engagements at writers' conferences from letters than I have any year since then. In my first such attempt, I knew no stale recipes to follow, so I cooked up something fresh. Hannelore Hahn, executive director of the International Women's Writing Guild, called to say, "A lot of people write to ask if they can present at our conference. But there was something in your letter . . . I'd like to have you lead a workshop at Skidmore next summer."

I'm tempted to compare letter writing with music, where those who love the art know the difference between someone who merely gets every note right and someone who speaks to them through the notes. But what we might call "charisma on paper" involves nothing comparable to lessons, practicing or holding your hands just so. Achieving one-to-one magic with letters requires mainly the courage to say it your way and unlearn ineffective habits.

Dare to Write Better Letters

Most people I asked could not recall having received any exceptional letters, ever. "Boring, trite and predictable" is the way communication specialist Ann Bloch of Lenox, Massachusetts, describes the state of American business letters. "Even visually they're stale. Open a typical letter and you see Courier or some other overused typeface and big gray blocks of type, starting with 'Enclosed please find' or some other unnatural phrase. Then you read a little farther and find yourself thinking, 'So what? So what?' If there's nothing in the letter you'd remember an hour later, it's failed." Our standard is so bland, so artificial, that imbuing a letter with real flavor has tremendous impact.

Traditionally, we construct letters like a sandwich. The salutation ("Dear _____:") and the close ("Sincerely,") serve as two slices of white bread. We slather mustard and mayo onto the bread with conventional openers like "I'm writing because . . ." and closing lines like, "I look forward to hearing from you soon." The nutritious, delicious stuff supposedly grabs taste buds from the middle. Must all of those components be present? Consider this letter, slightly shortened, that Ann Bloch wrote me after I interviewed her:

February 13, 1994

Marcia Yudkin
P.O. Box 1310
Boston, MA 02117

YOU ALREADY KNOW, MARCIA

Communications is such a bland term for all the words and sentences we exchange with each other in our quest to be understood. If only we worked as hard at listening, to *understand*.

Your book will fill a needed niche for business owners, judging by the repetitive "filler" correspondence I receive. Of course, I'm immensely flattered by your interview and encouraged by your supportive reaction to my opinions.

Most business writing needs more than "revising"—a boring letter, grammatically correct, is still boring. So I aim higher.

Thanks for seeking my opinion, and urging me to get going on my book. You're a great listener.

KEEP IN TOUCH

Ann Bloch

Bloch took several risks successfully in this letter, which I did remember one hour after reading. First, she dispensed totally with the salutation/close "white bread." Her "YOU ALREADY KNOW, MARCIA" and "KEEP IN TOUCH" surprised me, but seemed appropriate. Second, she eliminated the usual warm-up phrases and started right in with an interesting thought. Third, the whole letter exuded her personality. Instead of a professional mask, I got Ann Bloch. She advocates something else you can't see clearly in the above selection: using words that belong to our vocabulary but that we usually exclude from business letters, like "mollycoddle, "dither" or "panache."

Although I had never seen the letter format Bloch used, soon after I spoke with her I learned a name for it, from communication consultant Steve A. Glaser of Champaign, Illinois: the "billboard" style. Glaser also wrote me a follow-up letter to reinforce his main points. So full of good information and advice was this letter that I've decided to quote it almost in its entirety. See if you discern four additional risks he took.

> February 24, 1994—A great day to improve communications
>
> Glad to oblige, Marcia …
>
> with a sample Billboard-style letter. You'll note that I opened with a salutation that started the first sentence. This technique draws the reader immediately into the body of the letter, so I'm rather fond of it. Still, I might just as well have followed your name with an exclamation point and recast the rest of the sentence to stand alone.
>
> If you're thinking that the Billboard approach gives you lots of freedom in casting your salutation, you're absolutely right. Almost anything that leads promptly and logically into the purpose of the letter is fine. It's best, of course, if you begin on a positive note—even if bad news is to follow. But that's true for any business letter. Personal letters too, for that matter. It's also important that your salutation end with the recipient's name if you know it.
>
> Here I've given you an example of how you can play with the date line. You can tack a very brief thought to the date. Something to reinforce your message or build rapport. It can be quite effective when you have a sales letter making a limited time offer ("Sale lasts just four more days!") or when the date cries out for attention ("News you'll love for

Valentine's Day!"). I had fun with this on the date 8/8/88 and will again on 9/9/99. Feel free to join in!

By now I hope you've noticed how conducive this style is to a friendly approach. Of course, the way you write the body of your letter is critical to friendliness, but a Billboard approach helps you put that extra coating of personality into your correspondence. As a result, it's easier for your letters to build relationships. I'm sure I don't need to stress the value of good relationships in business, whether they're with customers, vendors or associates.

The simplicity, openness and friendliness also do a lot to help you stand out from the pack. That's another important edge for any business person.

But back to the format itself. The letter's layout is the same as a full block style, with everything flush left to create a crisp, modern, friendly but efficient look. *Don't* let your word processor justify your letters so that the right sides line up! It saps friendliness right out of your letter and, unless your word processor provides the subtle and precise spacing controls of a true typesetting program, probably makes it harder to read as well.

As for such things as margins, line lengths and line spacing, keep them comfortable to the eye. Don't be afraid of white space—it makes a letter easier to read. The easier your letters are to read, the better they'll be received.

Finally, strive for a meaningful complimentary close. Banish "Sincerely" forever, along with the salutation "Dear fill-in-the-blank." If nothing else comes to mind, "Thank you!" or "Thanks" usually works fine.

I hope you found this sample useful, Marcia. Please feel free to drop me a line with any questions I left unanswered. In the meantime, I hope you give the Billboard approach a sound trial. Breaking the Dear and Sincerely habit can feel a little odd at first, but I assure you that it will feel stranger to you than to your readers.

Let me know how it works for you!

Illustratively,

Steve A. Glaser

Marcia Yudkin
P.O. Box 1310
Boston, MA 02117

P.S. As you've already figured out, postscripts go here.

By Glaser's four additional risks, I mean these: (1) He added personality to the date; (2) he started the first sentence of his letter as a continuation of his salutation; (3) he included sentence fragments—incomplete sentences; and (4) he put my address at the end, out of the way, rather than at the beginning.

Don't worry if you don't feel ready to go as far as Bloch and Glaser in breaking letter-writing customs. I don't see myself adopting their style of salutation, for instance. After all, if we all started using a new standardized style, it would become just as stale as the old one in time. The most important principles underlying better letters, rather, are these:

1. Start with a grabber or an interesting statement rather than tired old phrases.
2. Concentrate on building rapport, not on sounding "professional."
3. Let your letter have personality, so that it sounds natural and relatively informal.

Since neither Bloch nor Glaser was really trying to sell me something, let's return to a sales letter situation to link these three principles with ideas discussed earlier in the book.

Persuading Your Audience of One

To craft a terrific sales letter, don't write a word until you think through the fundamentals of your sales situation. What specifically do you want the reader to do? What do you know about the reader that will allow you to gain his or her attention? How can you forestall and overcome objections? And how can you motivate the reader to take action? Ponder these questions at least overnight, so that your subconscious mind has the chance to contribute inspiration.

Here's how I did this not long ago. When the time came to approach people about writing a testimonial blurb praising my book *Six Steps to Free Publicity*, I began by trying to learn from my not-so-great prior results. For *He and She Talk*, I had written to six people asking for blurbs. I got the desired action from only one of the six, and his blurb arrived too late to put it on the book cover. At best that was a 16 percent response rate. Three of the six said they were too busy to read the book, and two did not reply at all. Obviously, I somehow had to overcome the busyness problem this time. I also realized that I hadn't felt as if I knew these six people well, and I'd approached them as if I were asking them to do me a big favor. While writing *Six Steps* I'd had the brainstorm that if I included people in the book whom I wanted to write blurbs, they'd have a personal incentive to be curious about the book at blurb time. I'd also feel more comfortable asking them to help me. Of the seventeen people on my blurb list now, I had quoted eight in *Six Steps*. All seventeen, however, were as busy as the people I had asked the previous year. I stirred all these facts into my mental pot and let it simmer.

As often happens with me, the inspiration came in the shower. By the time I was rinsed and dry, all I had to do was run upstairs to my computer and type it out. A few weeks later, my editor sent out seventeen versions of my letter with the bound galleys of *Six Steps*. By 2 p.m. the day after all these people received the package, my editor had already received three blurbs! Within one week, we had received ten altogether, and two more trickled in later. At this 71 percent response rate, my editor crowed; I laughed. I'll let you have a look at what I sent, then offer some observations about why this attempt tore right through the response barrier.

May 1994

Dear _____ :

Normally if you want your name on the cover of a book you have to write the book. Not this time! I'm soliciting testimonials for my forthcoming *Six Steps to Free Publicity*. Bound galleys are enclosed.

If you've never written a book blurb before, it's simple. Skim through the book (you don't need to read every page), figure out who would benefit from the book and why, and say so in two or three pithy sentences. My editor at Plume Books has provided an easy faxable release form for your comments. Fax it to her, not me, so she can pass it on to the cover artist as soon as possible. If you prefer to mail it, send it to her at Plume Books, 375 Hudson St., New York, NY 10014.

I guarantee that you'll find it a fun read. Thanks so much for your help.

Best wishes,

Marcia Yudkin

P.S. Naturally I can't *guarantee* that you'll be on the cover. But if you hurry and everyone else I've written to is a slouch, there you'll be. Why don't you begin by peeking at the manuscript right now?

Why did my sales letter succeed?

1. I had changed my attitude, so that instead of asking a favor, I was offering a credible benefit to my readers.

Approaching people with "Please buy" never works as well as "Here's an opportunity for you to . . ." To boost sales, some of you probably need more work on your self-confidence than your writing.

2. The letter built upon previously established rapport. A relationship with recipients explains why personal letters can blow direct-mail response statistics out of the water. Again, efforts beyond the letter itself pay off.

3. By explaining that they didn't have to read the entire book, I disallowed the escape hatch people had used before. I made the process of writing a blurb sound as easy, quick and unmysterious as possible. Can you make the action you want appear painless and clear?

4. From the first line on, I made the letter fun to read. See Chapter 4 on personalities on paper that help make the sale.

5. The "P.S.," the last thing they would read, gave them a reason to act at once. Remember that if people put the letter down thinking, "I'll do something about this tomorrow," you will have lost at least half your potential response.

In researching for this book, I examined three collections of model sales letters you're supposed to be able to copy for different situations. Because the model letters had to remain generic, I didn't find even one example that rose up off the page to grab the reader by the collar the way a dynamic personal letter can. I'm convinced you'll do much better to make up something nonformulaic that fits you, your target reader and what you have to sell. You'll find one more story about figuring out what to say in a letter in Chapter 20.

The Direct-Mail Courtship

Most of us know how to charm one individual, particularly someone we feel extremely attracted to. But few of us know how to make love to a crowd. It takes a rare talent to cast a spell over a large number of people at the same time, so that each one feels personally communicated to. But if it's difficult in a concert hall or stadium, imagine trying to be Sinatra or Streisand on paper! Using only written words, how can you speak personally to hundreds, thousands or even hundreds of thousands at once? That's the challenge of direct mail.

You might get a different impression from much of what's written by direct-mail specialists. Intimidating terminology abounds: "Bounce-backs," "lift letters," "traffic builders," "Johnson boxes," "conversion rates." Jargon has proliferated partly because elements of large-scale direct mail can be quantified, measured, tested and analyzed like no other form of marketing in this book. Practitioners have accordingly acquired vast stores of rules about what works better than what. (See Chapter 12 for some of these.) Yet most of the accumulated wisdom boils down to one basic principle: The more you create an illusion of pertinent one-to-one communication, the more powerfully your mass mailing persuades.

After all, why don't big companies simply stick their magazine ads into an envelope and send them to potential customers? We'd be puzzled and perhaps even insulted. We've come to expect letters in our mailbox because we respond to them. Though few of us are fooled that computer-generated missives were written personally to us, we enjoy personalization nevertheless. We prefer "Dear Gerry Glynn" (if that's our name) to "Dear Customer" or "Dear Madam." Even if the letter comes from a large corporation, we expect the signature of a named person. We respond better to a typewriter-style font with underlining than to italics and prefer ragged right margins to the squared-up sides of printed matter. We'd rather see a postage stamp than a box saying "bulk mail." We love a "P.S." and read it more than any other part of an impersonal letter. And apparently handwritten marginal notes in red and blue or on a self-stick note get our attention too.

The differences between the usual direct-mail package and a genuinely one-to-one letter begin with the envelope. If the mail piece looks at all mass-produced, direct mailers need something special to assure that the envelope gets opened. A message on the front and sometimes the back of the envelope that trumpets a benefit the recipient will learn more about inside may do the trick. Sometimes the envelope's "teaser" message provokes curiosity, as with a mailing I received—and opened—whose envelope copy began, "Money secrets: What your bank doesn't want you to know." To make recipients unsure about whether they can safely toss away a piece without reading, other envelopes use an enigmatic return address or none at all.

The letter inside the direct-mail envelope often contains something that derives from ads rather than personal correspondence: a headline. It may look like a headline, in larger, bolder type than the rest of the letter, or it may be boxed in or set off by asterisks. (Pros call the last of these options a "Johnson box.") Some effective letter headlines from my files include "How to Market Like a Millionaire on a Poor Man's Budget" and "Huge fortunes will soon be made by far-sighted individuals and companies who cash in on the hot trends of tomorrow. You can be one of them. . . ." The headline or boxed message, which precedes the salutation, serves to motivate you to read this missive from a stranger. Unless the letter is customized to read "Dear Vera," or whatever your name is, it reads "Dear Friend," "Dear Colleague," or "Dear Deep-sea Diver."

Direct-mail letters tend to be longer than most personal letters we receive. Designed to produce action, they grab the reader's attention and lead him or her through a highly orchestrated sales pitch that explains every benefit of the offer and attempts to defuse every possible doubt or objection to the sale. Of thirty-four letters labeled "classics" in *The Greatest Direct Mail Sales Letters of All Time*, half took up one or two pages, while half took up three to seven pages. "There's no such thing as a letter which is too long—just one that is too boring," says Richard Hodgson, editor of the collection. "There have been successful direct mail letters which are six, eight, ten and even twenty pages long. The role of a sales letter is to answer all the questions the prospect needs to have answered before he or she is willing to take the action requested. If it takes multiple pages to answer the questions, the letter can keep rolling until the last question has been answered." Other experts report that when they pit long letters against short ones for the same offer, the longer ones almost always win more orders. But what about our supposed short attention spans? Do busy people really read four- or seven-page letters? "Actually, I don't care if they read the whole thing," replies direct-mail copywriter Herschell Gordon Lewis. "Length makes a psychological impact. It inspires confidence."

Along with the main letter, signed by a president, publisher or manager of the sending company, recipients frequently find a second letter from another individual, folded over or sealed in an inner envelope bearing the legend, "Open this letter only if you have decided not to respond." According to direct marketing pioneer Bob Stone, this so-called "lift letter" usually increases response 10 percent or more by allowing the marketer to present additional clincher arguments. The traditional package generally also contains an order form and business reply envelope, as well as, sometimes, various "involvement devices" that readers are supposed to rub off or stick onto the order form. A carefully written, easy-to-follow order form boosts response too.

If I've made direct mail sound like a lot of trouble and expense, it can indeed represent a complicated, costly investment. Experienced direct-mail copywriters receive $5,000 and up to write complete packages, not including the cost of printing, list rental, preparation of the mailing and postage. But because this medium comes closer to a science than anything else in marketing, experts can also help you test copy and lists and project realistic returns on your investment. For instance, most warn not to expect more than one-half of one percent to one percent to respond to a "cold" mailing, where recipients do not know you. A good offer to your own customer list usually pulls better than that.

Should you venture into direct mail if you lack the money, time and patience to assemble the kind of complete package the professionals use? So long as you can put together a dynamite letter with a strong offer, yes. As with any great sales letter, start with a passionate desire to communicate what you're able to do for your audience. Craft a grabber of a headline or opening line, explain your offer and continue explaining everything the reader needs to know in order to be willing and able to grab onto it. Then study how other direct-mail letters are constructed and tinker with your letter until it flows smoothly and persuasively. Add an order form or clear instructions on the action you wish recipients to take, and send it out to several hundred people as a test. Remember that the criterion for the test's success is profitability. For example, while working on this book, I got an idea for a packaged consulting offer for which I had a perfect list—220 people who had attended a regional conference for professional speakers. Before I went ahead to write the letter, I calculated that I would turn a profit on the offer with even one positive response. Four orders materialized from the mailing, and four more people wrote or called for additional information. Although the whole project had proved a clear success, the very same rate of response for a cheaper service or product might just have broken even.

Note that I did not include a postage-paid reply envelope, a second color or a personalized salutation—all said to boost results, but expensive—in this profitable mailing. More proof that a well-executed simple approach can work comes from retired copywriter Howard Fisher of Dallas, who used to pull in business with one-page pieces on his business stationery that didn't even use the format of a letter. My favorite of four samples that he sent me runs as follows:

I MAY BE THE BEST BARGAIN IN DALLAS

That's what my financial advisor tells me. But he says not enough people <u>know</u> that. I'm too low-key, he says. I hide my light under a bushel, he says. So please remember: I'm a

Writer/Producer/Director/Announcer/Narrator/Thinker

Not necessarily in that order. I've done work (writing, production, consultation, talent) for 27 of the top 100 corporations in Dallas/Fort Worth. Eight of the top 10. I've helped several agencies pitch—and win—new business.

Recently, an out-of-town agency called; they were short on staff and needed help writing a year's campaign for a major account. A week (and two booklets, three TV spots, three consumer print ads, numerous headlines and trade ad ideas) later, the client said, "GOOD STUFF!"

I also function as broadcast/film producer for agencies and companies that are comfortable in print but uncomfortable in broadcast, film and audio-visual. Or staff is temporarily clobbered or on vacation. I understand agency and client points of stress. I also know what the dollars mean.

My financial advisor tells me that there are not many people like me—who are as <u>good</u>, or <u>qualified</u>, or <u>experienced</u>. He also tells me that since I do so many things so well, I may be the best bargain in Dallas—but bashful. That's why, he says, some of my friendly competitors who may not be as good are out-hustling me. If I were more aggressive, he says, I'd be rich and famous—like him.

Come to think of it, I must be doing something right. Otherwise I wouldn't need a financial advisor.

New Business/Marketing Proposals.
Advertising Campaigns and Copy.
Radio. Television. Films.
A/V Concepts and Scripts.

To me, this piece is so charming that I would do as many of Fisher's 1,000 to 1,500 recipients tended to do—file it and call him when I had something he might be able to help out with. Fisher recalls, "Only rarely would someone call and say, 'Hey, I got your letter. Come right over, I've got a job for you!' But months later, years later, I'd get calls—direct results of those Chinese water torture pieces."

Keep in mind that direct mail encompasses such flyers as well as coupons, announcements and postcards. So long as you have a decent mailing list, a targeted mailing with a benefit-rich offer, chock-full of memorable personality, should help keep business flowing your way.

CHAPTER 8

Newsletters and Publicity Materials That Build Your Reputation

Wouldn't it be great, I've heard people sigh, to be able to quit this damned marketing because people call all the time and say, "You don't know me, but I think you're the one who can solve my problem"? The dream of coasting on reputation alone becomes real for all too few businesspeople—even Oprah Winfrey, one of the richest and most prominent performers in America, still runs ads for her programs. But two strategies help build and maintain a reputation, and produce recognition and credibility out of proportion to the expense and effort involved. If you want to be viewed as an expert, the information in your advertising, brochures and direct mail gets discounted to a great extent because you're tooting your own horn. Both promotional newsletters and media publicity offer the opportunity to bypass the "I said so" onus.

Squarely in the "soft-sell" range of the facts-to-hype continuum (see Chapter 4), promotional newsletters and media publicity feel especially comfortable for professionals and others who shrink from selling that's too pushy. Let's start with newsletters, a marketing tool popular with an increasing number of businesses that do not always use them well.

Promotional Newsletters: The What, How and to Whom

Most promotional newsletters act like subscription periodicals in arriving regularly in the mail of a consistent group of readers. They also often look like subscription newsletters in having a nameplate or title banner across the top of the first page in an 11 by 17-inch size folded to 8½ by 11 inches, though they can take up just two sides of an 8½ by 11-inch sheet or use a smaller format. Unlike a subscription periodical, however, readers do not pay for or even necessarily request to receive it. In its purest form, a promotional newsletter contains information designed to be useful to a business's clientele and goes out to that clientele as a free service of the business. Smart companies also send their newsletters to prospective customers and the media.

Promotional newsletters vary greatly in their complexity. The simplest I've seen calls itself the *Happy Dog Newsletter* and exists on a 4¼ by 5½-inch postcard. Into that minuscule space, Wag & Wash, a dog-care service in St. Louis, Missouri, crams eight short items of interest to dog owners and an offer of $1 off if patrons bring in the newsletter on their next visit. *Personal Excellence*, from executive coach Nancy Yahanda of Boston, is considerably more elegant and elaborate, consisting of eight artistically designed pages of substantive articles, including a lead piece called "The Darker Side of Excellence," a book review and a guest column on transforming organizations.

Whatever length and design you choose, the more you include valuable information that shows off your expertise, the more your newsletter achieves these marketing goals:

1. It induces potential customers to spend more time in the virtual presence of your company than the seconds with which they speed through and perhaps toss away a typical brochure, ad or direct-mail piece. When prospects

feel they need to know you before they buy, the extra time builds your familiarity.

2. It gives clients something more substantive to save than a business card. The more they hang on to and refer back to your publication, the more likely they are to call you when they need your services. Besides including advice of lasting worth, you can encourage recipients to keep their issues by punching three holes in the margin or even providing customized binders.

3. It helps clients understand the range and depth of your capabilities. Someone who inquired about or bought just one product or service becomes exposed to other proficiencies of your company. Feature articles, explained below, can present your offerings in an especially engaging way not available in other kinds of promotional pieces.

4. For products and services whose benefits aren't easily fathomed, success stories, feature stories and advice columns allow other prospects to draw the conclusion that they may need to make a certain purchase too. For example, I provide editorial and marketing feedback to writers before they approach literary agents or magazine or book editors. But only a very small proportion of those who could benefit from that service understand that it could save them enough time, money and frustration to more than offset the cost. In a newsletter I could drive the point home through an interview with an agent or editor or a profile of a soon-to-be-published client for whom my advice clearly made a difference.

5. It positions you as a resource for your customer base rather than someone constantly asking for more business. Upon arriving in clients' mailboxes, the newsletter reminds them of your professional expertise in a classier way than a circular or sales letter.

On whether newsletters accomplished the above purposes better for existing clients than prospects, I encountered disagreement. According to public relations practitioner Mike Bayer, newsletters don't lure new clients anywhere as well as they help you keep existing clients and sell them additional services. "Clients are more inclined than nonclients to read the newsletter, particularly when you base the contents on client surveys that reveal the information that they want most." Desktop publisher and designer Louise Kursmark, however, got a boost of business from new clients when she "cold-sent" the first issue of her newsletter to prospects. Kursmark studied the street-by-street listings in the crisscross directory of her town of Reading, Massachusetts, keeping an eye out for bold-faced business numbers in what she knew were residential neighborhoods. She sent these five or six dozen presumably home-based businesses her newsletter and received immediate work from a pediatric dentist and two others that paid for her first three issues. Similarly, when Steve Glaser started his communication consulting business, he sent his two-sided $8^1/_2$ by 11-inch newsletter to prospects with excellent results. Now that he's more established, he sends it just to clients and those who've inquired about his services.

"My newsletter functions as a primary sales tool, since it demonstrates that I know my stuff," says Glaser. "Each issue includes one article in which I pontificate on a problem or aspect of communication, plus tips and how to get in touch with us. Usually I get an increase in calls the week after I send out an issue, and many of those people tell me straight out they decided to send me business because of something I wrote in the newsletter." Glaser's comments illuminate the particular strength of this promotional tool: to use a favorite phrase of writing teachers, newsletters allow you to show rather than tell. That is, instead of merely saying, "I can handle your negotiations diplomatically," a newsletter article demonstrates the ability by detailing methods of handling negotiations diplomatically. Likewise, an article describing how your investment product enabled a couple to retire early despite a modest income holds much more power than either claims to that effect or a two-sentence testimonial from the couple.

Plotting for Success

For best results from a promotional newsletter, you must walk a tightrope with your eyes fixed on the needs and interests of your market. If you use the newsletter format mainly to brag or peddle your stuff, you tumble into the swamp of "just a differently packaged sales pitch." You could provide precious and pertinent advice, though, without carefully selecting and slanting it to show off your firm to advantage. Then you'd get safely to the other side, but without doing much for your marketing objectives. Other dangerous traps include failing to keep to a schedule and undermining instead of bolstering your professional image through a poor verbal or visual execution. Success starts, then, with careful planning for a length, frequency and expense that you absolutely know you can stick with. (Tell readers your newsletter comes out "irregularly" or "approximately X times per year" only if you want to appear flighty or undependable.) Then, keeping your audience in mind, brainstorm a list of the general kinds of contents that might induce them to read and save the newsletter. Consider, for example, the candidates on this checklist:

Advice articles.
An accountant might run articles on midyear tax-saving strategies or record-keeping tips that rescue you at audit time. A car repair shop would provide value in a piece on how to interpret strange noises coming from the car while driving. A sculptor would win patrons' attention with tips for insuring art or keeping outdoor pieces safe from vandals. Guest contributors can lighten your writing burden and enhance your image as a well-networked resource.

Client/customer profiles.

Stories about real people bring dry information to life, says copywriter Alice Crane Kovler, who dramatized home equity loans for a credit union newsletter with a profile of the first family that signed up. If you manufacture software, relieve technical tedium with a piece describing how a small business sailed to success using your program. When you regularly include such stories, customers can begin to feel part of your community rather than having a buying relationship only with you.

Perspective articles.

Rather than offering advice, this kind of essay is a "think piece" on an issue of importance to a practitioner's clientele. For instance, a hypnotherapist might offer some reflections on the strange and wonderful healing powers of the mind.

List of new clients.

Brody Communications of Elkins Park, Pennsylvania, puts the proper soft-sell tone on this by heading its list "Welcome to Our New Clients." I think this works best as an occasional rather than regular feature.

Questions and answers.

Yes, you can become the "Ann Landers" of your field! In the beginning, you'll have to make up questions to answer, but when readers write or call with questions you'll know the newsletter has gotten them involved. Avoid questions that are so basic as to be boring or so specific that they don't apply to most of your audience.

Letter from the president.

Written as a letter, often signed, and often headed by a photo, this carries a message directly from the business owner to customers. Keep it friendly, not pompous, and substantive, not composed of fluff.

News and announcements about your business.

Make sure these items meet the "What's in It for Me?" test. If you've moved, don't give a lengthy explanation but emphasize "here's how to find us now." When you add new staff, use it as an opportunity to highlight the fact that you can now get orders out faster and better serve Spanish-speaking clients. According to newsletter expert Elaine Floyd, when customers have invested heavily in your high-tech product, it's easy to slant news about your product as news for them—they already feel a stake in its technological advances.

News for your market.

Here you offer professional updates and new developments that affect your readers and that they probably have not yet heard about. For instance, a pediatrician might cite a study showing that Lyme disease is often misdiagnosed; a furniture maker might pass on word about a new line of nontoxic cleaning and polishing products.

Interactive features.

At one San Francisco law firm, reports Mike Bayer, the newsletter had great success with a quiz on how to evaluate OSHA safety factors. "People had to call to get the answers faxed. That issue got spread around to other CEOs and resulted in new clients coming in," Bayer says. In Chapter 26 I've included a source for customized crossword puzzles. To get people to eagerly await the arrival of your newsletter, you could run a relevant puzzle, brain teaser or trivia question with the answer held back for the following issue.

Fillers and sidebars.

Boxed information items, called "sidebars" by journalists, fit the "quick read" nature of a newsletter especially well. Whether they illustrate a longer article with a list or graph or stand on their own, they get high readership.

Photos or art.

With photos, always include a caption carrying a promotional message. For example, instead of writing simply "Jennifer Smith" to identify your pictured client, write "Jennifer Smith holding up the orders that poured in after she used 'Marketing Magic.' " Captions get very high readership too. Commercial "clip art" programs furnish graphics, drawings and cartoons that you can buy inexpensively and customize for your newsletter.

Pull quotes.

If you're not including photos or illustrations, relieve visual monotony with extracts from your articles set off in large type.

Special offers.

You can indeed include discount coupons, a plug for a new product, a calendar of upcoming seminars or an announcement of a contest, so long as these don't overpower the newsletter's informational content. They're best isolated in a box or on a differently colored insert.

Coming attractions for the newsletter.

As in a magazine, you can announce the next issue's highlights to create a sense of continuity and anticipation.

Once you decide on the mix for a typical issue, you're ready to settle the newsletter's design. It doesn't cost much to have a competent designer draw up an imaginative, appropriate and visually coherent template for your newsletter. If you have and can use a desktop publishing program, you need pay the designer only once. You assemble particular issues yourself by fitting in the new contents on pages that are preset in the newsletter's style. Make sure the template includes a name banner, a place for the date or issue number, a masthead or box for the vital information about your company as publisher, big catchy headlines and, if the newsletter contains more than two pages, a place on page 1 for "in this issue" highlights. Decide ahead of time whether you're going to include photos, cartoons or illustrations, since you'll want to keep the look consistent from issue to issue. See Chapter 17 for additional suggestions on optimizing your work with a designer.

When you're ready to plan a specific issue, decide on particular topics from the point of view of their promotional value. Feature the service that needs more exposure rather than the one that practically sells itself. Turn your spotlight on seasonal needs. And instead of merely announcing a piece of news, consider how you can put it in some context that tempts readers to send you business. For example, here's a nugget I could have included in a newsletter in the winter of 1994:

> UNSLANTED: In March, two of my books, *Smart Speaking* and *He and She Talk*, were featured on *The Oprah Winfrey Show*.

I could use this fact as an opportunity to discuss my consulting services for those writing and hoping to publish books.

> SLANT #1: Clients often ask me if they should seek out large or small publishers. In February I had the opportunity to witness one of the advantages of the big, established operations. With only three days' notice, my coauthor of *Smart Speaking* and *He and She Talk*, Laurie Schloff, taped a segment for *The Oprah Winfrey Show*. Our publisher, Plume Books, immediately set in motion a set of procedures to produce more books, notify the sales representatives and get copies into bookstores by the time the show aired three weeks later. With small publishers you'll never feel like you're lost in a big lineup, but they might not be equipped to fully exploit such good fortune and get books into the stores in time.

Or I could put it in the context of my coaching for those seeking media attention.

SLANT #2: When you send your flotilla of press releases off to the media, you can't help but feel disappointed when weeks crawl by and no one calls. But don't give up hope, and don't give up trying. Sometimes you've done everything right, and it just takes the media a very long time to find a slot exactly right for you. In February the coauthor of my books *Smart Speaking* and *He and She Talk*, Laurie Schloff, received an invitation to appear on *The Oprah Winfrey Show—three years* after they received our information about *Smart Speaking*! Please be sure to let me know about your "hits" with the media, whether delayed or immediate.

Newsletter writing style is crisp and quick. Get straight to the point, and take special care to keep paragraphs short. You can end articles with a low-key call for action—"For more information on how you . . . , call . . ."—so long as that doesn't become a monotonous refrain. Pay special attention to fact checking and proofreading (see Chapter 18), since you want the newsletter to enhance your reputation rather than sabotage it.

Other Newsletter Options

Should you charge for your newsletter? If you're planning to fill it with valuable information, you may figure that's a logical step either to begin with or work toward. But as Bill Birnbaum, a strategic planning consultant in Costa Mesa, California, learned, that puts you in an entirely new business—or two or three or four. Propelled by meeting a guy who had one thousand subscribers for a $195 newsletter, he launched *Business Strategies Newsletter* in July 1984. "I now found myself in the editorial business—having to write articles; in the publishing business—having to take a master down to the printer; in the mail order business—trying to rustle up subscribers; and in the fulfillment business—making sure each subscriber got his or her next issue. On top of this, I was still running my consulting business. I was awfully busy." When the renewal rate for his lower-than-projected subscription base proved disappointing, Birnbaum turned it into a promotional newsletter and began breathing more easily. Instead of scrambling to satisfy subscribers who wanted information they hadn't read about in *Business Week*, he could write about the issues that come up over and over again in his consulting practice. And, as a marketing vehicle, it keeps clients informed about his capabilities and viewpoint.

But others don't mind those multiple roles. Ilise Benun started distributing her newsletter, *The Art of Self-Promotion*, for free, but two years later, after enthusiastic feedback, began soliciting subscriptions. She continues to hand out a lot of free issues, since the newsletter also takes the place of a brochure. Similarly, artists' advocate Caroll Michels began a ten-times-per-year newsletter for which she now charges clients a nominal fee. A simple two-page typewritten list of resources and contacts for artists, it takes just a few hours to assemble. Though Michels concentrates on making sure she screens out scams for her subscribers, she realizes she can also use it to remind clients of what she can do for them. "When I mentioned something about phone consultations, I got more appointments. I forgot that people forget what I do," she says.

If you like the promotional possibilities of a newsletter but don't have the time or inclination to produce it yourself, you have two options. One, you can hire a freelancer to produce it for you. See Chapter 25 for tips on farming out such work. Two, you can buy customized copies of a generic newsletter for your industry to send out to your best clients. The easiest way to find these newsletter producers is through your industry association. "You're best off working with the provider to insert a few articles from you and use their stuff as filler," advises Elaine Floyd. "People can sense if you're just slapping your name on something packaged." And unless the packaging deal includes some sort of geographic exclusivity, this option could backfire. Imagine the impact on your reputation when a prospect receives two copies of substantially the same newsletter—one with your firm's name on it and the other branded with the identity of a competitor.

Soft-Sell to the Media: the Publicity Route

Nothing beats media publicity when you want to create a stir about a product or add a halo of legitimacy to your services. People who might otherwise doubt claims coming from you are more likely to trust, respect and pursue what they read or hear about in the nonadvertising sections of newspapers and magazines, radio and television. This occurs because people know that no one can buy editorial coverage. But relatively few understand how a creative, professional presentation on paper can win that opportunity for you no matter how obscure you've been.

Sam Caine, president of IDR Technology, Inc., in Atlanta, Georgia, mounted a publicity campaign in 1993 for Life-Fax, a new product designed to help travelers in need of emergency medical help. For no more than the cost of paper, time and postage to about 150 media outlets, Life-Fax achieved mentions in *Harper's Bazaar*, *Conde Nast Traveler*, the *Miami Herald* and the *Atlanta Journal*, with other media passing on the information after reading it here or there. As a result, IDR received more than one thousand phone calls, leading to several hundred sales and numerous valuable contacts. Here is one of the press releases that helped launch his product:

For: IDR Technology, Inc., P.O. Box 501136, Atlanta, Georgia 31150
Contact: Charles McKay/ Julie Abrams, 404-552-4140

FOR IMMEDIATE RELEASE

**LIFE-FAX CARD PROTECTS TRAVELERS
AND MOTORISTS,
ASSISTS HOSPITAL PERSONNEL IN EMERGENCY**

ATLANTA, GA, April 26, 1993—By making extensive and up-to-date personal and medical data available to hospitals and emergency personnel, Instant Data Retrieval (IDR) Technology, Incorporated's Life-Fax Emergency Response Card helps protect travelers and motorists if they are involved in an accident or any other type of medical emergency. The immediate availability of vital medical and personal data assists emergency room personnel in quickly and properly treating patients.

According to IDR's President, Samuel Caine, "Over 1.5 million people are injured and 40,000 people are killed every year in auto accidents alone. Unfortunately, most do not prepare for these life-threatening emergencies, and that delays notification of loved ones, and sometimes delays proper medical treatment. Life-Fax aids people if they are involved in an emergency. It is essential for travelers, family members, people with any type of medical condition and anyone taking any type of medication."

When a Life-Fax member is in need of emergency medical attention, hospital personnel simply call a 24-hour, toll-free number and enter their fax number. Within seconds, vital information on the card-holder, such as emergency contacts, complete medical history, current prescriptions, insurance information, organ donor information and an actual copy of their living will is sent by fax to the hospital, saving valuable time.

Life-Fax members can update their information as often as needed with just a phone call. Members also receive free semi-annual newsletters containing information such as consumer tips, travel, health and well-being information and personal financial planning information.

The Life-Fax Emergency Response Card is only $29 for a single one-year membership, and as low as $22 per member for a family of four, and is available directly from Life-Fax by calling 1-800-487-0329.

For further information regarding the Life-Fax Emergency Response Card or sample cards, please contact Charles McKay or Julie Abrams at 404-552-4140.

Note that the tone of the release is objective, with the single selling adjective ("essential") occurring within a quote attributed to Caine. The release worked because it answered the key question of any media gatekeeper: Why would our readers (or listeners or viewers) be interested in this now? Concisely but thoroughly it explained specific benefits of the new product to specified and even quantified groups of people. The magazines and newspapers that published the information thus understood almost at a glance that this was something new and beneficial for their audience, not an advertisement in disguise.

In contrast to Life-Fax, whose newsworthiness was fairly obvious, you may have to reach for your ingenuity to come up with an angle on your business that would meet the media's criteria for news. Sometimes you succeed in catching their attention with something very tangential to the way you normally present what you do. Use this checklist of tried-and-tested ideas:

1. *Announce something new.* Besides releasing a new product, this might include winning an award or contract, posting record profits, relocating the company, or adding personnel or services. Many trade magazines and local newspapers are happy to proclaim minor changes to their public for you. The more momentous the "new" part, the greater your chance of major media coverage.

2. *Set your business apart as distinctive.* Personal trainer Jeff Rutstein of Boston landed in the pages of the *Boston Globe, Vibrant Life, Club Business International* and *Sober Times* by explaining in his press release that he stressed the psychological along with the physical benefits of exercise for those recovering from drug or alcohol abuse. The resulting articles made a big deal of the fact that no one besides Rutstein was doing this.

3. *Describe an upcoming event the media can latch on to.*

Even if the event is as mundane as a free talk at the public library, it transforms your business from something that there's no more reason to cover this week than next to something relevant right now. An unusual or especially colorful event, like an attempt to beat something in the *Guinness Book of World Records*, usually proves irresistible to the media.

4. *Piggyback on what's in the news now.* As the Tonya Harding/Nancy Kerrigan saga stretched on for weeks, a real estate agent on Long Island situated close to the intersection of Harding Road and Kerrigan Road decided to make hay out of the connection. If your food packaging company had been supplying rations to the military since World War II, the fiftieth anniversary of D-Day might have been an excellent time to remind the media of your existence.

5. *Celebrate a special day, week or month.* In 1993, I sent out announcements of the first annual No Resolutions Day on December 31, and received coverage that included mention of my creativity newsletter in the Spokane *Spokesman-Review* and the *Boston Herald* and on the New England Cable News. You only need to fill out a simple form to get your special day, week or month listed in *Chase's Annual Events*, the major reference for such things.

6. *Entangle your offerings in the timeliness of a larger trend.* Tell the media why increased sales of your eggs forecast a steadily improving economy. Show how your tours satisfy the yearning of city folks for contact with primeval nature. Explain how you're implementing the dream of the "paperless office."

7. *Be funny, dramatic or surprising.* These "human interest" factors lure the media because they appeal to readers, listeners and viewers. Sometimes even marginally quirky businesses get wide coverage because some publication or program has extra space or time to fill.

Newsweek once filled an entire column with "Gee whiz, here's a whole newsletter about copy editing!"

8. *Can you provide useful tips for a certain audience?* This approach works especially well for service providers. With a strong benefit-oriented headline, your press release can list three to five tips on a subject of importance to your market. Some media outlets will use the release almost as you wrote it, some will file it until they're doing something on that topic and others, convinced of your expertise, will call you for an on-air interview.

In writing up and formatting your release, you'd do well to use the Life-Fax one as a model. If not printing the release on your company stationery, begin with a "for" line indicating the source of the information. The next line provides the name and phone number of the person you've designated to furnish further details to the media. Then comes the headline, which can take up to three lines to present the newsworthy angle of the release. Start your first paragraph with a newspaper-style dateline, and then fill it with the main facts about your angle. The second paragraph is a good place to bring the facts to life or put them in perspective with a quote from a named person. Use the remaining space for further explanations, and end with the practical how-to-get-in-touch or where-to-go details. Keep the release to one page if possible, two pages at the most.

After checking it over to make sure you have a newsworthy angle, have kept your writing in the soft-sell range (see Chapter 4) and have eliminated typos and wordiness (see Chapter 13), you're ready to send it off. Chapter 26 lists several reference books you can find in most public libraries that contain up-to-date names, addresses and fax numbers for magazines, newspapers, newsletters, radio and TV shows and the wire services. For radio and TV you'll be approaching show *producers*, not hosts. As you select recipients for your press releases, remember to zero in on publications and programs that reach the market for your goods and services. In other words, if you produce memory expansion boards, forget *Donahue* and think *Info World*. When Mike Van Horn, director of The Business Group in San Rafael, California, wanted to spread awareness of his coaching groups throughout the San Francisco Bay Area, he successfully targeted business editors of just the newspapers in that geographical area.

Try an alternative to the press release when your purpose is so precise that you can isolate a few media outlets you want to concentrate on. A "pitch letter" uses a regular business-letter format to set out your case that that specific outlet's readers, listeners or viewers would benefit from learning about you. Herman Holtz recalls writing such a letter years ago to the business-news reporter of the Washington *Star* explaining that he helped clients win government contracts, in contrast to the generalized help offered by most marketing consultants. After emphasizing how uncommon his service was, he said he'd be glad to be interviewed. The reporter got his editor's OK and ran a quarter-page story and photo on the business page of the *Star*. "Afterward," he says, "several more newspaper stories and magazine articles were spun off by other writers who called on me, and I appeared on the TV news also." Holtz adds, "I think others can do what I did quite easily, by showing the other party how it is in his or her interest to do the story."

Multiplying Your Media Impact

As Holtz's story shows, one key media story can snowball into an avalanche of exposure. But even if that doesn't happen spontaneously, you can take steps to stretch your fifteen minutes in the spotlight into a lasting glow of fame. Collect and file the originals of any print articles about you and clip and paste them up nicely, with the date and publication name indicated and neighboring advertisements cut away. Send the reprints to key clients with a self-stick personal note, and include them in a folder when corresponding with prospects. Begin a media list of your appearances in print and on the air, and include that along with clippings, a photo, your brochure and your business card when someone requests your "press kit."

Most importantly, one media coup will beget others if you take the trouble to nurture relationships with media representatives. Have a helpful attitude when reporters call, and get back to them promptly! Ask producers assembling a panel if they'd like suggestions of other experts. Send or fax them additional information about your area of expertise whether they ask for it or not. Your goal: to have them think of you the next time they work on a story you might fit into. For your personal press list, get the name and address of media people who call you—sometimes they're freelancers who write for several publications. By following these guidelines, Manhattan psychotherapist Linda Barbanel amassed a list of media appearances that in double columns and small print goes on for more than twenty pages. Not listed there are the results of that exposure, which have included clients who read about her or saw her on TV, higher fees, more visible speaking engagements, an invitation to write her own piece for the *New York Times* and the opportunity to write a book for a major publisher. "The right attitude is the biggest hurdle," she says. "Once you've got that, the sky's the limit."

CHAPTER 9

No-Sell Selling with White Papers, Tip Sheets, Columns and Articles

In six years of teaching my seminar "So You Want to Write a Book" at adult education centers in New England, three times before I even said "Hello, class" someone approached me to announce that he'd brought along a book proposal or manuscript he wanted to hire me to evaluate. The first time this happened I was shocked. The second time I still felt knocked off balance. Why didn't they need to see me in action before deciding I was qualified to help? The third time it happened, I began to comprehend that to these folks, the simple fact that I was teaching the seminar proved I had the authority and expertise that they were looking for. Presenting that class positioned me to get hired as a consultant even before I opened my mouth and revealed that providing feedback on manuscripts was one of the things I did. Although my mentioning that I worked one-on-one with people on their writing would often motivate class participants to ask if I could help them, in those three cases I sold without any verbal selling on my part at all.

In this chapter I discuss a few kinds of writing that put you in the lucrative position of an expert. Unlike newsletters and publicity materials, these forms of writing persuade by offering apparently impartial perspectives. Although these pieces may issue from a calculated promotional strategy, the reader feels he or she is reading neutral, valuable information from an on-high authority. The disinterested tone makes all the difference in the world here; without it, you turn no-sell selling into no sale at all.

White Papers

This communication format takes its name from nineteenth-century practices in the British Parliament. Apparently official government reports were usually presented to Parliament on blue paper. Whenever someone produced a corrected version of the document, however, that revised report appeared on white paper. In this country, "white paper" has thus meant a position paper—a short treatise packed with facts and figures that argues for a policy or point of view. Political action groups produce them to influence the media, the public and key decision makers. For instance, Patricia Bario, president of a public relations agency in Washington, D.C., that bears her name, produced one for a coalition of small business owners who favored an employer mandate for funding health insurance reform. "It had a few pages of dispassionate exposition, then a few pages of Q & A, in which we took on the arguments of our opponents and responded to them," Bario says. Outside of politics, white papers compile background information on an issue or technology of central importance to a company or firm, but without any apparent selling of their wares.

New Jersey copywriter Bob Bly wrote one once for a company marketing software security systems for mainframe computers. "For this complicated a purchase, costing up to $120,000, a brochure is too promotional," Bly says. "You need to convince buyers of their need for computer security and persuade them of the superiority of the company's general approach to the problem. I wrote a white paper that laid the groundwork for the sale without once mentioning the product. When you've done it right, people read the white paper and agree, yes, this is the way to do it—and lo and behold, your product is the answer. Go for the sale, however, and you destroy your credibility." Bly says you also lose credibility by omitting competing approaches. "Then readers think you don't know what you're talking about. Instead, mention all the options and explain why the others don't work as well as yours."

White papers work especially well for expensive products and high-end services requiring trust or commitment. Indeed, a poll of law firms reported in the *Wall Street Journal* named white papers as their fourth most important promotional tool, below media exposure, client newsletters and sponsorship of seminars, and above brochures. A dentist might pen one on the pros and cons of removing mercury fillings, while a franchise broker might focus on how new legislation has affected the success rate of franchises. On a heated-up topic, a white paper must come across as a cool voice of reason. "When we put together a white paper on wireless LANs, we tried really hard *not* to appear biased toward our client's particular way of getting something done," says Alan Weinkrantz, who heads a PR firm in San Antonio, Texas. "It can be hard to substantiate their direct effect, but we have won support and praise long after the initial media hoopla blew over from editors, writers, analysts and gurus, thanking us for supplying a concise and well-written take on our subject." In the terms of my schema in Chapter 4, white papers sit as far away from hype as possible.

Once you write a white paper—which can represent a real challenge, warns Weinkrantz—what do you do with it? The one Bob Bly wrote on software security systems was presented at a computer conference, then offered as a "bait piece" in direct-mail and print ads. Readers who wanted information on the subject wrote or called for their free copy and thereby identified themselves as prospects for the product. Of course, they also received promotional literature about the company's product, but this was separate from the detached analysis in the white paper. Weinkrantz places his in press kits for new products and distributes them to anyone who is anyone in the computer industry. The dentist might send or offer his to holistic medical colleagues in a position to refer patients, while the franchise broker might tuck hers into information packets for potential franchise buyers.

Tip Sheets

Whereas white papers convey their neutrality best with a simple, almost typewriter-style layout, the next no-sell selling tool might look as slick as a well-designed flyer or brochure. A "tip sheet" consists of a set of "how-to" information in a neat, quick-read format. It might be as short as a page, or as long as an eight-page booklet. Tip sheets also go by the terms "report," "special report," "pamphlet," "fact sheet" and "handout." Typical titles flaunt the practical payoffs prospects get from reading them:

- Six Myths about Job-hunting in a "Buyer's Market"
- Ten Pitfalls of Poor Pest Control
- The Field Guide to Containing Packaging Costs
- How to Choose a Colorist
- Five Free Ways to Keep Your Car Alive

Compiled properly, tip sheets represent brag-free guidance for your prospects. Used wisely, such pieces position you as an expert to those who would benefit from your services or products.

Tod Maffin, a media technology consultant in Vancouver, British Columbia, tapped into a swell of public interest when he composed a tip sheet titled "Profiting from the Information Super-Highway: Ten Expert Tips on Using Today's Business Marketing Technology." His ten points included "1. Set up your own online service" and "6. Make your old E-mail do

new tricks," with enough explanations and examples on each
to whet, though not satisfy, a business person's curiosity. Point
#10 read like this:

> 10. And . . . call us. Now that you know what's possible,
> you need someone with the expertise to put all the pieces to-
> gether. Let us start working on your custom solution today. Call
> today . . . you can be connected to the future tomorrow!

Because this promotional blurb sits below a cascade of useful
information, it comes across as another helpful tip for readers
rather than as a sales pitch. Indeed, if Maffin had said nothing
about where to seek help implementing tips #1–9, the tip sheet
would have seemed incomplete. Another effective way to end
a tip sheet is with a third-person bio that motivates people to
call. For instance, at the end of a six-page tip sheet called,
"How to Round Up Customers Online Without Raising Hackles," I wrote, in part:

> Marcia Yudkin, Ph.D., is a Boston-based writer, consultant
> and seminar leader who provides fresh perspectives on commu-
> nicating creatively. She has achieved publicity on the front page
> of the *Wall Street Journal*, in local newspapers from the *Anchor-
> age Times* to the *Boston Globe*, in magazines from *Business
> Startups* to *Across the Board*, and on the New England Cable
> News. Through her edit-by-fax service, she helps clients target
> and polish press releases, articles and book proposals. For more
> information, call (617) 266-1613 or write to her at P.O. Box
> 1310, Boston, MA 02117.

Again, because readers have a natural wish to know about the
source of the guidance they've received, this does not stand
out as a hustle for business.

Tip sheets are the most valuable tool I know of for attracting auspicious prospects. Maffin created his in conjunction
with his appearance on a local radio talk show, where he spoke

about the Internet and E-mail. At the end of the program, he gave out his phone number so people could call and request a copy of the information. "In the hour it took me to drive from the studio to my home, callers had completely flooded my voice mail, with two hundred messages recorded and another two hundred pending. Fifty-five more called while I was taking the information off the voice mail—altogether six hundred or seven hundred calls, mostly from around British Columbia. This produced two dozen good leads and a dozen signed contracts. It was a godsend." Since Maffin had designed his tip sheet as one faxable page, his only costs were the time it took to write it, do the radio program, get callers' information from his voice mail and fax the material to respondents.

I have successfully gathered a gaggle of clients through tip sheets in conjunction with print publicity. Five times, in fact, I did it this way. First I created the tip sheet, usually in the form of a booklet. Then I wrote a press release announcing the availability of the tip sheet and highlighting its juiciest items. Respondents had to send either just a self-addressed stamped envelope or a dollar or two. I mailed the press release to magazines and newspapers and sent the whole booklet with a personal note to a few key magazines and newsletters. When I offered the tip sheet as a freebie, sales of products and services more than covered the cost of copying or printing, whereas charging a small fee enabled me to turn a profit while building up my mailing list and attracting follow-on business. For a booklet called "Six Steps to Free Publicity," which led to my book of that title, I received more than 6,000 requests!

Besides offering them as a lure through media publicity, you can use tip sheets as seminar handouts, add them to information kits about your company, turn them into published articles or incorporate selections into a brochure. Wally Bock, an Oakland, California, seminar leader and publisher of *Cyberpower Alert!*, uses tip sheets in the form of booklets to test-market concepts cheaply. "I used to develop whole courses with handouts and all only to discover that the market really

wasn't interested," Bock explains. "Now I begin by quickly
creating a booklet and then I set out copies at events I'm
speaking at and mention it on-line. Depending on the response,
I either develop the material into a for-sale item in the form of
a tape, book or other product, include it as an add-on to other
for-sale items or let the booklet live out its life in that form
when the market gives a collective yawn."

Bob Osgoodby, owner of Mcar Appliances in Asbury
Park, New Jersey, used the tip-sheet principle of selling via
nonpromotional information through Prodigy, the online service. After combing through Prodigy membership lists for
people located within ten miles of his store, he electronically
sent them what he calls "alerts." In late November, his message ran along these lines: "Hey guys, it's going to get real
cold soon. If your washing machine is on an unheated porch,
it's time to take care of it by taking it inside or draining it."
Another time he told people it was time to clean their dryer
vents and explained the dangers of not doing it. Another time
still he offered tips on how to keep refrigerator doors sealed.
Of course, at the end Osgoodby provided information about
his store. "Some people sent thank-you notes, some called for
a repair, and one guy who didn't follow the advice about taking in his washer came by a few months later to buy a new
one. Though we said we'd take people off the distribution list
upon request, no one asked. I think people appreciated getting
information without any sales pitch or obligation."

Barbara Winter, who discusses tip sheets in her national
workshop "How to Establish Yourself as an Expert," passed
on to me a creative variation on the informational format. A
company called Greenway Products produced a brochure-
sized pamphlet in the form of a quiz called "How Green Are
You?" It invites you to rate yourself on whether you take specific steps to save water and electricity, cut down your garbage
production, avoid hazardous substances and use environment-
friendly products. On the back, it ties its promotional message
to your quiz score: If you totaled thirty points or more,

"You're close to perfect! Become a Greenway distributor now!" If you scored below ten points, "Phone a Greenway distributor while there's still time!" Then there follows a short profile of the company and, stamped in a box, the name of the Greenway distributor who'd given the piece to Barbara Winter. All in all, a clever way to get the involvement of precisely the people who'd be most interested in the company.

Columns and Articles

Another avenue for offering information that puts you in the position of an expert is writing a regular column for a magazine, newspaper or newsletter. Carolyn Woodie, an Annapolis, Maryland, consultant who helped small businesses computerize, wrote a biweekly column on computers for four years in the late 1980s for a local paper, *The Publick Enterprise*. "It gave me name recognition and credibility—just what I was looking for as a new consultant," Woodie recalls. "One day, for example, I went to the local Computerland to buy something, and when I handed over my credit card, the salesperson said, 'Wow! You're the one who writes the column!' I almost didn't fit through the door on the way out, my head had swollen so. Even five years later I run into people who remember me as the columnist." As with any other marketing vehicle, the column worked for Woodie because she made sure it worked for her readers. "I knew that my audience was people who had computers at home—the boating crowd, retirees, professionals on vacation. It wouldn't work to be evaluating high-end software for people who read the *Washington Post* and the *Wall Street Journal* but have no time to read the neighborhood paper. I made sure I wrote on small programs that do a lot, like Calendar Creator Plus, and other topics like computer maintenance, viruses and local user groups that were relevant to novices."

Like Woodie, Dixie Darr says that her column on home-based businesses yields more indirect benefits than direct returns. Darr, based in Denver, profiles local small businesses, discusses the local business climate and offers advice on marketing for readers of the *Colorado Small Business Review*. Whereas Woodie receives a display ad in *The Publick Enterprise* in exchange for her column, Darr gets a promotional blurb at the end of her article which reads, "Dixie Darr is a freelance writer in Denver and publisher of *The Accidental Entrepreneur* newsletter. Order a copy or tell us about your home-based business by calling Dixie at 303-433-0345." Primarily, she says, the column has made it easier to wrangle invitations to speak before crowds of potential subscribers, like at Small Business Development Centers. "The column has helped establish me as a small business expert in Colorado and, to some extent, nationally."

Pharmacist Allen Bunn of Hartman Pharmacy in New Egypt, New Jersey, gets increased traffic in his shop through a hybrid column/ad every week for the *New Egypt Press*. "The column has made me a celebrity in my community," Bunn says. In each piece, he discourses enthusiastically and informatively on a topic of interest to pharmacy customers, such as the pain-reducing power of a traditional remedy—urine—and its equivalent in inoffensive ointment form. Because Bunn's chatty discussion leads up to a special sale offer at the pharmacy, the piece is presented as an ad, with the words "This is a paid advertisement" at the top. But he pays only for the space that the offer takes up—around $40, and most weeks the resulting extra profits shoot much higher than that. A column about the dryness of indoor winter air sold over $1,000 in humidifiers. A column about diet aids sold dozens of bottles of chromium and amino acid supplements. One about blood pressure monitors seemed to stick in people's minds and still got people asking about the devices months later. Despite the explicit labeling of the column as an ad, I believe three factors influence readers to experience it more as an editorial column. First, it looks like an article, with a headline, subhead and byline; second, it is printed in the same typeface as the rest of the paper; and third, Bunn writes in the voice of a well-informed, personable guy. The special offer comes along in that same voice, not in ad-ese.

Although I've authored a whole book on how to publish articles and get paid for them, I believe that for marketing purposes, you get a greater payoff from writing a regular unpaid column than from selling one-shot articles. Because most readers pay more attention to the content of articles than to bylines, few notice or remember when you write one isolated article. But so long as you follow these guidelines, over time column writing builds up valuable familiarity and credibility in your target market:

- *Carefully choose the publication you approach about a column.* If it targets your prospects, it's good for you. Otherwise, keep looking. If you provide legal services for small businesses, *The Small Business Gazette* makes more sense as a home for your column than *Connecticut Real Estate News*.

- *Write in a personal voice.* The more readers feel you're talking to them, the more eagerly they seek out your contributions in future issues. As I explained in Chapter 4, this doesn't mean talking about your cats or your CAT scans, but coming across as a trustworthy, approachable individual.

- *Avoid promotional statements about yourself in the column.* Paradoxically, when you convey useful information because you really want them to know and understand, you sell them on thinking of you when they need, say, your veterinary services.

- *Offer fresh, pertinent information.* Reveal the scoop on in-window air-conditioning that they won't get from the average dealer. Share your theories on why everyone in-

evitably has bad hair days. Decipher terms and procedures that baffle most of your accounting clients.

• *Don't be bland. Take a stand!* Readers want your informed
judgments. Back them up with reasons and explanations,
and respect people who disagree with you. If this provokes
letters to the editor, good! They prove people are taking
you seriously.

Once you've come up with a focus for a column, seek out
an appropriate publication that reaches your intended audience
and could use coverage of your topic. Write the editor a business letter explaining the rationale for your column and providing a list of six to eight column topics as well as at least one
completed sample column. A safe length would be in the range
of 800 to 1,200 words. (Length needs to be fairly consistent
from column to column.) Mention that you'll gladly provide
the column for free in exchange for a display ad and/or a biographical paragraph at the end of the column that includes contact information. Offer a photo to accompany the column in
case they want it, since that increases reader involvement and
response. And if one publication turns you down, shop it
around to the next.

One-shot articles call for a somewhat different approach.
You're best off writing a proposal letter about the piece you
have in mind, rather than submitting the completed article.
This allows the editor to have you tailor the length and content
to that publication's needs. Make sure you propose a distinctive, specific and appropriate article rather than something
vague or generic. *Northern Lumber Mill* wants "How to Cut
Mill Maintenance Costs," not "How to Cut Operating Costs,"
for any industry from interior decorating to carburetor manufacturing. Yes, that requires you to learn enough about lumber
mills to include lumber-mill examples and suggestions. Two
bonuses may follow such research: people you interview
sometimes turn into clients; and having published something

for that industry gives you great credibility in soliciting other lumber-mill prospects for business.

By the way, all three of our featured columnists mentioned psychological benefits from their regular writing. Both Darr and Woodie said their column boosted their self-confidence. Woodie went on to contribute to two WordPerfect manuals and create a newsletter reaching more than 1,200 subscribers. Allen Bunn said, "I learn so much from writing the columns, which helps me when I am counseling clients in the pharmacy." Considering that effective marketing requires believing you have valuable skills, products and services to offer your market, there's great value in writing's power to spread success to seemingly unrelated facets of your business.

CHAPTER 10

Advertisements That Bring in Steady Business

In 1982 or so, while riding the subway in New York City, Peter Baxter happened to glimpse an ad across the train that overturned his thinking. The ad for a Tandy computer, on the back page of someone else's *New York Times*, said it cost only $699. Believing it was a misprint, Baxter nevertheless grabbed his own copy of the paper and eagerly turned to that page. Apparently not a misprint, Radio Shack was announcing the first affordable computer he had ever heard of. "I became captivated by the idea that I could have my own computer," recalls Baxter, now president of the Business Solution Group in Lenox, Massachusetts. "At that time only big companies had computers, because they cost at least $100,000. That ad about a low-cost computer got me dreaming about having a scaled-down version of a minicomputer for my business. It produced an epiphany like no other ad I'd seen."

The shock wave Baxter experienced upon seeing the ad, and his motivated action in heading to Radio Shack the first chance he had, represent every advertiser's dream. Ironically, he didn't purchase the Model 1 in the ad because he discovered that it wasn't a serious business machine. All fired up then to find a system for his needs, he bought something from another company that didn't work as promised. He ended up going back to Radio Shack and purchasing their newer and more powerful Model 2, spending several times more than that $699.

Given that every ad competes with more than two thousand others every day for a typical prospect's attention, it's not easy to break through to the kind of impact Radio Shack achieved with Peter Baxter. And the challenge mounts when we factor in the often incredible expense of advertising—the priciest of all the marketing formats I'm covering. Misfires here can precipitate an abrupt about-face in your march toward profit. And it seems I hear a lot of stories about low responses. Kevin Cooter, for example, paid $5,000 a month for three months to place a ¹⁄₆-page ad for Ultrastat, a static-elimination device for computers, in *PC World* magazine, said to reach a million readers. "It was definitely a flop," he wrote me at the end of the first month. "We got two responses the first week, four the second week and thirty-six the third week, and out of those forty-two, only six purchased. Grrr! We were expecting sales of at least a hundred units a month to break even. Since we have a great closing rate whenever we can demonstrate the product in person, we're going back to trade shows, which have always paid off for us."

Because advertising may not be the best vehicle for you to find and motivate customers, I'll first review the criteria for appropriately choosing to place ads. Then I'll discuss how to do it right, so that your debut in the ad pages becomes not a debacle but a triumph.

When Advertising Makes Sense and Why

The principles here are simple. Unless you have mile-deep pockets, advertise only when (1) you view it as an investment that pays you back over time and (2) when you know who you're trying to reach, how, what about and when.

Advertising tends to accomplish its mission best through repetition, over time. To understand this, consider what would have happened if Peter Baxter, after having had the sudden awakening advertisers dream of, had had to rush off the train before reading the ad carefully. If he's like most of us, he would have chased down the Radio Shack computer only after a second ad reminded him of the first. Now think about the somewhat larger pool of readers who noticed the same ad but found it moderately impressive rather than electrifying. Checking out the Model 1 wouldn't have had high priority for them, but each additional exposure to the ad might bolster their intentions until they reached the threshold of action. Now add in the still larger group of prospects who passed right on by the ad, either because they were busy turning to the sports section or because they didn't think they needed a computer— but later do. If the Radio Shack ad isn't repeated, these potential buyers drop out of the respondent pool as well. In fact, many professional marketers swear by the "Rule of Seven," which holds that the average prospect must notice an advertising message seven times before he or she responds.

For a payoff from advertising, then, you must plan from the beginning for a campaign, rather than a one-shot ad. You must also have enough nerve to keep the campaign going long enough for the repetition to do its work. As circus promoter P. T. Barnum put it, "Advertising is like learning—a little is a dangerous thing. If a man has not the pluck to keep *on* advertising, all the money he had already spent is lost." Precious few of us can maintain that pluck, however, when those advertising dollars that appear to be accomplishing naught bring us closer and closer to a cash-flow crisis. The "do-or-die" mentality of someone desperate for results will almost always sabotage the success of advertising, whether the danger of financial collapse is real or only imagined. Paradoxically, the more comfortable you feel with the idea that all your advertising expenditures might bring you nothing, the better position you're in to generate profits from your ad costs. Katie Hickey, owner of KT Creative in Anchorage, Alaska, adds that you have to be willing to spend enough to get the ad that's appropriate for your company. "For instance, a clothing store that wants to sell to high-end customers but doesn't want to pay for better art and a more sophisticated-looking ad is in for trouble. When people are shopping by price, schlock is good, but when they're shopping for an image, the image has to be there in the execution of the ad."

The other prerequisite for successful advertising—knowing your audience, your message and its optimal timing—enables you to place the right ad in the right print media at the proper time. By knowing who your prospects are and when the best time is to reach them, you can easily narrow down possible outlets for an ad. Let's consider timing first: Daily newspapers have the shortest lead time and the shortest life span. That is, while you can get an ad to newspaper readers within a couple of days, each newspaper ad hangs around only about that long as well. Weekly papers have a slightly longer lead time and life span, while monthly magazines require you to plan several months ahead and allow you to reap responses for considerably longer, since magazines hang around for months and even years in bathroom racks and waiting rooms. Yellow Pages and other directories have the longest lead time of all, and a life span measured in two or three years. (Everyone doesn't toss out the old directory when the new one comes.) Unlike newspapers and magazines, though, a directory actually "reaches" people not when it arrives but whenever someone takes their fingers walking through it on the way to a phone call.

Because their survival usually depends on attracting advertising, newspapers, magazines and directories can give you a very precise breakdown of the age, income, sex, professions, interests and geographical distribution of their readers. Don't go by assumptions—ask! For example, you might suppose that a magazine called *Executive Female* circulates mainly to high-ranking corporate women, when in fact most of its readers work much farther down the corporate ladder. Basically you want to find the best matches between your market profile and publications' readerships. You'll get media leads worth checking out by asking current customers or appropriate prospects what they read. Without a specific description of who you'd like to reach with an advertising message, any commitment to ads constitutes a very expensive test. But after formulating a target such as "office managers within a twenty-mile radius of Homeville" or "physically active professional women in their twenties and thirties," you're ready to focus on the ad itself.

Composing Your Ad

Chapter 5 coaches you on developing three of the five main components of a typical ad—the headline, the offer and the middle or body. When you leave out the offer, you have created what's known as an "institutional ad" or "image ad," which helps spread awareness of what you do but does not sell. Unless you represent a well-heeled, mass-marketing institution like Pepsi or Holiday Inn, I do not recommend that approach. You must also include identifying information about the advertiser, usually in the form of a "signature" or logo plus locating information. Optionally, an ad contains an illustration, photo or other visual as well.

When it comes to incorporating pictures in your ad, remember that the old adage "a picture is worth a thousand words," applies only to illustrations and photos that reinforce your message. One kind of illustration that always grabs me is "before and after," whether the pair of photos shows a transformation from stringy, shapeless locks to glamorous hair or from bulging fat to a waistband that has become six inches too big for its wearer. In these cases, pictures supply proof. Since photos and sketches, especially of people, tend to involve the viewer more than words, they help humanize an abstraction, such as a financial planning company or an airline. Occasionally a picture supplies a captivating visual metaphor, like a Rolm ad showing a desk telephone from which extrudes a cash-filled open drawer, beneath the headline "Considering how our phone systems affect revenues, perhaps we should consider a new design." Or an illustration can bolster the double meaning of a headline, as in a British Airways ad that says "Nonstop to London. Showers expected upon arrival" above a composite of a metal showerhead raining water across a cloud-specked blue sky. And of course, pictures also help prospects visualize a product—especially vital for cars, clothing and other items where style comprises much of the appeal.

Pictures get you into trouble, however, when they distract from your offering, mislead about what's being advertised or simply fail to connect with the copy. The worst offender I found was a Logitech ad dominated by a close-up of a black-and-white speckled dog holding a black rectangular object in its mouth. White typed words in the upper right-hand corner call attention to the dog:

Man's best friend
- retrieves
- comforts
- guards

Inconspicuously in the lower left-hand corner of the photo, corresponding white type against a busier background points to the black rectangular object and says:

Businessman's best friend
- scans
- copies
- faxes

The sad-eyed dog has so much prominence in the ad that it took concentrated study for me to figure out that the thing in the dog's mouth, not the dog, was supposed to be the focus of my attention. I doubt that one reader in a thousand understood at a glance that this was an ad for a scanner rather than some kind of tribute to a loyal dog.

As for the wording of your ad, how much do you need to tell in order to sell? Partly this depends on whether your strategy involves one-step or two-step selling. With the former, you attempt to sell directly from the ad, while the latter generates leads that you follow up by mail, phone or in person to clinch the sale. One-step selling requires a similar strategy to a direct-mail letter: You must describe the benefits and features of what you're selling, address the most obvious questions and doubts and tell readers how to buy. A coupon with prominent dotted lines increases orders from your ad, as does the strongest guarantee you can afford. For example, a full-page black-and-white one-step magazine ad for a video called *Sexual Positions for Lovers* features an attractive couple half-wrapped in towels and the headline "Sex Education for Me?" I imagine that the most common questions asked about such a product are: What's in it? Is it educational or pornographic? Can it be shipped in a plain brown wrapper? Is it guaranteed? The ad answers all four, by pitching know-how as an aphrodisiac, describing the credentials of the video's narrators (presumably a Harvard Medical School sex educator would not be involved in pornography) and listing some of the kinds of techniques illustrated therein by four "typical couples." The copy also explains that it's shipped unmarked "for your privacy" and carries a no-risk guarantee. A mail-in coupon occupies the lower right-hand corner, along with a toll-free 800 number for credit-card orders. Altogether, a complete order-generating ad.

A two-step ad might be as short and simple as a classified: "Ninety-seven-pound weakling? Become the muscleman of the beach with new foolproof bodybuilding method. Free details: 1-800-555-5555; P.O. Box 199, Hometown, ST 00000." Or it might be as elaborate and well-designed as the sexual video ad, but without an invitation to order. Instead, the two-step ad asks people to call a certain number for more information, or send for a free brochure, booklet or prospectus. "Don't be afraid to turn the wrong people off in the first step of two-step marketing," advises marketing consultant Sherman Robbins of Fort Lauderdale, Florida. "You shouldn't judge results by the quantity of responses but by the quantity of *quality* responses." Robbins once created an ad for the trust division of a bank which was only interested in serving "old wealth." To get across that message, the ad showed a family grouped on the lawn of a huge estate, saying implicitly, "If this isn't you, don't bother." You can also qualify prospects via copy, says Robbins—for example, by saying, "If you have more than $5 million in assets, we can . . ."

Those with experience say that for items costing about $10 or less, you can get away with a one-step classified ad. To pack in the most selling power at the lowest cost, mercilessly excise unnecessary words, like "the," "and" or "of." And don't underrate these diminutive marketing notices. For eight years, Jay Levinson earned about $500 a month from a classified ad that sold his forty-three-page book called *Secrets of Successful Freelancing*. After figuring out which of eight publications he tested gave the best return, and the ideal frequency for the ad, he just kept running and running and running it, and profiting and profiting and profiting. "Classifieds are inexpensive to try, and inexpensive to fail at," says Levinson. "But the results from that ad never tailed off, and I stopped it only because my plate became too full with other things."

At the opposite end in copy length from classifieds lie "advertorials," or advertisements in the form of an article. In Chapter 9, I described how pharmacist Allen Bunn negotiated a minimal fee for his column/ad, but even if the publication charges you for the whole space, you may find the format pays off better for you than an ordinary display ad. Advertorials work especially well for service providers because you have the opportunity to present your approach in more depth or to offer tips of value to your target audience. An accounting firm might create a series called "Small Business Success Tips," or a printer a piece called "How to Find a Conscientious Printer." Some community papers include a periodic advertorial as part of an advertising package—for every four weeks your space ad runs in their service directory, you get featured with a headline, photo of your business and a short feature article written at no cost to you by a staff writer. Since most readers take this spread as editorial copy rather than advertising, the format gives you credibility. When she worked for the *East Side Monthly* in Providence, Rhode Island, Louise Gordon wrote a piece like this for an elder care agency that doubled its caseload that month.

And let's not forget the Yellow Pages, a specialized advertising vehicle that can make a huge difference in the number of calls you receive from new customers. "If your competitors have big Yellow Pages ads, you must have a big one too," says Kathy Murtagh, who worked in sales and marketing for the Southern New England Telephone Company (SNET) for more than thirteen years. Not only does greater size translate into more attention from prime prospects, in most directories, the largest ads appear first in each section. "And it helps to put your company under multiple headings like 'heating' and 'furnaces' for a plumber, in addition to 'plumbing,' " says Murtagh. "But you don't need a huge ad under each heading. You can say, 'See our ad under ____.' " The best checklist for what a directory ad should include comes from journalists' "5 *W*'s": *Who* are you? *What* services do you provide? *Where* are you? *When* are you available or open? *Why* are you special? Because the Yellow Pages place you chock-a-block with your competitors, creative ads stand out, although directory publishers may have stringent restrictions governing what you must or may not do in your ad. In Connecticut, for instance, Murtagh says that SNET would not allow undocumented superlatives, such as an unexplained "fastest delivery," or more than 50 percent of an ad in reverse type. Movers had to list their ICC license number, and attorneys had to provide proof that they had passed the bar.

Although people tend to use compact, staccato "ad-ese" in smaller ads, Jay Levinson reports superb results from longer text in warm, cushy language. "Classified ad takers know all the abbreviations that save you money, but neophytes reading the ads don't recognize what they mean," he says. "When I went to London all the housing ads said 'CCFF,' which meant 'carpets, curtains, fixtures and fittings,' but I couldn't guess that. Abbreviations frighten people because they think they'll be dealing with a technonerd. Be different. Put warmth and humanity into your ad—make it sound like a person talking." Advertising consultant Laura Lee Lemmon recalls several of her clients showing her an ad in a horse-breeder magazine that used imaginative language to sell the services of a stallion at stud. At the top a clipping, like from a personal ad, began, "Single father looking for many dates. His children have won . . ." Then it listed awards his offspring had won and finished off with a photo of the horse and how to contact the owner.

Checklist for Advertising Success

Does it grab attention—of the right people?

A targeted headline and appropriate illustration accomplish most of this work. Keep in mind that being noticed is not an end in itself. Dog lovers who lingered over Logitech's spotted hound were not necessarily good candidates for buying a scanner. An unexciting way to attract the people you want is simply to call out to the: "Job-hunting?" "Attention aging athletes," or "For women who are tired of yo-yo dieting." Pedestrian though this technique may be, it works.

Is it clear what you sell and what your company does?

Richard Ott warns not to assume that people recognize and remember your business when the company name doesn't spell it out. "A radio ratings survey once revealed that some people thought 'K-93' was a new bug spray. Others thought it was an automotive lubricant. The radio station brass had to be scraped off the floor. It had never occurred to them someone might not know what 'K-93' was," says Ott.

What message does someone get who passes over the ad without paying close attention?

I've already mentioned the chance that an illustration confuses people into thinking that you're, say, a dog trainer when you really sell computer equipment. When you picture or mention a competitor in a comparative ad, you run the risk of glancers thinking you are touting rather than criticizing your rival. When you fail to mention your company name and product or service prominently, you probably make no measurable impression on inattentive readers at all. Even when you believe you're doing everything right, people sometimes radically misperceive your message. Remember the Energizer rabbit on TV whose batteries kept him going and going and going? Despite the evidence of their eyes and ears, early viewers of this commercial thought that the bunny was fueled by *Duracell* batteries—perhaps, says adwatcher Michael Finn, "because Duracell had a history of using battery-operated toys in its commercials, and consumers perceived the Energizer bunny as just another in the line." Prevention: Show people your ad for a few blinks and then snatch it away and ask them what it was all about.

Do the graphic elements and copy enhance each other?

If by subtracting the graphics you would diminish the ad's impact, you've done an excellent job of integrating words and pictures. On the other hand, if a photo, cartoon or drawing seems like it might have wandered into your ad space by mistake, get rid of it.

Is the pith of your message prominent?

Copywriter Dick Dunn says that marketers have a tendency to "bury the news"—that is, to hide a message that would be surprising and welcome to prospects inside a camouflage of humdrum copy. Locate your "news" and position it more conspicuously. For instance, a workshop ad from Mark Barnard of Bos'n, Inc. headlines the name "Pinnacle Workshops," and just below that in a box: "This unique program is designed for experienced sales professionals and executives who are committed to reaching the ultimate levels of sales performance." Neither the title nor the purpose statement motivates or intrigues. But near the bottom, the idea "Help your prospects sell themselves" come across as fresh and interesting, as does the second of five bulleted points in another box: "How to sell more by 'selling' less." Either of these phrases would stand out brightly as a headline. Unfortunately, good ideas don't get the chance to show their real colors when packed in amongst a bunch of gray.

Is the message timely?

The second week of April, I noticed an ad in my local paper: "Tax-Time Troubles? Procrastinators call today, extensions available." I'm sure that did better than any generic we-do-taxes ad that week. Besides tying in to seasonal events, consider piggybacking on current news. After millions watched O. J. Simpson's low-speed flight from police along Southern California highways, all Ford dealers had to do was feature the word "Bronco" to cash in on increased interest in the car people had seen on their TV screens throughout the chase. Though you don't have to be obviously up-to-the-minute, at least don't use outdated language, photos or illustrations without a special rationale.

Is the message clearly focused?

According to Sherman Robbins, beginning advertisers often try to cram too much into each ad. "Stick to just one point per ad, and emphasize and expand on that point," he says. "If you have a lot to say, create several ads and rotate them." When trying to drum up listeners for a New York easy-listening radio station, Robbins found that only two elements had to come across in each ad—the dial position and the format. "So our whole ad was 'The lite at the end of the dial: 106.7.' Nothing else mattered."

Does the message fit the medium?

Two ads in the same issue of *Working Woman* magazine made me wonder who had fallen asleep at the watch. The Wharton Business School's executive education program ran a full-page ad featuring a Harley-Davidson motorcycle, headlined, "Malcolm Forbes learned to ride a motorcycle at 50. What have you learned lately?" This was supposed to appeal to *women*? Inside the back cover, Whirlpool pitched its dishwashers by expressing empathy for the multiple roles women have to fulfill in today's society. (The dishwashers save time and bother, it said.) But of the ten pictures of the same woman meant to represent those multiple roles, every one depicted a domestic task. And *working* women were supposed to see themselves in this picture? Whoever arranged for placement of these ads either hadn't seen them yet or hadn't thought about the appropriateness of a generic ad for a narrower audience. Dangerous, dangerous!

Have you told the reader what to do and how to do it?

That is, have you included an offer as well as complete and accurate contact information? It's easy to forget these essentials, says Laura Lee Lemmon, who displays an example at her seminars and asks participants what is wrong with the ad. "It shows a beautiful stallion and says to contact such-and-such farm—no address and no phone," Lemmon says. "People exclaim about how beautiful the horse is, and it takes them quite a while to realize they wouldn't be able to find the horse unless they already knew that farm."

Might your ad offend people you can't afford to slight?

Though I don't have any Italian blood, I was bothered by a Gateway computer ad that seemed to rely on ethnic stereotyping. Using the premise that Bonanno Pisano might have been able to design a non-leaning Tower of Pisa had he had a Gateway P5–90, the ad said in part, "Mamma-mia! What'sa matta me! That'sa last time I buy a kit from the Tower-R-Us catalog. Never get enough cement mix. So, I used my mother-in-law's linguine sauce as extra cement. Oh boya, I no like how that turned out." Sure, some will laugh. But what about those whose backs go up? Besides sexist, racist, age-ist and other such sins of commission, stay watchful for significant omissions. Do your photos, testimonials and copy reflect the diversity of your customer base and those you hope to attract?

Do you have a way to track the effect of your ads?

See Chapter 14 for suggestions on ways to keep tabs on which ads are doing what. But don't be too quick to conclude you've wasted your money. Advertising often has indirect effects. Kevin Cooter, CEO of Ultrastat, who had initially expressed disappointment with his ad in *PC World*, wrote me later with an update. "Though responses averaged about forty a week after Week 4, turning into only ten sales or so per week, the ad apparently gave us credibility in the eyes of potential distributors and dealers who have started buying from us. That should eventually pay for the running of the ad. Also,

because many who bought only one unit are in organizations
that have thousands of computers and we have a 50 percent re-
order rate from satisfied customers, we anticipate getting more
money back from that—just not right away." Remember, advertising makes sense only as an investment.

CHAPTER 11

Other Formats, Innovative and Traditional

The most thrilling television show I recall from my childhood always started with a message selling a particular mission. After a tape described the details of a dangerous assignment that would save Western civilization, both the tape and the tape player self-destructed in a hiss of smoke. This technology didn't exist apart from the *Mission: Impossible* show, of course, but I was sold on it.

Although the 1990s still haven't brought us tape machines that disappear without a trace, we do have new marketing media that allow business communication to transpire without paper. In this chapter I cover the promise and pitfalls of some cutting-edge communication tools as well as media and formats that simply didn't fit in previous chapters. Besides billboards and radio and TV advertising, which have nonpaper traditions of their own, I'm eager to see your other examples of innovative marketing, either using paper or some substitute medium.

New Marketing Media

Fax

As of December 1992, federal laws in the United States explicitly prohibited unsolicited faxing. So forget about gathering fax numbers and advertising that way to strangers. But as a communication aid for business relationships in our snap-your-fingers-and-get-what-you-want age, you can't beat facsimile machines. In the selling process, faxes have two advantages over phone calls that you should keep in mind: They give your prospect something tangible to be acted on, referred to again and perhaps filed, and they come as less of an interruption, because people pick them up whenever they feel ready to deal with them. Compared with materials on paper that have to travel through the mail, they can make an instant impact. But since faxes using thermal paper tend to fade away to illegibility within months, don't use this vehicle for contracts or a brochurelike information piece intended to stay in someone's files. Here are some additional tips for courteous, effective marketing via fax:

- Conserve recipients' paper. You don't need a whole page to convey identifying information about you and your recipient. Either design a half-page cover sheet bearing your company logo or buy compact fax routing forms at an office supply store. The latter should have a plain white background and no graphics more complicated than straight lines.

- Design follow-up materials specifically for faxing. According to newsletter expert Elaine Floyd, small italic type looks almost illegible when faxed, while 14-point or larger sans serif type (see Chapter 16) gets your message across most clearly. Since fancy graphics, photos and shading all slow down transmissions, devise simple, clean fax order forms and information sheets. A two-column format may allow you to fit more onto a page legibly than long lines all across the page. Always create material for faxing with the 8½-inch dimension across the 11-inch dimension down. Prevent crowding with plenty of white space. Test your fax forms by copying them on the fax machine, then copying the copy twice—can you still read everything?

- For important marketing messages that get no response, call to make sure the fax made it to your prospect. Once my editor said there was still nothing in the fax bin when I'd faxed something and then refaxed it twice. It turned out that, unbeknownst to her, the machine had a memory and stored messages when the paper ran out. Remember that people away from the office can more easily pick up phone messages than retrieve faxes waiting for them.

- Mass faxing. If you have time-sensitive information that needs faxing to many people at once, consider a fax broadcast service. You'll need a modem as well as a fax machine to construct, update and communicate the distribution list, but once the system is set up for you, you could send in something in the middle of the night to be faxed to everyone on your list instantaneously, without any human intervention. "Because of our huge volume, we get enormous discounts from the phone company, which we pass on to customers," says Gary Aili, president of Karat Interactive Network in Boulder, Colorado, which might charge less than $5 to fax your document to thirty recipients. Internationally, the savings of time and money are even more dramatic.

Fax-on-demand

With special equipment, you can set up a system where customers can fax to you, press numbers on the keypad corresponding to specific information they want and watch it roll out of their fax machine automatically during the same fax call. Para

Publishing founder Dan Poynter, whose fax-on-demand system in Santa Barbara, California, receives an average of thirty to forty calls a day, calls it "serving your customers while you sleep." Of course, if you're awake while these information requests get fulfilled, the system allows you to handle work that can't be automated or delegated. The four-page fax-on-demand menu that Para Publishing customers receive includes valuable resources, like lists of attorneys specializing in publishing—not only its own promotional information on products, events and services. "Giving out these documents helps educate people and leads them into buying more from us," says Poynter. "We appear extremely generous, but in fact, after setting the system up, it saves us a lot of time and all it costs is the monthly basic telephone line—about $15 a month." Poynter spent less than $500 for the software and special board he needed to run the system, which he installed on an old computer he had hanging around.

Although numerous fax-on-demand service bureaus will handle the whole thing for you on a fee basis, Poynter says many charge more per month or quarter than it would cost you to buy your own simple system. Catalog publishers use fax-on-demand so they can run shorter product descriptions and invite customers to fax in for detailed specification sheets. Restaurants free up their phone lines by offering their menus and a map with directions via fax-on-demand. Newsletters provide sample articles and subscription information to snare prospects immediately after they become aware of the publication's existence. Fax-on-demand makes the most sense if you serve a business group with easy access to a fax machine. Poynter estimates that at least 70 percent of his customers, primarily publishers, have their own machine. Once you've set up your system, be sure to publicize the number in your advertisements and correspondence.

Computer bulletin boards

According to media technology consultant Tod Maffin, a very small investment can set you up with a twenty-four-hour computer bulletin board system (BBS in techie jargon) to which people can dial in to receive your product information or resource files from electronic menus and leave you orders. "Most of the software you need for such a system is virtually free, and you don't need a separate phone line or a computer any more powerful than a '286,' " he says, estimating a cost of just $60 to $90 for software and utilities and at least $150 for a consultant to set up your system. Maffin cites an online résumé service and a graphic design firm that successfully created their own BBS's for customers to electronically drop off and pick up work. Companies could use BBS's much as those described above use fax-on-demand. Maffin adds, "All customers need is a modem," but even though upwards of 70 percent of new computer systems are sold with modems, non-techie BBS users also need some bravery to dial in for the first time. Fax machines intimidate people less than computers, I think. Until modem use catches up with, say, the prevalence of word processing, I'd recommend a customer-oriented BBS mainly if you sell to a technologically comfortable crowd.

Online services

I've generated a good deal of business for myself through networking on CompuServe and Prodigy. Along with GEnie, America Online and Delphi, these commercial services offer electronic forums in which you can carry on conversations with other members. Since most of the services outlaw solicitations in the forums, you need some cunning to put out the word to their well-heeled businessfolks and consumers while staying within the rules. All of the following tactics are safe and effective:

- Ask for advice and help. If you say, "I'm putting together a marketing plan for my new Flibberdeboojee. Does anyone have a list of trade shows in the Southwest?," someone is guaranteed to come online and ask,

"What's a Flibberdeboojee? How much does it cost? How can I get one?" You're free to—indeed expected to—answer such questions in detail.

• Offer help. Cruise around for people asking questions in your area of expertise. In answering them, describe your product or service briefly. Serious prospects will pop up, wanting to know more. You can also initiate a discussion topic where you offer to answer questions about business plans, investing in fine art or whatever your specialty is.

• Leave informative articles in the libraries. Write a brief collection of tips for your target market. Most of the online services have a special area, open to all contributors, for such documents. End yours with a paragraph about your services or products and how people can get in touch with you. Post a public message on the relevant bulletin boards announcing your new contribution to the library and where to find it.

• Provide statistics, facts, references. If you're good at collecting information, start your own regular feature, like "Job-Hunting Statistic of the Week" or "Little-known Resources for Desktop Publishers." Keep it brief, and either before or after your tidbit, introduce yourself. Something low-key like "Here's something I ran across while consulting on customer service" nevertheless markets for you. Remember that many people need to run across your name seven times before they trust you.

• Repeat your message after people respond. When people have requested to read only new messages, they can come upon—and then ignore—the cryptic middle of your conversation. Every time you reply to a reply, restate the context you established earlier, as in, "I'd be glad to send you information about reconditioning your laser printer. Look for it in the mail."

Most of the services also offer, for a fee, electronic classifieds. As with print classifieds, before you invest a lot of
money, check their effectiveness by tracking how many advertisers continue to pay for postings there. I've heard mixed
results about online ads. Whether in the forums or the classifieds, though, the skill of writing compact, descriptive headlines helps. Avoid hucksterish wording (see Chapter 4) and
long stretches of capital letters, considered the electronic
equivalent of shouting.

Beyond the online services stretch the vast, only partly
charted seas of the Internet, the anarchic, unowned worldwide
network. The above guidelines should help you make connections there as well without getting "flamed" (heaped with electronic abuse). But because the distinctive culture of the
Internet evolved from universities and the government rather
than from the business world, you may find it harder to convert
Internet connections into paying clients and customers. Inter-
netters expect the good stuff they can access through their
computers to be free.

The latest rage on the Internet involves the World Wide
Web, an easy-to-navigate system that displays graphics and
text to visitors in a sort of electronic billboard. Unfortunately,
many business people are replicating the mistakes that are
rampant for brochures in this brand-new medium. Just as a
brochure most commonly (and ineffectively) opens with the
name of the company, followed by a profile of its capabilities,
many World Wide Web business sites bear a headline pro-
claiming the company name, followed by an explanation of
what the company does. When designing a "home page" to
showcase your business, apply the lessons you learned
throughout this book, particularly the necessity to think
through the needs of your audience and to keep the emphasis
on "you, you, you" rather than "I, I, I" or "we, we, we." Using
the "tip sheet" (see Chapter 9) approach would pay off far
better here, I believe, than a "da-da, here's who we are" song
and dance.

Brochures on disk

Some marketers call disk-based marketing materials "interactive brochures," but of all the samples I reviewed, only one offered significantly interactive features. The rest required you to load files onto your hard disk—hogging a *lot* of space, by the way—and then simply click to get to the next screen. One company mentioned that they could send a version of their electronic brochure by modem, "which gives immediate gratification." As a novelty item, brochures on disk probably do appeal to customers who love to try the latest toys. But it takes imagination to produce more than, in essence, a computer slide show. I was relieved that everyone's loading instructions were easy to follow, but I noted that only one of the companies included its contact information on the disk label. The rest apparently assumed I wouldn't mind reloading the disk to access their address and phone number included within the program (wrong), that I would keep the program on my hard disk (wrong) or that I would keep the disk with the folder of other information they sent (right, but why take such chances?).

The one sample that impressed me came from a firm called Virtual Creations in New York City, whose marketing disk for a product called "The Virtual Machine" allows you to select which features of a screen representation of a machine you'd like more details about. Another set of options allows you to browse among sets of descriptions of the benefits and features of the product. In full color, this truly interactive demo was beautifully constructed and designed, without a touch of home-grown, first-try flavor in it anywhere.

Audiotapes

Prior to the mid-1980s, audio lost cachet to video, but according to Laura Moore, a Cambridge, Massachusetts, producer of audiocassettes and compact discs, the introduction of the Sony Walkman and certain inherent advantages of audio made it bounce back as an attractive marketing vehicle. First, unlike video, the audiocassette format is standard around the world. Second, "Audio respects people's time more than video"—since people can listen while exercising or driving. Third, says Moore, "Without the expense of video, audio allows you to communicate in your own voice, which is especially valuable in building trust. You can also choose to use a professional actor to set the proper mood for your message." Compared with printed brochures, audiocassettes have advantages as well. "No one files or piles audiocassettes," Moore notes. "They stay on people's desks for a long time. People perceive them as a gift. And since few people use audio for marketing, sending a cassette sets you apart from the competition even before they hear your message."

Although technologically it's feasible to use CD's as well as audiocassettes, Moore doesn't see that as appropriate quite yet. Once CD players match the popularity of cassette players in cars and homes, the newer medium might make sense. And if you believe that the medium of audio appeals primarily to men, you're wrong. "Producers originally geared audio to men because they didn't understand the market. Seventy percent of audiocassette purchasers in New England are female," says Moore. "Whether you're marketing to men or women, it's best to send promotional cassettes to people who've already expressed interest in information about your business."

For the smoothest delivery of your message on tape, prepare and practice a script. Some people edit recordings of live presentations, splicing in introductory and bridge material. Follow the basic principles discussed elsewhere in the book, such as getting the audience's attention first with benefits, using specifics rather than generalities and ending with a call to action. I recommend a soft-sell to medium-sell approach (see

Chapter 4) that includes educational information of value to the listener, not something akin to a radio ad.

Videotape catalogs

What do you do if still photos and words can't capture the dynamic magic of your offering? Perhaps the continuity and movement possible with videotape provide the answer. Sculptors Harvey Rattey and Pamela Harr of Bozeman, Montana, bypass the flat single views of the bronzes possible in their newsletter catalog through the all-around perspective achievable in their video catalog. They've also spliced in personal insights about the artwork and segments from TV interviews. To keep their costs down and send the videos only to serious prospects, Rattey and Harr request a $15 deposit, fully refundable on the video's return.

Self-stick notes

Although Post-it Notes and knock-off brands have been popular for years, it's only recently that companies have exploited their marketing potential. In Chapter 26 you'll find a supplier of customized self-stick notes, which John Collins of Hartford Toner had made up in bulk with his company logo. "Customers called up asking if they could have some. Now I give pads of them out to people on the least excuse. They only cost 30 cents each, and every time people use them, they help spread awareness of Hartford Toner." I don't give away my own 3 by 4-inch Post-it Notes, custom-printed with my name and phone and fax numbers, but they save me gobs of time and make a classy impression. I now write about 20 percent as many formal business letter as I used to. Instead, I handwrite a simple marketing message on the Post-it Note and slap it onto my enclosures. Recipients tell me they appreciate that personal touch.

And Let's Not Forget . . .

Postcards

While postcards can serve as the vehicle for a direct-mail message or even a newsletter, they can also be used for more creative purposes. From chiropractor and motivational speaker Jenna Eisenberg of Wheaton, Illinois, whom I once met at a conference, I received a large postcard photo of a green, purple, gold and blue poster reading "Born to Be Wild." On the reverse, in an eye-catching layout, was a story about how Eisenberg uses the poster to motivate herself during aerobics workouts. "Were you taught to be mild, but born to be wild?" the story ended. I found the story evocative and the whole postcard so intriguing that I wrote to find out how she used the postcard. As I suspected, it's a way for her to stay in touch with her mailing list of patients and seminar participants. A previous postcard shared a story about her sister trudging through the snow to a neighbor who had a sign by the pool, "If you don't visit me in January, don't visit me in July!" Eisenberg ended that story, "What action can you take today so that your life is filled with things you love to do and people you love to be with?" In her letter back to me, she wrote, "I know I don't use these mailings to directly promote myself. But I love putting these pieces together. I love staying in touch through these pieces. I love sharing stories. And I love hearing from people who tell me they enjoyed what they received and it made them feel good." I have a hard time believing that this doesn't translate into business!

For a less unusual but still effective use of postcards, bring your client list along and buy a bunch of cards when you travel to an exotic locale on business. No secretary would fail to pass on a handwritten greeting on a postcard from Amsterdam, Nairobi or Bogotá. During those inevitable dead hours of delay, think up a message that connects your business and the destination, such as, for a thinking styles consultant visiting

London, "I'm planning some new research on whether the British are more right-brained because they drive on the left. Not knowing which way to turn my head before I cross the street makes me *no*-brained! Regards . . ."

Envelopes

Direct mail commonly emblazons a marketing message or teaser on envelopes, but there's no reason you can't use that space on your "regular" business envelopes too. Barbara Levine, author of *Your Body Believes Every Word You Say*, had customized envelopes made up featuring the title of her book. "It didn't cost extra, and you never know who will see it," she says. The most creative marketing on a general-purpose envelope that I've seen comes from speaker Patricia Fripp, who in 1991 won a much-bigger-than-lifesize ad on a San Francisco billboard by raising more money than anyone else for the Leukemia Society of America. Along the left-hand third of a 9 by 12-inch white envelope, she reprinted a black-and-white reproduction of the billboard—every bit as arresting as the outdoor version, yet not scheduled to vanish after a month. And don't overlook the customizable portion of a postage meter imprint as a chance to get a brief sales message in front of the eyes of several people besides your recipient. Envelopes that get metered at the American Kennel Club in New York City go out with the message, "Make Time for Responsible Dog Ownership" to the left of the meter mark.

T-shirts, buttons and posters

Whoever first came up with the notion of getting people to pay for and then wear or post their advertising deserves our applause. In a creative twist on these walking advertisements, author Patricia Gallagher made up T-shirts for her three young daughters that read "Have you read my mommy's book?" "Ask me about my mommy's book!" and "My mommy wrote a book!" The author of *Working Solo*, Terri Lonier, had a small full-color version of her book cover laminated and backed with Velcro so that she can wear it on her chest, where it generates visibility for her business. "It breaks the ice, helps people remember the book and starts people on conversations that lead to great business deals or fresh ideas that I can use in my writing." Writing consultant Gary Blake of New York City turned a profit *and* gained publicity in office corridors by selling two-color posters featuring easy-to-grasp rules for punctuation and grammar along with a subtle plug at the bottom of the posters for his firm.

Calendars, magnets and other "freemiums"

How can you establish a constant presence in someone's kitchen or study? If you give people something they'll want to keep around, and your message is on it, they'll remember you. Computer consultant Barbara Boudreau sends out calendars imprinted with her name, tag line and phone number at the turn of the year, and says they work better for her than customized pens. Herschell Gordon Lewis introduced me to the term "freemium," which denotes an advertising trinket such as a refrigerator magnet enclosed in a direct mailing. Since its purpose is to prompt people to send you business, make sure it includes how they can reach you. When I called *Making a Living Without a Job* author Barbara Winter to find people to interview for this book, she mentioned a creative local business, then said, "Let's see . . . No, they're not listed in the Minneapolis directory. Wait, I have them right on my refrigerator! No, there's no telephone number on their magnet, either . . ."

After marketing consultant Jeff Slutsky published his first book, *Streetfighting*, he experimented with using the book as a "freemium." "We figured it was sacrilegious to throw away a book," he says, and he was right. After beginning to mail out five a day to a select list of top-level managers, calls started coming in. "Some wanted to buy more copies of the book.

Others wanted to hire us for speaking and consulting. It really helped to get things moving for us." Slutsky says that to lure prospects with a more expensive gift, the item should be valuable enough that it won't be tossed at first sight; affordable enough so it won't bankrupt you; something prospects want; and something that ties in with your products or services.

Creative delivery

Sometimes the way a marketing message gets delivered makes it memorable. To announce the fourth anniversary of the founding of the agency she was working for, Nancy Michaels of Concord, Massachusetts, dropped off bags containing a piece of cake and a press release at the offices of clients and prospects. Artist Peter Anton, who creates objects that look like food, came up with a bold way to get attention when business was slow. He put some leftover brochures about his art in personal pizza boxes from a restaurant-supply house, customized them with address labels resembling take-out forms, and sent them to galleries. They ate it up! As with all bravura acts, make sure that such dramatic gestures fit your business image.

Poems

Since 1986, my sister Gila Yudkin, a freelance tour guide based in Jerusalem, has sent a Jewish New Year's greeting every fall in the form of a page-long poem to the American ministers and tour organizers who have brought groups to her in the past. She spends dozens of hours every summer writing and polishing a new poem that describes newly opened and favorite sites in the Holy Land and invites the readers to come back. "As far as I know, I'm the only Israeli tour guide using a poem for promotion," Gila says. "Note, though, that if I sent it at Christmas time, it would get lost. No one responds immediately, but when tour leaders write to tell me that they are returning and to reserve dates, they almost invariably begin their letter by saying how much they've enjoyed reading my annual poem. When one pastor recommends me to another, he has usually kept the poem in his files. One tour leader/minister I had never guided for wrote and asked for permission to print my poem in his travel newsletter, so I know that it gets passed around too. All in all, I'm not sure the poem keeps the clients, but it sure is the best method I've come up with for helping tour leaders remember me and find me—much, much better than a business card."

Directory listings

Most professional associations publish directories that give members an opportunity to describe their qualifications and areas of specialization. Few people use their allotted space effectively as a marketing tool. For example, here's a hypothetical listing in a trainers' association directory that would not entice buyers to call:

> Dynamic, inspiring speaker and seminar leader on sales training and other topics you'll love.

Of these fourteen words, four are empty boasting, three are fillers, three are redundant and two are ridiculously vague. Can you figure out the only two words that do help—just a little—to distinguish this trainer from the thousands of others in the directory? ("Sales training.") Differentiation, not self-administered accolades, does the trick in directories as elsewhere. Wherever you have the chance for such a listing, edit it ruthlessly so that every word contributes to pulling in referrals or bookings.

In addition to membership directories, investigate the compiled directories that circulate in libraries and are described in a master reference called *Directories in Print*. It includes more than 15,000 published sets of listings from the *Burwell Direc-*

tory of Information Brokers to the *Virginia Insurance Directory*. Most reference directories require you only to fill out a form to be listed; some require you to submit references; and a few, such as the *Yearbook of Experts, Authorities and Spokespersons*, ask for payment. Because Marilyn Ross of Buena Vista, Colorado, performs a lot of different tasks in the publishing process, she has no less than eleven listings in *Literary Marketplace* for her company About Books, Inc. "Once you've gotten in there, it's pretty painless to be continued to the following year's edition," Ross says. "We use every bit of space allowed us to show how we solve people's needs. By appearing everywhere, we look like a big, established company, and we get about 10 percent of our customers from that one source."

Packaging and instructions

If the customer has a chance to see your product before buying, the writing on the package as well as its aesthetics can promote or jettison the sale. Tom Chappell, founder of the all-natural personal-care products company Tom's of Maine, used product labels to initiate a personal relationship with customers. "We always tried to imagine the customer as someone we could actually talk to, face to face," Chappell has written. "From the first package, we had communicated with customers in a letter on the label, informing them about the source and purpose of our ingredients (for example, saying we use fluoride in toothpaste that is found in the sea and prevents cavities), ending with the invitation, 'Please write and let us know your experience. Your friends, Tom and Kate.' Immediately we got letters from enthusiastic customers." Similarly, the outrageous success of Smartfood popcorn—until being taken over by Frito-Lay— had much to do with the sassy copy on its black-and-yellow package. In my opinion, it's the best-tasting cheese popcorn on the market—but copy like this fractured Shakespearean quote, "Alas, poor Yorick, he never got to try Smartfood . . . ," even more than the flavor, helped give the product personality.

According to home business expert Barbara Brabec, hand-crafted merchandise always fetches higher prices when it includes a decorative "hang tag." Artistically executed, it can offer tidbits about the making of the item, its maker or its care—or even a little saying that simply reinforces the buyer's feeling that the item is special. These cost just pennies to add to products but pay off in many dollars. For books destined to be sold in bookstores, the back cover copy makes such a difference in sales that Dan Poynter in *Is There a Book Inside You?* even recommends you write that copy before writing the book!

For other products, the written directions for use strongly influence customers' degree of satisfaction with the product. Not everyone is willing to suffer through the muddled English and enigmatic diagrams we associate with Swedish furniture. In Chapter 2 I mentioned a computer company that slid into bankruptcy because customers frustrated by an instruction manual returned the product en masse. I came very close to returning a game called "Mindtrap" because after three readings I could not understand the play instructions. Remember to take any copy accompanying your product as seriously as you would the copy that precedes the sale.

Handwritten notes

Are we all rebelling against over-proper mothers? Most of us no longer practice the rule drummed into us and enforced when we were children: Write a thank-you note whenever someone does something nice for you. Because this gesture has become rare, it makes a big impact when you do take the trouble. For a properly personal touch, handwrite your message on a postcard, a high-quality stationery note or notepaper headed with your logo. To make sure that her assistant can enclose a handwritten note with every product shipment, professional speaker Patricia Fripp sits in front of the TV when she isn't traveling, signing note after note, "Thanks for your order! Patricia Fripp."

PART III

◇

APPRAISING
YOUR WORK

CHAPTER 12

Using Trade Secrets
from the Masters

A few months before the scheduled weekend of my twentieth college reunion, I sent postcards to my four best buddies from back then, reminding them that they had promised to attend. All four showed up. Jack Smith, who drove all the way from Michigan to Rhode Island for the event, told me that the way I worded the postcard made a difference to him. "If you'd asked, 'Are you still planning to come?' I would have said no," he said. "But you said, 'Don't forget . . . No excuses accepted.' So I came."

With any kind of persuasive writing, small alterations in wording can produce great increases or decreases in results. Ditto with substitutions of color, paper, format, timing and a myriad of other factors. Although you should constantly test refinements of your materials, you can also benefit from the discoveries of those who have made it their business to learn what works. For those professionals who have truly devoted themselves to this craft, no punctuation mark, no manner of folding is too trifling to pay attention to. Here are a slew of subtleties they've been willing to share. As in any field of expertise, renegades constantly come along and disprove principles most specialists took as irrefutably established. So take these tips as provisional ways to improve your marketing materials, not gospel.

Choosing the Right Words

To corrupt a phrase by Mark Twain, the difference between the right word and the almost right word is the difference between a sale and a beached whale. While no checklist can infuse you with the skill of a wordmaster, these points can keep your copy lively and compelling.

Choose short, powerful words over longer ones

Your ads, brochures and sales letters are no place to show off an imposing vocabulary. Most of the time, substituting a shorter alternative equivalent in meaning adds vigor to your prose. For instance, John Caples reports that changing a headline from "How to Repair Cars—quickly, easily, right" to "How to Fix Cars—quickly, easily, right" increased orders 20 percent! Other examples:

INSTEAD OF: concerning, furnish, request, subsequently
USE: about, give, ask, later

Consider how words sound

Columnist William Safire once sponsored a "Miss Word Contest" and awarded beauty pageant honors to "mellifluous." Other top contenders included "sunset" and "lavender." The ugliest word, he decided, was "glut." More people salivate at the offer of a "plump" grape than a "round" or "fat" one, partly because the repeated *p*'s make it sound more interesting. Indeed, according to Michigan State University advertising professor Bruce Vanden Bergh, most of the top brand names include at least one of the so-called "plosive" sounds—*k, p, b, c, d, t, ch* and *j*. According to an ad of the Marsteller agency, words can sound feminine or masculine, confident or worried, round or oblong, fast or slow:

Feminine: slipper, peek, flutter
Masculine: socks, cartel, rupture
Confident: lavish, demand, Brooklyn
Worried: pill, stomach, Bronx
Round: Bob, bubble, Oslo
Oblong: obscure, Michigan, Ontario
Fast: brash, violet, astringent
Slow: damp, purple, hamburger

If these categorizations of words bewilder you, don't worry. But if they sensitize you to word headlines so that they embody dependability or ceaseless motion, great.

Be sensitive to words' connotations

Former president Jimmy Carter learned the hard way that words can be technically correct, yet wildly inappropriate because of common associations. In 1989, he was mystified when guests at a party said hello and then covered their crotches. One guest laughingly explained that in Carter's book *An Outdoor Journal: Adventures and Reflections*, he had written that on one fishing trip a salmon took "a ferocious leap at my fly." Mortified at the misinterpretation, Carter arranged for all the warehoused copies of the book to be doctored so that the salmon instead took "a ferocious leap at my lure." A more mundane example: After I got no response to a flyer for my editing service headlined "Constructive Critic on Call," I realized that the word "critic" carried associations of pain for most people. Similarly, I advised an investment advisor who wanted to pitch his products as "so predictable and profitable they're boring," that "boring" conveys unpleasantness. To maintain the allure of his message, I recommended saying something

like, "so predictable and profitable you'll be able to spend
more time playing golf."

Indeed, some words have such positive connotations that
they usually boost response. Jay Conrad Levinson, for one,
lists these magical attractors:

- Free
- New
- You
- Sale
- Introducing
- Save
- Discover
- Results
- Proven
- Guaranteed

The following words, however, detract from any headline.
Even in what you believe is a positive context, suggests Levinson, they poison the atmosphere.

- Buy
- Failure
- Bad
- Sell
- Loss
- Difficult
- Decision
- Death
- Cost
- Order

Choose emotional words over intellectual ones

Even accountants and rocket scientists would rather have
you "explain" something and "help" them than "disclose"

something and "aid" them. In most cases, the emotional words from this roundup by Herschell Gordon Lewis encourage a clearer mental picture than the more distant, more abstract intellectual versions:

Intellectual word	Emotional word
accelerate	speed up
completed	finished
for	because
intelligent	bright
learn	find out
reply	answer
wealthy	rich

Prefer present tense to future or past

What's more powerful than a promise? A result that exists right now. That's why your copy pulls in more orders when you say, "We *delight* our customers with same-day service" than when you say "We *will delight* you with our same-day service" or "We *have delighted* customers with our same-day service for fourteen years." When trying to make a sale, writing about what your product *will* do or what the buyer *will* receive creates a tiny space for doubt. In proposals, sales letters and brochures especially, you sound more confident when you write about what the product *does* and what the buyer *receives*.

Avoid conditional and hypothetical statements

COMPARE: If you join our health club, . . .
WITH: When you join our health club, . . .
The latter shows more poise, without being presumptuous. Similarly, compare the power of the second, nonhypothetical scenario:

BEFORE: Suppose you lost your wallet. Would you know how to notify all your credit card companies?

AFTER: On your way home from the movies, you realize your wallet is gone. Do you know how to notify all seven of your credit card companies?

Richard Ott suggests readers identify more with your copy when you describe a situation where the reader already enjoys your product or service.

BEFORE: Come experience the beauty and serenity of an Alaskan vacation.

AFTER: In Alaska, you are surrounded by beauty and bathed in serenity.

Transitional words and phrases keep people reading

Create a smooth flow in your copy by beginning some sentences "And," "But," "Yet" or "Even so." If your fifth-grade English teacher's rule against the first two bothers you, tell yourself you've graduated into the real world, where that rule has all the force of the 55 mph speed limit.

Allow redundancies for impact

Copy crafters who respect the English language know that "free gift" and "absolutely, positively" make the same point twice. Still, because these repetitions get better results than just "gift" or "absolutely," they use redundancies for emphasis of key selling points.

Choose numerals or numbers in words strategically

Even buried in the middle of a paragraph, far down a page, "$500" sticks out more than "five hundred dollars." Consequently, copywriter Dick Dunn recommends that if price is a selling point, use numerals. The same price in words, however, plays down the amount and gives your piece more class. Likewise, "$500" seems more sophisticated and smaller than "$500.00."

Cashing in on the Psychology of Buying

Some marketing experts have passed on observations that help you persuade prospects teetering with indecision to pull out their checkbook or their credit card. The greater the commitment you are asking of buyers, the more you need to relieve their fears and doubts.

Reassure prospects with guarantees

According to Marilyn Ross, the stronger and longer your guarantee, the fewer your returns or requests for a refund. A ninety-day guarantee inspires fewer returns than a thirty-day guarantee, while the fewest returns of all come from a lifetime guarantee. That's either human perversity or procrastination at work!

Head off "That's too good to be true"

With great justification, Herschell Gordon Lewis calls our era the age of skepticism. Most customers who encounter an offer that appears too good to be true shy away, sure there must be some hidden catch. Thus if you've cooked up a juicy offer, explain how you're able to do so much or take so little. Whenever your promotions come to the attention of regular clients and customers, you must prevent them from drawing the conclusion that they can hang back from buying until your once-a-year inventory sale. A unique, unrepeatable reason for a discount or special offer, such as "We're overstocked" or "To celebrate our 10th anniversary . . ." can do that.

Use your address to bolster buyer confidence

Research shows that people trust a street address more than a post office box. If you add your street address *above* the line that says, "P.O. Box XXXX," you win reader trust without redirecting any mail from your box. Direct-response specialist René Gnam finagled the ultimate—a street name that matches his business to the "R." Was it serendipity that enabled him to locate at "1 Response Road" in Tarpon Springs, Florida? Nope, he says. "I named it. Why not? I own it." Naturally, he also calls his property "Response Ranch."

For greater credibility, choose photography over illustrations

We believe what we see in a photograph more than comparable information in a drawing or diagram. Except in a catalog, where you should highlight the products for sale, photos of people draw more attention than those of things.

Write something to reinforce buyer confidence after a sale

According to Richard Ott, the fungus of doubt grows where buyers don't know how to judge the results of a product or service. By providing perspective in a follow-up letter or an information piece that accompanies the sale, you increase the odds that customers whom you served well feel satisfied. For example, if my piano seemed out of tune two weeks after it was tuned, I might think the tuner did a horrible job—except that he explained why the fact that it hadn't been tuned for years meant that it might not hold the correct pitch as long as it otherwise would. Another instance that comes to mind is a woman whom I helped with a press release who complained that "only" eight out of fifty outlets that she sent it to contacted her. Belatedly I assured her that with a 16 percent immediate pickup rate, she was actually doing remarkably well. Ott uses the example of a company that refinishes hardwood floors, which could hand out a brochure after the sale explaining how the process works, how to judge results and how long I should expect my shiny new floor to last. Even better, the company could also guarantee the work and provide me with a special number to call if I had any questions or comments. "Isn't it odd how each of us receives a ton of literature before the purchase, but little or none after?" Ott asks. "You feel the marketer abandons you right after you've decided to embrace him. That's not a good feeling."

Appropriately appeal to wants or needs

According to Bob Bly, when we buy as private individuals, we would rather indulge a yen for something we fancy than a cold-blooded judgment that this is something we should have. But in the realm of business, we spend more readily for needs than wants, since we normally have to justify expenditures—if only to ourselves. Hence when selling to consumers, stress wants more than needs, and for business customers, turn the emphasis upside-down.

Prevent "I'll-do-it-later-itis"

These proven techniques encourage people to act now:

- limited quantities
- reward (premium) for fast reply
- deadline rubber-stamped on a letter
- discount for fast response
- multiple methods of responding, such as phone, fax, mail and E-mail

The following principles also help demolish barriers to the sale:

- A fill-in-the-blanks coupon or order blank boosts your response rate 25 to 100 percent in ads, direct mail, newsletters.

- Include your contact information somewhere else besides the coupon, so a second person—or the first person, later—can find you.

- A toll-free number triples your response rate; use the
  words "toll-free" and not just "1-800-. . ."

- Accepting credit cards beats out cash or check required
  at least two to one.

Profitability Formatting Your Piece

Finally, here are some miscellaneous tips for setting up
your marketing pieces for maximum response.

1. *Break copy up with subheads.* Subheadings—subsidiary
   headlines throughout a piece—preclude a dense, forbid-
   ding look. They also help get your message across to
   browsers, and improve the pulling power of direct mail,
   ads, newsletters and brochures.
2. *For letters, end pages in the middle of a sentence.* This
   is not the place to be a neatnik. Forcing people to turn
   the page to find the end of a thought beats formatting
   each page to look self-contained.
3. *Indent.* Whether in a letter, ad, brochure, press release
   or newsletter, indented paragraphs get read more than
   blocky nonindented ones.
4. *Use "drop caps."* According to one study, larger initial
   capitals increase readership 13 percent.
5. *Keep paragraphs short.* When you organize copy into
   columns, this dictum becomes harder to obey, yet
   more vital. As in newspapers, feel free to break up
   what you wrote as one paragraph into two or three.
   Seven lines or less per paragraph is the consensus of
   the experts.
6. *Always caption photos, graphs, diagrams.* Experts agree

that four times as many people read captions as read body copy.

7. *Organize selling points with bullets.* Lists arrayed with oversized dots make your points stand out. Numbering the points in a list gives them more emphasis than bullets. For even greater spotlighting, give the list a title through a headline or subhead.

8. *Don't end a headline with a period.* As David Ogilvy points out, the other word for a period is, appropriately, a "stop."

9. *Keep columns narrow.* Up to forty characters wide keeps it readable. Beyond that, people struggle to find the beginning of the next line.

CHAPTER 13

Editing for Crisp,
Clear—and Correct—Copy

"Writing is hard work. A clear sentence is no accident. Very few sentences come out right the first time, or even the third time. If you find that writing is hard, it's because it *is* hard. It's one of the hardest things that people do."

So says William Zinsser in his classic text, *On Writing Well*. And to illustrate the pains that even highly skilled, experienced writers take with their work, he provides a facsimile of his fifth and next-to-final draft of that very chapter of his book. Of 513 words on his two-page spread, 119 lurk beneath crossouts, destined for the trash. Apter, simpler words replace them here and there, and curvy lines show how to link the beginning of one thought to the ending of another, leapfrogging across the rubber in between.

Zinsser's craftsmanship deserves emulation, whether you are writing for your hardware store customers or readers of *The New Yorker*, as he has been known to do. With persuasive copy you need to wield an editing pen as ruthlessly as a landscaper uproots weeds, and as judiciously as a surgeon slices out cancers. Your goal: clean, uncluttered prose that sends your message straight to the understanding of your prospect.

Don't let Zinsser intimidate you into believing that the realm of clear communication lies far beyond you, though. Even as a beginner, you can measurably improve your initial drafts just by applying a few basic principles.

Guidelines for Effective Editing

Writing is a process

Rather than expect crystalline clarity on your first try, allow for improvement through a succession of drafts. Work on refining your concept and basic approach first before worrying about things like paragraphing and word choice. Leave correcting the grammar and assuring the accuracy of details for last. By attending to the larger issues first, you avoid getting the words perfect in a section that later proves unnecessary.

Extra words—and extra paragraphs—obstruct your message

I agree with Zinsser that "clutter is the disease of American writing." Always imagine that you must cut at least 20 percent of your words, and you'll be amazed to see your message become sharper. Watch these before-and-after transformations, for example:

UNEDITED: Pioneerland, the largest in acreage of any American theme park except Disney World, is scheduled to present its opening ceremonies just after New Year's Day, on January 2.

EDITED: Pioneerland, America's second-largest theme park, opens January 2.

UNEDITED: As a general rule, we offer our services to clients located in areas ranging from the Southeast to the Northwest through the vehicles of the postal service, facsimile machines, telephone and personal meetings.

EDITED: We serve clients nationally by mail, phone, and fax as well as in person.

Hunt for excess verbiage, especially at the beginning of your brochure, ad or newsletter article. Do you start off strongly, or do you spend a few sentences warming up? Writing teachers call such slow starts "throat-clearing." Now that you know the name of this common phenomenon, make sure you sweep your unnecessary noises off the page.

Specifics communicate better than generalities

Stay on the lookout for empty adjectives like "marvelous," "indispensable" or "unique." Transform vague verbiage into copy that sells by substituting precise, named qualities for broad descriptions or indefinite accolades.

WEAK: Best-selling author Tom Wallabee has done it again with *Three Cheers for Wally*.

BETTER: Tom Wallabee's previous books sold more than 120,000 copies. The *Miami Herald* has already acclaimed his new book, *Three Cheers for Wally*, as "destined to become a children's classic."

WEAK: Cape Cod Cascades is the affordable seaside vacation.

BETTER: For just $129, less than the cost of a year's daily newspaper, your family of four can enjoy a memorable beach weekend at Cape Cod Cascades.

If it sounds good but doesn't further your purpose for your audience, it needs to go

You don't—shouldn't—want compliments on your fine writing in your marketing piece: you want appointments, orders or sales. Effective persuasive writing does not call attention to itself.

Energetic writing keeps readers alert and interested

Sometime before the age of twelve, you undoubtedly learned the term "passive verb," as in "The ball was hit by Bob," in contrast to the active verb in "Bob hit the ball." What they probably didn't tell you back then is that passive verbs strangle the life out of your writing if you allow them into your prose. To keep your sentences vibrant, say *who* is doing *what* to *whom*, rather than *who* is being *whatted*. The other great deadener is "is," along with cousins "are," "was" and "were." Though this may take some thought, replace these with more specific verbs wherever you can. Your writing will perk up like an always-just-plugged-in coffeepot.

DEAD: Complaint letters are discussed every week.

ALIVE: We discuss complaint letters every week.

DEAD: The G.R.T. program is designed to get customers calling you.

ALIVE: The G.R.T. program encourages customers to call you.

DEAD: The reason for failure is usually laziness.

ALIVE: Laziness usually accounts for failure.

DEAD: Your result is satisfaction.

ALIVE: You achieve satisfaction.

A fresh approach enlivens an ordinary message

Predictability bores, whether in a combination of words anyone can complete if you stopped in the middle (otherwise known as a cliché) or in a promise people have read a million times before. To avoid provoking yawns, toss one unexpected word into a formula or substitute an original image.

BORING: Accountamatics, Inc., has made tax preparation a whole new ball game.

BETTER: Accountamatics, Inc., has made tax preparation a simply-punch-in-the-numbers game.

Positive wording persuades more than negative

Negative phrasings usually lead readers away from the action you want them to take. For instance, what idea would this letter opening from a real estate company put into your mind?

BEFORE: Mrs. G. has asked me to write and give you the first right of refusal on the sale of the condominium you are currently renting.

When I see "first right of refusal," I think about saying no—but that's not what the letter writer wants. The following rewrite gets me thinking in a more positive vein:

AFTER: Mrs. G. asked me to write and let you know that you now have an outstanding option to buy the condominium you are currently renting.

Pass your copy through the Literal Reader test

Think about this claim: An ad said that General Motors cars had the "best overall injury loss experience." A literal reader, taking each word in its usual meaning, would interpret this to mean something like "GM owners had the most fun while their cars were being wrecked," which I doubt the copywriter intended. So-called mixed metaphors create even more havoc when you try to picture the action they evoke in your mind's eye: "Our personnel handbook keeps the long arm of the law from raining down on you." (Have raining arms ever been a problem for you? I didn't think so.)

Intention counts for little; reception is all

A consultant in one of my classes acted like I was dumb when I asked how much the seminar advertised in her brochure cost. She'd written, "Fee: $300/person," then four lines below that, "INTRODUCTORY PRICE: $150." I see-sawed back and forth: So was it $150 or $300? If a member of your intended audience missed the point, assume the fault is yours. "But that's not what I meant! Look, it says right here . . ." is not an appropriate response when someone misconstrues your headline or your promise. Seek a clearer way to get your meaning across.

It takes practice to anticipate all the astonishing ways people fail to get what's perfectly clear to you, so you'll need plenty of feedback (see Chapter 14) and plain old trial and error to achieve clarity when you're starting out. Imagining a perverse reader may help you root out ambiguities like this one:

BEFORE: Some people want coaching on an hourly, as-needed basis. Others choose to meet regularly for an extended period of time. (Does "extended period of time" mean longer-than-one-hour sessions, or regular sessions over a period of months, or both?)

AFTER: Some people want coaching on an hourly, as-needed basis. Others choose to meet regularly for a morning or afternoon at a time.

Simple and straightforward never offends

When you use jargon—buzzwords bandied around by insiders—you run the risk of turning away otherwise good prospects who have no clear idea what you are talking about. Even if you think appropriate customers *should* know your lingo, roll out the welcome carpet by including a definition or an alternate characterization of what you are talking about in layperson's terms. You can do this inconspicuously, without alienating those in the know, so don't worry that you can gain one group only by losing another. "No one ever lost a sale because they were too easy to understand," notes technical copywriter Bob Bly. Here are some examples that show how to count everyone in instead of excluding through your use of jargon:

BEFORE: Yankel, Yankel & Gray represent parties in an exchange relationship in the business environment that experience a breach in the terms of commercial conduct.

AFTER: We help settle buyer-seller disputes.

BEFORE: Through instruction in effective electronic document management, we dramatically increase the productivity and effectiveness of knowledge workers. (For me, reading this sentence is like reading French—I have to guess at a few of the terms' meanings and am not sure I grasped the overall intended message.)

AFTER: By teaching new computer strategies, our seminar increases the productivity and effectiveness of those at your company who create correspondence, communicate company policies or file, retrieve and manipulate information.

Though brevity is an important communicative virtue, you're always better off going longer if you add clarity along with additional words.

Inclusive nonsexist language fits the '90s

Unless you're writing to a male military or police officer, eliminate "Dear Sir" from your letter-writing repertoire. If you don't know your respondent's name, substitute a classifying or descriptive term, such as "Dear garage owner" or "Dear new home buyer." Or, as I illustrated in Chapter 7, try leaving off the salutation altogether. Also avoid assuming in your choice of language that certain groups are composed of members of one sex or the other when that isn't necessarily true.

NO: When an electrical engineer needs temporary on-site assistance, he calls ElecTemps.

YES: When electrical engineers need temporary on-site assistance, they call ElecTemps.

NO: In their convention off-time, nurses and their husbands can enjoy visiting the famous sites of San Francisco.

YES: In their convention off-time, nurses and their spouses [or "families"] can enjoy visiting the famous sites of San Francisco.

Note: In my books, I use the strategy of sometimes using a generic "he" and sometimes a generic "she." For people taking in the whole book, these balance each other and create nonsexist prose.

You Can Prevent the Top Eight Copy Crimes!

If you want to impress readers as competent and literate, eliminate the following clearcut goofs from everything you write.

"It's" instead of "its"

An easy rule keeps this Number One offender from marring your copy. When you can substitute "it is" and retain your intended meaning, use "it's" (the apostrophe signifies the missing *i* in "is"); otherwise, use "its," which indicates the inanimate version of "his" or "her."

WRONG: Here's what Great Green never told it's customers. (You do not mean ". . . never told it is customers.")

RIGHT: Here's what Great Green never told its customers.

WRONG: Its easy to save money with Top Tix on your team. (You do mean "it is easy," so . . .)

RIGHT: It's easy to save money with Top Tix on your team.

Lack of agreement

Verbs that do not match their subjects convey carelessness. For every action word, find the person, place or thing performing the action and make sure they agree in number with the verb. Ignore all the words between the subject and the verb, which often provoke the mistake.

WRONG: Handmade buttons like the one pictured below is our specialty. (The subject of the verb "is" is "buttons." You wouldn't say "Buttons is . . .")

RIGHT: Handmade buttons like the one pictured below are our specialty.

Watch out especially for these words derived from Latin, which are all plural: media, criteria and phenomena. Their singular versions are, respectively, medium, criterion, and phenomenon.

WRONG: What does the media say about auto consultants?

RIGHT: What do the media say about auto consultants?

Misused semicolons

Used properly, a semicolon (;) normally brings closer together two sentences, each capable of standing on its own. To test, read each side of the semicolon out loud and ask yourself if it makes a complete thought.

WRONG: All business owners must concern themselves with the constant changes occurring in today's economy; moreover, the new provisions in the Revenue Reconciliation Act of 1993. (The "moreover" side of the semicolon isn't a complete thought.)

RIGHT: All business owners must concern themselves with the constant changes occurring in today's economy, as well as the new provisions in the Revenue Reconciliation Act of 1993.

Misplaced or missed apostrophes

"It's" is not the only culprit when it comes to apostrophes. If you've used an apostrophe, it belongs only in two cases: (1) It indicates letters left out, as in "you've" for "you have," or (2) In "thingamajig's doohickey," it indicates possession—which can always be restated as "the doohickey of the thingamajig." Be extra careful when turning a plural noun into a possessive: "the doohickey of several thingamajigs" becomes "the thingamajigs' doohickey."

WRONG: A product who's time has come. (You do not mean "who is time," so . . .)

RIGHT: A product whose time has come.

WRONG: Better than your competitor's ads. (Correct only if

you have just one competitor. For more than one competitor, you need . . .)

RIGHT: Better than your competitors' ads.

WRONG: Taking better care of childrens teeth. (You mean the teeth of children, right?)

RIGHT: Taking better care of children's teeth.

Conflict between setup and follow-through

Whenever you say, "There are three remedies for this problem," you must list exactly three, not two or four. Sound obvious? This copy crime can take much more subtle form.

WRONG: Is your inventory investment being managed wisely, or are you experiencing costly stock-out or overstocking problems? Unless you can unequivocally answer yes to this question, you owe it to yourself to speak to us. (Your prospect can't do as you ask, because that is not one yes-or-no question.)

RIGHT: Is your inventory investment being managed wisely, without costly stock-out or overstocking problems? (Now your prospect can unequivocally answer yes or no.)

Inconsistencies of detail

With some elements of punctuation, spelling and formatting, you have a choice. You can use roman numerals or Arabic ones; write "M.I.T." or "MIT"; capitalize "President" or not; use British spelling or American. But if you begin a list with "I" and "II" you shouldn't continue with "3" and "4"; you shouldn't write "M.I.T." and "IRS" in the same piece of writing; you shouldn't call one person the "President" and another the "third vice-president"; and you shouldn't name "gray" (the American spelling) as one of your paint "colours" (the British version). Most readers won't notice these mishmashes consciously, they'll just feel vaguely uneasy, as when an orchestra plays just a bit out of tune. The longer your document, the more you need to keep track of your choices. Professional editors create a schematic list called a style sheet to achieve consistency. See the book on copy editing in Chapter 26 for more information on this.

Compounded modifiers

A fast-talking style sometimes piles up a lot of adjectives in front of a noun. In writing, however, this style usually creates ambiguities or confusions that must be clarified by either restructuring the sentence or marking the compounded adjective with hyphens.

WRONG: My newsletter continually exposes the undermining financial integrity facts about stocks, bonds, and mutual funds. (People read this as "exposes the undermining . . ." and have to backtrack when they get to "facts.")

RIGHT: My newsletter continually exposes the facts about stocks, bonds and mutual funds that undermine their financial integrity.

WRONG: We deliver knocks your socks off service. (Sounds at first as if you deliver knocks.)

RIGHT: We deliver knocks-your-socks-off service.

OR: We deliver service that knocks your socks off. (Don't use this line if you sell shoes.)

Dangling modifiers

When a description followed by a comma leads off a sentence, the reader takes what follows the comma to be the thing to which the introductory description applies. These crop up all the time in bios, sometimes leading to ludicrous characterizations.

WRONG: A veteran talk-show host, Jones's guests are always at their best. (This says that the guests are the host!)

RIGHT: A veteran talk-show host, Jones is known for eliciting the best in her guests.

WRONG: As director of The Pottery Project, Mary Lou's

charitable works won acclaim. (According to this sentence, Mary Lou's charitable works served as director. A neat trick!)

RIGHT: As director of The Pottery Project, Mary Lou won acclaim for her charitable works.

CHAPTER 14

Getting Helpful Feedback and Testing Effectiveness

In 1979, after I had completed the first draft of a novel, I attended a prestigious writers' conference in Vermont. One well-known author duplicated my first three pages to discuss in class, and began the session by inviting me to read it out loud. After I sat down, the author delivered his criticisms from the podium to the more than 100 people assembled. "This is a perfect illustration of why you should never write in the first person. The narrator is utterly unlikable, the language is fuzzy—she says 'home' instead of 'house' . . ." He went on and on, unrelentingly negative.

Then the author's sidekick, who had also published several books, went to work. Sneering at his copy, he stabbed me even deeper. "Well, if there was at least *something* interesting about it—the plot, the language, the characters . . ."

I cried for days and walked around for weeks in a state of shocked disheartenment.

When I told this story years later as a teacher of a writing class, someone asked how I was able to pull together and write again. I began to wonder about that too, and came to the conclusion that it was partly because those butchers were not able to explain their objections in a way that I could understand. *Why* is "house" a better word than "home"? They had no interest in helping me improve my story. Instead of offering constructive feedback, they had orchestrated an occasion to show off their superiority. Since they had not really communicated with me, the attacks eventually rolled away without taking permanent hold.

I've learned a lot about constructive feedback since 1979, both as a recipient from a highly skilled teacher and coach, and as a giver to my own students and clients. There's actually much you can do to ensure helpful comments on your writing, including setting the stage for fruitful assistance and avoiding people who only know how to display their egos.

Getting Reviews You Can Use

The ideal people to give you feedback on your marketing piece had no role in its creation and know nothing about the thinking that went into it. Thus they can tell you, pure and simple, what the words on paper communicate. Solicit their comments after you've polished it all you can, but before you take it to the printer. To help them help you, mentally prepare them and yourself.

Mentally prepare them by telling them what they will be looking at, the target audience you wrote it for and specific questions you'd like feedback on. For example: "This is an ad I wrote that's going to appear in *Modern Keyboard*. I'm trying to get intermediate-level classical piano players to send away for my home-study jazz course. If you played classical piano, would this grab your attention? Did I convince you that you can learn jazz from my course? Is it clear how to order, how much it cost and all that kind of stuff?" I've seen a lot of people who normally say just "Looks great" or "Good job" become more discriminating and articulate when told what to look for. Explain that you're trying to fine-tune your approach.

Once a woman in a writing workshop complained that she only ever got negative comments on her work. The oddness of that response stuck with me, and I later asked her what she told feedback givers when she handed them something of hers. "I tell them, 'Please be totally frank—be brutal. I can take it!' " she replied. I couldn't help laughing ruefully. Usually you get what you ask for!

Mentally prepare yourself by remembering not to take any suggestions or criticisms as personal attacks but as data that can help you get your message across. If you were thinking earlier in this chapter that ad and brochure writers don't invest as much of themselves in their work as novel writers, you're wrong. Written copy about your product or service naturally deeply concerns you. Besides, most people finish any kind of writing task convinced that they have said exactly what they intended to say. When they reread it, their intended meaning bounces right back to them from the words they see on the page. Since the glow of your intentions distorts perception of your own work, you need objective opinions the same way a singer needs someone to check how well her voice carries to the back of the hall.

When the feedback comes, bite your tongue except to probe for clarifications and explanations—"What do you mean, it seemed cold?" or "Which part went on too long?" not "But look . . ." If you feel your hackles going up, smooth them down again. Decide whether you have to discount the positive or negative tone of the comments. A Bostonian now living in Nova Scotia told me that local Canadians would never tell him if they didn't understand something, while many from the Northeast United States would. On the other hand, you may encounter someone who takes pleasure in ripping good work apart. Someone who makes blanket condemnations like "The whole thing is dumb" probably enjoys being savage, and should be crossed off your list for next time.

If you have the opportunity to watch people read your marketing piece, what you see can furnish valuable clues. Where do they laugh? Where do they furrow their eyebrows? How do they skip around? How quickly do they seem to get it? If your materials often sit out somewhere, observing walkers-by can be just as rewarding. Do they pass right by your ivory handout for the fuchsia one? Do they pick up your ad sheet, turn it over quickly and put it back down? Do they pause thunderstruck at your headline, grab your brochure and immediately look around for a pay phone? (We can always hope!)

Even better than soliciting feedback from friends is asking friends who owe you a favor to show your piece to a few of their friends, let them glance at it and then ask what it was about. You want to find out if your message comes across to people who are not paying close attention. According to Richard Ott, author of *Creating Demand*, roughly 80 percent of people exposed to the typical ad pay no conscious attention at all to it. If those who tune out nevertheless get a fleeting and accurate impression of your business, that boosts your effectiveness. But if your ad for no-stink athletic socks makes browsers think you're plugging laundry soap, you have a problem. I say more about this danger for ads in Chapter 10.

Communications consultant George Berman remembers objecting when a client of his, a real estate broker, wanted a full-color photo of one of his agents in a green blazer. "You're selling real estate, not blazers," Berman said, insisting that the distinctive color would distract casual readers. As this example shows, you want to invite comments on the layout, graphics, color scheme and photos as well as the words. Whoever failed to do this at my health plan had to run this apology in the members' newsletter: "In last fall's issue, we were so eager to show you the delightful face of a young member Ashley Champlin riding her bike in our story about asthma, we left out something very important—Ashley's bike helmet. Wearing a bike helmet is not only smart (helmets reduce the risk of head injury by 85 percent), in Massachusetts it's now the law." If columns need straightening, if type seems smudged or illegible, if a decorative swirl looks unintentionally like a swastika, you certainly want to know.

You also want to know if any wording is awkward or any sentences are hard to comprehend. Test this by setting your copy aside at least overnight and then reading it out loud. Any place you stumble indicates something that needs to be fixed. Even better, suggests advertising great John Caples, have someone who has never seen your piece read all the words out loud. "You know which words to emphasize in order to bring out your meaning," Caples explains. "You know how to make a long sentence sound simple by pausing at the proper places. Another reader does not know these things. You can tell by the smoothness of his reading whether your copy is clear." Listen for things like accidental rhymes, choppy sentences and a clumsy rhythm. Although normally readers won't recite your copy out loud like second graders, such glitches do slow people down and have a subtle negative impact.

Even after a piece is printed, you can continue collecting useful feedback. Ask a sampling of people who responded to an ad or your newsletter what inspired them to act. Ask long-time clients if your introductory materials aptly portray what they know of your service. Compare accolades in fan letters about your product to the benefits you stressed in your publicity and brochure. Ask friends who seem well attuned to the times if anything you've used for a while seems outdated. Or, imitating the focus groups of professional marketers, invite half a dozen people from your target audience to a fun lunch and get them talking about key words and concepts in your promotions.

Measuring and Testing Effectiveness

All of the above gives you qualitative information—ideas about what people like, loathe or disregard. Whatever you're selling, you should collect quantitative data too—numbers about how much business comes in from each marketing vehicle. On the most basic level, measuring effectiveness involves correlating incoming orders, appointments and requests for information with the sales and promotion materials you put out into the world.

When business comes in by phone, tack one short question onto the end of every conversation with someone who never called before: "How did you hear about me [or us]?" Have a system, on computer, in a notebook or on a bulletin board, for recording answers and periodically tallying them up. The results may surprise you—and enable you to save money. The staff of Hartford Toner in Broad Brook, Connecticut, use a standard form whenever a call from a new customer comes in. "Within a minute in the first conversation, I ask, 'How did you hear about us?' with a little music in my voice, so that it sounds spontaneous," says John Collins, president of the company. "We write it down, file these sheets, and once a month my wife adds them up. I had thought our newspaper ads were working, but only one customer in three years had come in from seeing our ads in the newspaper. Forty to 50 percent of new customers come in from our radio ads, so even though it's expensive we know it gives us a good return." Yet a curious phenomenon indicates a certain margin of error for customers' answers: Six people said they'd seen Hartford Toner on TV—though Collins has never run a single television ad. "It's probably just because we have so many different ways we market the company," he says.

You can go whole hog tracking and evaluating results using computer analysis. A relatively new kind of computer program called "market mapping" software can create a display in map form showing where geographically your responses are coming from. Other software can analyze things like where your top 20 percent of customers, who may account for 80 percent of revenues, heard about your firm. With an ordinary spreadsheet program, you can produce nifty graphs that help you make sense of a lot of data. How many days after sending out a direct-mail piece does response peak? Do mass mailings of your brochures bring in more or less earnings than personal referrals and networking?

But these low-tech methods also make tracking a lot easier:

1. Add "Ask for Brenda," "Department 68" or "Extension 7392" to your action statement. When no one named "Brenda" works for you, and you have no real department numbers or extensions, the person answering the phone knows for sure that a particular marketing piece using that subterfuge did its job.

2. Try adding a department number for a mail offer, but this works less well. If your ad runs in *Window Management* magazine, and you ask people to write to "Department WM," that's such a transparent code that many respondents know you'll receive their correspondence without it. (I usually think, "Why should I do their marketing research for them?" Some people, it seems, are irremediably rebellious.) A craftier system may be necessary for serious tracking.

3. Vary your address for certain offers. I get mail at my post office box without the name of the post office on the envelope. But when an envelope shows up with the extra line, "Back Bay Station," I know that a request for a specific booklet sits inside. When my name appears on the envelope as "Marcia Yudkin, Ph.D.," I'm also pretty sure what's in there. Similar variations I have thought of for mail offers include adding a middle initial to my name and adding a letter or two after the box number. Add a suite number if you use a street address occupied by you and you alone. Be sure to alert your letter carrier or box mail sorters if you decide to use a new company name altogether as your signal.

4. Require people to send back a card or a coupon. Something on the card or coupon should distinguish it as belonging to that campaign.

5. Use entirely different phone numbers or box numbers. With voice-mail companies or non-USPS postal offices, this doesn't cost much or obligate you beyond

about three months. You'd have one offer go to one voice-mail box or suite box and another to another.

The ultimate testing for ads, brochures and direct mail involves what's called a split run. Half the copies of a publication run one version of an ad and half run another, or you send one version of a mailing to half your list and another to the other half. You use one of the above systems to see which headline, approach, color or graphics pulls better. John Caples's books on advertising (see Chapter 26) contain fascinating examples of headlines and complete ads tested against each other. For the most effective testing, vary only one element at a time.

Sometimes you can learn what works and what doesn't by tracking other people's marketing, for free and with little effort. When serious money is involved, marketers repeat those ads and mailings that work and quash the ones that don't. For ads, look at eight to twelve consecutive issues of a publication. You can assume that any ads in two or more nonconsecutive issues worked, while the one-shots did not. Direct-mail pro Herschell Gordon Lewis does much the same for mailings. Using about 30 variations on his name, he gets onto major lists and analyzes the direct mail he receives for clues. "Comparing what comes to the different names, I can see what people are testing. Then I wait to see which version I get three months later. Obviously, that one worked."

Unless you're selling events or some other offer that evaporates after a certain time, you may draw mistaken conclusions about the impact of a particular promotion because results take time to show up. My sister Gila says that she took ministers off the list for her promotional New Year's poem when five years went by without her hearing from them. Then a tour leader who hadn't been in touch for seven years requested her as his guide and arrived in Israel with a full busload of fifty-one pilgrims. "At the airport, he asked if I had stopped writing my Rosh Hashanah poem. I was embarrassed. I had crossed him

off my list two years earlier." John Caples tells a similar
story of a man who read a Steinway ad, decided that was the
brand of piano he would buy and walked into a showroom
to do so—ten years later. Besides the circumstances being
right in being able to take another trip abroad or afford a grand
piano, some people just take ages to make up their mind.
Richard Ott puts it this way: "Ninety-five percent of the
marketing you do fills the bucket but might not be enough to
activate the decision-making mode in many people. Five percent of the marketing you do is the final drop that activates the
decision-making mode and makes 100 percent of your expenditures effective."

CHAPTER 15

Legal Constraints
to Be Aware Of

There's one kind of response you definitely do not want to receive when you're sending out your printed darlings to hustle business for you: a "We hereby inform you" letter from the attorney for another company or a customer, or from the government. "If you're not careful, you expose yourself to the possibility of fines, damages and even court orders requiring you to stop distributing materials or selling a product," says Fred Steingold, a small business lawyer in Ann Arbor, Michigan, and the author of *The Legal Guide for Starting and Running a Small Business.* "And that's not to mention legal fees and damage to your reputation, which is perhaps the most significant consequence of all."

Since running everything you write past a lawyer would cost you dearly, the most cost-effective way to stay out of trouble is to inform yourself about legal danger zones, take care to avoid common traps and consult an attorney when you're wondering if you've wandered into a scarlet-tinged area. Though I've done my best to be accurate here, I am not a lawyer, so please do not take the following as legal advice for your particular case.

How Do You Spell Protection? R-E-S-P-E-C-T

After studying what lawyers have said about the danger zones, I think the key is developing five kinds of respect.

Respect others' privacy

If you use someone else's name or photo without permission, you could be guilty of invasion of privacy. To stay out of trouble, make sure the permission is written. A standard release form states that you have the right to use that person's name, words or likeness without compensation. This applies not only, say, to candid photos you take of customers at your store or trade booth but also to the photos and comments of employees, loyal longtime clients, relatives and friends. Brian L. Smith, a lawyer in Gallatin, Tennessee, who publishes a newsletter on copyright and intellectual property, gives the example of including a photo of an employee in your company's annual report. "Suppose that employee leaves and you don't have written permission to use his picture. Hell has no fury like a disgruntled employee. You might get a letter from his lawyer saying, 'You know those annual reports you're passing around with Joe's picture in it? You didn't get Joe's written permission to do that, so you'd better throw them in the garbage can.' They can do that."

An overlapping legal concept to the right to privacy is called the right of publicity, which holds that celebrities and other public figures have the sole legal right to profit from their name, identity and likeness. In *An Ounce of Prevention: Marketing, Sales & Advertising Law for Non-Lawyers*, Steven A. Meyerowitz explains, "An unauthorized commercial appropriation of a person's identity converts the potential economic value in that identity to another's advantage." That is, if Julia Roberts showed up at your art opening—and maybe even bought one of your fiber hangings—you would be violating her right of publicity to include her photo, or her name as a buyer, in an advertisement or brochure. Interestingly, in many states a celebrity's right to publicity continues fifty years after his or her death. A car mechanic in my area who uses a photo of Elvis Presley on an advertising flyer for his repair shop might thus be opening the door to a lawsuit from Presley's heirs.

Respect others' reputations

By outlawing libel, the law prohibits you from writing something that unjustly injures another person's reputation. To take an extreme case, if you decided on the slogan "Humboldt County's only honest auctioneer," you would be implying that your competitors in that area were all dishonest. You had better have iron-clad evidence that they had all, say, been convicted of fraud! Note that libel laws apply not only for formally printed materials but also to a mass-distributed direct-mail letter and to public messages on an electronic bulletin board.

Things get really sticky when you decide to compare your products or services with competitors' in your advertising. According to Meyerowitz, on the one hand comparative data on competing products or services could serve as valuable information for consumers. On the other hand, when you portray a competitor in an unflattering way, the competitor is more likely to get upset and initiate legal action. Since the relevant law forbids making materially false representations about another company's goods, services or commercial activities, your best protection, says Meyerowitz, is to "be truthful, objective and able to substantiate the claims made in the ad."

Respect readers of your materials

Basically, tell the truth and make only promises you will be able to keep. Laws against deceptive advertising bar not only factually false statements, but also anything that, taken as a whole, might mislead an average person. Be ready to provide proof of any of your claims if challenged, advises Frank Grazian, executive editor of *Communications Briefings*. "If you say, 'You'll make at least $50,000 a year,' you have to be able to prove that the majority of participants, not just an occasional one, makes that much money. Furthermore, how you meant what you wrote is irrelevant. If a naive person would develop a mistaken expectation from what you wrote, you're liable. One ad said that with their product, you'd lose inches, but the copy didn't indicate that the loss would be temporary. They got in all kinds of trouble."

The Federal Trade Commission has several important guidelines about the word "free," one of the most attractive words in marketing. You have to state any conditions qualifying "free" conspicuously and clearly at the outset of the offer, not in fine print elsewhere. For example, a headline reading "Free video!" must mean "no strings attached," says Fred Steingold—not "You get this free video when you order our $295 deluxe set." The FTC specifically says that you can't refer the reader to a footnote qualifying what you mean by "free." Nor can you slap a sticker on a shrink-wrapped product saying "Free one-year supply of whoosits—details inside." A customer must be able to learn the details of the offer without buying. Naturally, you can't mark up any product or service someone has to buy to cover your costs for a "free" item.

According to a law called the Uniform Commercial Code, you don't have to use the words "guarantee" or "warranty" to create a promise a prospect has a right to rely upon. In a precedent-setting 1932 Washington State case, Sam Baxter successfully sued a Ford dealer and the Ford Motor Company when the windshield of his Model A Ford shattered under the impact of a pebble and shards of glass flew into Baxter's eye. Ford's catalogs and brochures had characterized Ford windshields as made of shatterproof glass that "will not fly or shatter under the hardest impact." Other cases have made it clear that even pictures can create so-called express warranties; unless otherwise informed, a consumer has a right to expect that a photo in a catalog accurately represents the product she will receive upon ordering. If you do want to offer some sort of guarantee, don't say just, "Money-back guarantee." Spell out the terms explicitly, as in, "If you're not 100 percent satisfied, let us know and you'll receive a refund on all unmailed copies of your subscription." Without any amplification, words like "satisfaction guaranteed" mean that the buyer has a right to a full refund upon request, with no "ifs," "ands" or "buts."

Watch out too for the following words that could get you in trouble with various authorities:

- *banish, rid, stop, end, correct, remedy, cure:* These all imply to readers that your product or service will make a problem go away permanently.

- *safe, harmless:* Since even a penny isn't a safe product in the wrong hands, these words invite liability suits.

- *science, scientific, evidence, proof, research:* These imply laboratory-type experiments or strictly controlled studies.

- *like new:* This phrase means your product performs no differently from one completely fresh and unused.

Respect buyers

Under the Federal Trade Commission's thirty-day mail order rule, unless your literature specifies a longer delivery gap, you must ship a product within thirty days of taking the customer's money or give the customer the choice of waiting further or receiving his money back. Another FTC rule says that if you advertise an item in your store, you must have reasonable quantities on hand. If a particular item sells out, the law says you can't unilaterally substitute another item to fill an order, even if the substitute item costs more.

Respect others' intellectual property—and protect your own

Complicated copyright, trademark and unfair competition laws govern your use of other people's material, but they boil down to something you probably learned in the third grade, says Brian Smith: Don't copy. "It's one thing to look at other people's work for inspiration, but another to imitate it too closely," Smith warns. "A dairy that wanted to get into the frozen yogurt business took a container to a graphic artist and said, 'We want something like this.' There was a $1,200,000 verdict because the court ruled that the package was likely to cause confusion between the two products." Here are some other kinds of appropriation to stay away from:

- Using a published cartoon on any sort of sales piece, in a newsletter, on a slide at a training session or on a fax cover sheet without permission. The same goes for reprinting a quiz, crossword puzzle or recipe in your newsletter without permission. Don't be lulled by the fact that "everyone" seems to do this and get away with it—a judge can levy penalties for unauthorized exploitation of copyrighted material *per copy distributed*. Here as elsewhere, giving credit to the copyright owner does not take you off the hook. Ask a reference librarian how you could track down the copyright owner—or, if that's too much trouble, just don't use anyone else's work.

- Using someone else's slogan, even for a very different product. Slogans are usually trademarked.

- Quoting without permission any part of a song or poem written in the twentieth century. When you do ask for permission, you're likely to meet a demand for a steep fee to use even one line. It's usually not worth it.

- Using any portion of a recorded performance in your audio or video without permission. Though works of long-dead composers like Beethoven or Bach aren't covered by copyright, specific performances on tape or video are. The American Society of Composers, Authors and Publishers (ASCAP) can come after you if you play a popular song over the sound system while you walk onstage or off during a talk that is recorded and sold.

• Scanning a photograph or illustration into your computer and printing it, whether altered or not, in your newsletter, brochure or company calendar without permission.

• Using the names or likenesses of copyrighted characters such as Mickey Mouse, the Jolly Green Giant or the Lone Ranger without permission.

• Using a business name that someone else has already registered within the geographical area where you do business. Before you launch a national service or product, you could save yourself a lot of grief by hiring an intellectual property or business lawyer to search existing trademarks and register yours as soon as the lawyer says that the coast is clear for it.

Should you similarly place a copyright notice on all of your brochures, ads and sales letters to stop copycats? Brian Smith says that's only prudent. Since it's not common practice, however, Steven Meyerowitz says that it may tell people that you're inexperienced, immature or overly litigious. "Consider whether you have something valuable to protect there, and whether there may be a benefit from not copyrighting your work—maybe you *want* people to spread your news around for you. If so, you could write, 'Permission is granted for anyone to copy this so long as you indicate the source.' " Although I'm normally a strong advocate of copyright protections, I lean toward Meyerowitz's view, especially for brochures. First, the year necessary in a valid copyright notice can date your materials sooner than anything else, and second, if your product or service is truly distinctive, you will have easily developed copy that wouldn't make sense when used by a competitor. Meyerowitz adds that without a copyright notice on a piece, you might still be able to get a plagiarizer for unfair competition. Finally, note that because of some million-dollar lawsuits, some shops will not copy stuff marked "Copyright 1995 Paula Johns" for anyone besides Paula Johns.

Staying Within the Lines of Postal Regulations

Since the U.S. Postal Service holds a monopoly on the delivery of first-class and bulk mail, its rules virtually carry the weight of laws. Run afoul of its regulations and you could find an expensive mailing embargoed or customers complaining about receiving your stuff marked "postage due."

Some of the most frequently violated rules cover size. The lower rate for postcards covers only those cards up to $4^1/_4$ by 6 inches. Exceed either of those measures by a little bit and you have to pay full first-class fare. Similarly, the one-ounce letter rate applies only to pieces that measure less than $6^1/_8$ inches tall and less than $11^1/_2$ inches long. Even if your 9 by 12-inch envelope weighs just half an ounce, it gets charged extra for being oversized.

A rule of thumb that stood me in good stead during a dozen years as a freelance writer is that you can send five sheets of paper in a business envelope for the one-ounce letter rate. If you're near the edge of a weight category, make sure you weigh a sample on an accurate scale *with* a stamp, staple or press-on tab and a mailing label, if you plan to use them. Nothing breaks your budget more stupidly than a mass mailing that's one-sixteenth of an ounce into the extra-postage zone.

Special regulations govern international mail, as I learned this year when I tried to send a self-mailer into Canada. Verboten! Self-mailers aren't allowed to cross national borders. So I went home and sealed the Canada-bound materials into one of my 9 by 12-inch first-class envelopes with green triangles around the edges that I'd imprinted with "Creative Ways" by the thousands. Also verboten! Those green triangles aren't allowed outside the country either. What I've learned most about what's OK and what's not is: Don't assume. Before you commit yourself to jet-black envelopes or odd-shaped postcards, get them certified as kosher from the person at the post office who's most up on such stuff. Your local postmaster may refer you to specialists at the Postal Business Center serving your area.

If you plan to be mailing in huge quantities, study the free guides provided by the postal service to bulk mail, bar-coded mail, business reply postcards, and so on. You'll learn about the maximum skew you can have with crooked labels or crooked bar coding, about recommended and nonrecommended typefaces and many other delightful guidelines.

Other Trouble Zones

- If you hold any sort of professional license, your marketing materials may have to adhere to rules promulgated by professional licensing boards or the state. For example, Brian Smith told me that in Tennessee a lawyer is not allowed to say that he specializes in a particular area of the law. Those regulations aren't as fierce as they were before the 1970s, when just about the only advertising a doctor or lawyer could do was hang out a shingle and hope someone would notice—"a great way to starve to death," Smith notes.

- Be careful about using the words "Better Business Bureau" in your marketing. Anyone can register their business for free with the Better Business Bureau, but that does not entitle them to mention their registration in an ad or brochure, warns Barbara Brabec. "They're very strict about the use of their name—you'll end up in court," she says.

- If you produce or package food, the Food and Drug Administration has plenty of rules for you on labeling your product.

- It's currently a felony to use a life-size color reproduction of money in any of your materials. Currency reproductions can only legally be in black and white, and either less than $3/4$ actual size or more than $1^1/_2$ times actual size.

- Using the word or initials "FBI" in an ad is a misdemeanor.

- You can't use the words "Association" or "Institute" for a private company, or any business name that falsely suggests your operation is a part of the government.

PART IV

◇

YOUR IMAGE
ON PAPER

CHAPTER 16

What Do-It-Yourselfers Need to Know About Graphic Design

I can still remember what happened when I marched into my neighborhood copy shop, having decided to create my first official letterhead. After I showed the guy at the counter the words to typeset and my simple design, he pulled out a chart crammed with different styles of letters. "Which typeface do you want? Do you want it in all capitals or upper and lower case?" he asked. My confidence drained away as I stared at the chart. I could see that the styles were different, but I could no more imagine from the chart how my letterhead would look than I could make a speech in Turkish using a tourists' phrase book.

If you don't know a serif from a cherub, take heart. Desktop publishing software makes it infinitely easier than in the days of typesetting to experiment and learn to construct simple, effective designs. Although I still consider myself artistically challenged, I can now recognize Times Roman on sight and produce simple brochures, flyers and booklets that provoke compliments and orders from my customers. Once you've absorbed a few basic design principles and mastered some tools of typography, you'll be able to stay on the civilized side of good taste. Even if you decide to leave layout, graphics and type to your designers, this chapter will bone you up so you can intelligently guide and judge their output.

Your No-Sweat Guide to Looking Great on Paper

Get your concept clear before fiddling with the design

Since design is a vehicle for communication, not vice versa, know what you want to say, and to whom and how you want to say it instead of starting with, "Gee, wouldn't it be great to use Tabby's picture in my ad for the pet food sale!" According to Roger Parker, author of *Looking Good in Print*, a lot of people begin worrying about white space and choosing type before they ask themselves what they want to accomplish and what action they want the reader to take. "Once they define the purpose of the publication," he says, "the design usually falls into place."

Don't use a computer feature just because you can

When desktop publishing burst into popularity in the mid-1980s, design-savvy folks had to shield their eyes from the horrors resulting from overenthusiastic uses of new features. Always have a reason for using your unusual options. We still see a plethora of typefaces in one document, fancy fonts that can't be read and squared-up right margins that have no rationale besides wanting to show off. If you get feedback like, "Oh, I see you got some new equipment," you have probably fallen into this trap.

Break your typewriter-era habits

Certain substitutes that developed to compensate for the deficiencies of typewriters produce poor results with higher-capability software. Except in direct-mail letters where you want a typewritten look, avoid underlining in favor of its proper version, italics. Instead of two hyphens for a long dash, learn how to create what's called an "em-dash" (the dash that equals the width of that font's letter *m*). Similarly, whereas typewriters have just one key to produce one kind of quotation mark, with desktop publishing you can and should distinguish beginning and ending quotes through distinctive opening and closing quote marks. Likewise, instead of double spaces between paragraphs—your only option on the typewriter—create more visually pleasing paragraph breaks in desktop publishing that equal more than one but less than two spaces. I've also heard that asterisks should not be used to mark a list, as they take the place of those filled-in dots called "bullets," now available as a special character in most word-processing programs. And finally, for typeset quality hit the space bar only once after a period, not twice as on a typewriter.

Position elements for the scanning eye

According to those who study such things, people looking at a page generally scan it in the shape of a *Z*, starting in the upper left-hand corner, moving to the upper right, then to the middle and finally along the bottom from left to right. Hence the upper left quadrant is the best place to put whatever should be seen first, such as the headline, while the lower right is the spot of choice for a coupon or information on how to respond. Trying to defy these expectations would be a prime example of misplaced creativity.

Group related items closer to each other

Instead of either spreading elements out all over your available space or arranging all the information in one unit, analyze which elements belong with which and with what relative importance. Then create visual groupings that reflect those

conceptual relationships. Notice the improvement, for example, in this concert announcement, adapted from Robin
Williams's *The Non-Designer's Design Book*:

BEFORE: CHAMBER CONCERT SERIES
Shanghai String Quartet
Mozart, K387, Bartok #3, Beethoven, Opus 59, #2
Hu Mi & Hua Na, Violins; Ji Weizi, Viola; Qiao
Pei, Cello
March 17, 8 p.m., Tinghao Center
Hals Trio
Mendelssohn, Opus 49, Beethoven, Opus 97,
"Archduke"
Fritz Hals, Violin; Gretchen Gogh, Cello;
W-W Neder, Piano
April 3, 8 p.m., Jaynes Center

AFTER: **<u>CHAMBER CONCERT SERIES</u>**

Shanghai String Quartet
Mozart, K387, Bartok #3, Beethoven, Opus 59, #2
Hu Mi & Hua Na, Violins
Ji Weizi, Viola; Qiao Pei, Cello
March 17, 8 p.m., Tinghao Center

Hals Trio
Mendelssohn, Opus 49, Beethoven, Opus 97,
"Archduke"
Fritz Hals, Violin; Gretchen Gogh, Cello;
W-W Neder, Piano
April 3, 8 p.m., Jaynes Center

You'd improve your piece further by increasing the size of
type for the name of overall series and the names of the performing groups in line with their relative importance, and ad-
justing the leading (see below), or spacing, between the
concert groupings.

Strive for a unified, consistent look

Within a single brochure or ad, you achieve unity most easily by using no more than two typefaces, one for headlines and another for text, and repeating some of the following throughout the piece:

- boldface elements
- horizontal lines ("rules")
- graphic motifs and illustrative doodads, including bullets
- indentations
- alignments
- accent color
- reverses (inked boxes containing words in white)

With communications that repeat, like newsletters and series of ads, keep the basic format the same from issue to issue. Among all of your marketing communications, there should be enough of a distinctive family resemblance so that if they were spread out on a table along with other companies' materials, someone would be able to pick out yours without reading any of the words or having to hunt for your logo. Murray Raphel, owner of Gordon's Alley, a pedestrian mall in Atlantic City, tells the story of the day the newspaper left out the name and address of his clothing store from his ad, yet he still sold seventeen of the men's jackets announced in the ad as being on sale. After speaking with customers, Raphel realized that using the same page position, typeface and design style had paid off. Regular readers of the paper knew it for a Gordon's ad without being told.

Avoid unbroken blocks of gray

In *Alice in Wonderland*, the heroine's misadventures started when she wandered away from her bookworm sister, thinking, "What is the use of a book without pictures or conversations?" In the real-life business world, all too many adults share Alice's attitude. Your misadventures in printland could get rolling if you force readers to confront line after line after line of unrelieved regular text. Instead, provide visual variety with photos, cartoons, clip art or original illustrations, graphs, boxed sidebars or pull quotes—excerpts from the text printed in larger type. Even in letters you can add interest and respite for the reader's eye with subheads, bulleted lists, phrases in bold and inset paragraphs. According to Frank Grazian, text in indented paragraphs gets higher readership than paragraphs starting at the left-hand margin and separated just by extra space. Secretarial schools started the less readable nonindented style, he says, because it allowed them to type faster. To attract the reader to the beginning of your sales pitch in an ad or an article in a newsletter, try using oversized, stylized initial capitals. And instead of text so wide the reader's eye gets lost trying to locate the next line, divide your message into columns.

Give your layout space

"White space is the gravitational force that holds elements in your layout together," says Elaine Floyd in *Advertising from the Desktop* (see Chapter 26). While too much white space in the middle tends to undo the unit, white space around the perimeter of an ad helps the design hang together as a whole. Roger Parker recommends turning the page upside-down to analyze more easily whether you've included enough blank area. Don't skimp on this powerful ingredient just to get your money's worth. Too little white space affects the reader like a nonstop bore who talks whether he's breathing in or breathing out. The amount of white space also helps telegraph class. Like property that includes a tremendous yard, lots of white space signals "I can afford to have more than I need" and helps you market expensive products to well-heeled individuals. A crowded layout with paltry margins, on the other hand, conveys a lower-class image. Both princesses and paupers, however, appreciate your providing enough space for their information on an order form or coupon.

Grab more attention through heightened visual contrasts

Robin Williams puts it this way: "If two items are not exactly the same, then make them different. Really different." Even simple amplifications of contrast like making headlines darker, rules wider, type size larger and smaller instead of almost the same add pizzazz. When a page is interesting to look at, explains Williams, people are more likely to read it. The contrast should also make the organization of your information clearer at a glance.

Crop photos strategically and use captions

Don't assume because you went to all the trouble to take or get a photo that you have to run it exactly as is. A simple process called cropping allows you to zoom in on the all-important face or trophy. Just explain to the printer where you want the borders of each photograph to appear. When you scan a photo into your computer, you can perform the same magic of changing the borders and sizes yourself. Through another process called silhouetting, you can even get rid of the telephone pole seeming to grow out of the bank president's head. By hand, place a piece of tracing paper over the photo and draw lines that indicate where the printer should eliminate the background. Or, on the computer, delete an area of a scanned-in photo using a photo manipulation program. Whenever you include a photo in a marketing piece, make sure an informative caption runs beneath it or beside it. Studies have confirmed captions as the second most read element, after headlines, of a brochure or ad.

Communicate with your printer, copy shop or service bureau before finalizing your piece

Otherwise you may be innocently including a feature that forces a choice between advanced reproduction techniques (and higher costs) and lousy results. See Chapter 17 on features to be especially cautious about, such as "bleeds"—printing to the very edge of the paper—how and where you plan to add color and "reverses"—large dark areas that allow the color of the paper to show through in the form of letters.

By all means, swipe!

Most graphic designers maintain what they call "swipe files," examples of interesting techniques they can browse through when they need inspiration. Designer Howard Munce says he keeps a file just for different styles of ampersands ("&"). You too should collect pleasing samples of whatever format you're trying to create to use as models, especially samples from a different geographic or professional area. For a Yellow Pages ad, for instance, study telephone directories from across the country at your library. For a brochure on your home knitting machines, stockpile product sheets given out by, say, home health care companies and appliance stores. So long as you don't copy a direct competitor or plunder both the words and the design, swiping is no more than learning by example, not something that ought to weigh on your conscience.

Your Typographic Toolkit

Typefaces or fonts

Although some software companies use the word interchangeably with "font," "typeface" properly denotes a designed set of letters and numbers that can be scaled in different sizes and printed in a regular or roman version, italic or bold. Like pets, typefaces have names, such as Baskerville, Garamond, Optima and Bookman. Also like pets, they not only have telltale differences in detail from other typefaces, they have distinct personalities. Futura has the stylish slimness of a moving mannequin; Palatino wears the subdued refinement of banker's gray; ArchiText looks like the hand lettering of an artist trying hard to keep the lines regular and neat. Typefaces with relatively shorter lowercase letters tend to look more classic and formal, while those with relatively taller lowercase letters come across as more casual and relaxed. If you're like me and can't perceive their spirit except in an expansive sample, you have three choices. First, save samples that you know are in a particular typeface, or keep a design book on hand that includes pieces in lots of typefaces. Second, use your software to convert a section of your piece into different typefaces and print them out for comparison. Or third, tell a designer the personality you want the piece to have and ask to see your piece in two or three typefaces consistent with that image.

Another big factor in choosing a typeface concerns the difference between serif and sans serif faces. (Since "sans" is French for "without," I used to think I'd be cool and pronounce "serif" so that it rhymed with "Omar Sharif," but I was wrong. "Serif" doesn't come from French and rhymes instead with "sheriff.") Serifs are additional strokes projecting from the ends of letterforms found on traditional typefaces such as Times Roman, Goudy and New Century Schoolbook. They aid readability by leading the reader's eye horizontally across each line. Sans serif typefaces such as Helvetica and Univers look cleaner and more modern but require more effort from the reader. Since even the most ill-educated eye registers the contrast between serif and sans serif typefaces, people commonly use a serif face for main text and sans serif for headlines and display type. I should also mention script typefaces, such as Zapf Chancery, which simulate handwriting and belong only in invitations and short, emphatic bursts of copy such as headlines and subheads.

One more factor to keep in mind when choosing is how a

typeface uses space. Elaine Floyd calls some faces like Tiffany and Avant Garde "pudgy space hogs" because their wide letters take up much more space per line than, say, Times Roman, which was specifically designed to be readable but horizontally compact.

Type style and weight

Most typefaces come in a range of styles, including roman, the regular style; italics, which puts the letters on a slant and often also makes them look more elegant; and bold, which thickens and darkens the letters, making them stand out more on the page. A "reverse" option makes letters appear white against a dark background, while "outline" or "shadow" styles create a fancy three-dimensional effect. Some typefaces include additional options for gradated weight, ranging from Helvetica Light or Ultra Light, whose letter strokes become slender and slight, to Helvetica Black, even darker and thicker than bold. "The light faces fade out quickly and don't reverse well," notes Roger Parker, "while the heavy ones can overpower a page. Use those for logos, not for text." If you plan to run more than a line in italics, test how it looks first, because some faces lose readability from italics' extra curlicues. Some type families include a version with the word "Condensed," especially designed to improve the weight and blackness of headlines while hogging less horizontal space. Don't use these for running text, only for headlines.

Type size

Any desktop publishing program and most word-processing programs allow you to select different sizes of type for different portions of your text. They use a measure called "points," which refers to the vertical height of the letters. (Approximately 72 points make up one inch, and 12 points make up another measure called a "pica.") The standard range for easily readable text is 10 to 12 points, although you can get away with 9-point text in certain uses. I would not recommend type any smaller than 9 points if you want people to read it—especially over-fifty prospects whose eyes don't work as well as they used to. On the other hand, for disclaimers or other information you must include but want to downplay, 8-point type is perfect. Reserve type larger than 12 points for headlines and other brief messages.

Not all 12-point type *looks* the same size, however. The heavier the weight of the letters and the higher the so-called "x-height"—the height of lowercase letters like *x*, *o*, and *a* in relation to those like *b* or *p* that contain ascending or descending strokes—the larger the type appears. According to Elaine Floyd, typefaces with tall x-heights appear more contemporary and informal than classic typefaces with shorter x-heights.

Case

Most beginners need to learn to go easy on capital letters—called "uppercase" in typesetting lingo. The longer a stretch of capital letters continues, the more it slows the reader down. More than one line all in capitals can make even the most sympathetic reader recoil. "People recognize letters by their shapes," explains Roger Parker, "and when you set words in uppercase type, they lose their shape—they become simple rectangles and harder to read." So if you've been automatically setting long headlines in all capitals, consider your other options. Capitalizing just the first letter of each word except for "a," "an," "the" and prepositions alleviates the readability problem for headlines. For an equally readable, slightly more formal look, substitute so-called "small caps"—smaller capital letters, an option in most typefaces—for the lowercase letters. For a more informal look, capitalize just the initial word of a headline and leave the rest of the line in lowercase letters—a surprisingly common style, as you'll notice once you start observing such things.

Alignment

When you have more than one line of type, you can align it either along the left-hand margin only ("ragged right"), along the right-hand margin only ("ragged left") or along both margins ("justified"). Without a high-end, near-typeset-quality system, justification produces uneven spacing within the lines that slows down readers. In the belief that it looks neater or more advanced, some desktop-publishing novices become too fond of using justification when ragged right would get a better response. Justified type does appear more buttoned-up than un-justified type, but its formality is out of place for letters and many brochures. If you've been justifying your documents for no special reason, release your right-hand margins and compare the resulting readability and image.

Leading

This word, which rhymes with "heading," denotes the amount of space between lines. With larger-sized type, longer lines or italics, you need more leading to maintain readability. Most desktop publishing programs have a default automatic setting that you can override for either a lighter, more spacious look with more leading or a denser, heavier appearance with less. The longer your lines and the smaller your type, the more you need extra leading to preserve readability.

Dingbats

Many desktop publishing programs including these small decorative arrows, bursts, boxes, hearts and other symbols as a font automatically linked to the abc's and numbers on the keyboard. Try them out—sparingly. "I try to use dingbats like triangles or pointing fingers in moderation so it doesn't look tacky," says Judy Madnick of A-1 Office Assistance in Albany, New York.

Produce Precise, Pristine Printouts

Did you ever get lousy copies from a printer or copy shop only to be told the problem lay in your original? Sometimes that's true. Do-it-yourselfers need to understand that printers and copy shops can't deliver top-notch results unless you give them a first-rate printout. Here are some factors in your output that can spoil the results from a copier or a printing press:

Skew.

Unless I carefully check the way I've loaded the blank paper on my laser printer, it may emerge with margins one-sixteenth of an inch off from straight. If the copy-machine operator in turn is less than perfectly precise, I may end up with perceptibly crooked materials. If it's partly my fault, I have less justification for a complaint, and less of a chance of getting the job rerun for free. Sometimes even with operator precision, a different texture or color of paper makes a skew more noticeable and sloppy-looking than on the original.

Later generations.

Always print or copy from an original, not a copy or printed version that looks the same to you as an original. With each generation of reproduction (copy-of-a-copy, copy-of-a-copy-of-a-copy, etc.), the ink tends to spread and makes letters and graphics fuzzier.

Poor lettering.

Never use even a good dot-matrix printer for originals you plan to duplicate. Also, examine closely the rounded portions of large letters. If you can see zigs and zags in *O*'s or *C*'s with the naked eye, you probably need the better output available from an imagesetting machine at a service bureau. These firms, usually found in the Yellow Pages under "Desktop Publishing," produce sharper versions from your computer files with more dots per inch than you can get from the machines currently found in the typical office. Or, seek out a freelance desktop publisher with a high-resolution (800 dots per inch) laser printer.

Broken type.
Never fold originals, since that can cause toner to crack and look damaged when reproduced. This applies especially when you are submitting camera-ready ad copy by mail or sending originals off to a mail-order printer. Pay the extra postage necessary for a larger envelope, with your original sandwiched between sheets of cardboard.

Inadequate margins.
Many duplication technologies need margins of at least three-eighths of an inch; stuff any closer to the paper edge gets truncated.

Dirty or colored originals.
The "eye" of a machine perceives differently from yours. Although you may be able to see type from the other side of the paper when looking at your original, the machine's flash probably will not pick that up. However, a slub of correction fluid or a speck of debris that your eye does not notice can produce a spot on the reproduction. Paper any color but white for originals may sabotage your attempt to get clean, clear results.

Photos.
To reproduce a photo clearly, you should convert it to a version composed of tiny dots, called a "halftone." Printers do this for you, for a small extra charge. Just give them a glossy black-and-white photo of any size and describe the placement and size of the picture you want in your piece.

CHAPTER 17

....

How to Work with Designers and Printers

"I strongly urge you not to do your own graphic design," says Terri Lonier, whose book *Working Solo*, published by her company, Portico Press, teaches lone-wolf practitioners how to thrive. "Prospects are visually sophisticated nowadays. I have a masters of fine arts degree, but when it came to designing the cover of my book, I knew my limitations. A professional brings a fresh viewpoint and trained creative skills. For my *Working Solo Newsletter*, I would fax an idea to my designer and she'd zip it back having taken it light-years farther. Remember that a client's first impression of your business may come from your printed image, not your smiling face or your cheery voice. Of all the hats you might wear in your own business, design is one you should almost always pass off to another professional."

If you're a die-hard do-it-yourselfer, then skip ahead to the section of this chapter on dealing with printers. But if Lonier's advice makes sense to you, read on to learn how to find and get the best results working with a design professional.

Working Effectively with the Right Designer

The easiest way to find a qualified designer for your printed materials is to check your Yellow Pages under "Graphic Design." Probably the best way to find someone compatible with your tastes is to ask other businesspeople whose stuff you like who designed it. For the cheapest help, call the art department of a local practically oriented college (i.e., not Harvard) and say you're looking for a student with graphic design skills who is interested in building up a portfolio. Also, most printers and desktop publishing service bureaus have a designer either on call or on staff at least part-time. If barter appeals to you, graphic design is probably one of the services you can exchange your own skills for in a local barter exchange. (Check the Yellow Pages under "Barter.") Because you'll probably need at least one face-to-face meeting to work together effectively, I'd recommend restricting yourself to candidates within comfortable driving distance.

Since you want to make sure that a particular designer produces work you like, matches your budget and can understand your needs, your first step should be a brief introductory meeting at which you review the designer's portfolio, explain your needs, desires and constraints and inquire in general terms about pricing. If all of that warrants a "go," then you're ready to make a deal with respect to timing, design goals and price for the specific job you currently need. But if you feel uneasy with the style, experience, communication skills or fee of that designer, search on. When I created my subscription newsletter, *The Creative Glow*, I knew I wanted someone who would create a prototype I could adapt on my own computer for each issue, and I happily found Best Impression of Reading, Massachusetts, in the telephone book under "Desktop Publishing."

"For best results, tell the designer who your client base is and the purpose of the piece you want designed," says Christine Reynolds, owner of Reynolds Design and Management in Somerville, Massachusetts. "Do you expect it to go on file for reference? Will it be given out or mailed? What kind of impression do you want to make about your business—forceful? Well established? Innovative? Which of these three is most important to you: the perfect design, the right timing or the optimal budget? You can satisfy one or often two of those ideals, but rarely all three. Do you want the designer to deal with the printing for you? If so, she'll check the proofs for you but will probably mark up the printer's charge somewhere from 5 to 20 percent. Do not expect the designer to come up with the marketing concept, the strategy and wording of a piece unless she says that's part of her scope of services."

Bring the designer examples of things you like and hate, suggests Louise Kursmark, owner of Best Impression and designer of my newsletter. "You don't have to have the final copy ready, but it's helpful if the writing is close to finished." If, like me, you would like to have the design on disk as well as on paper, now is the time to establish systems and software compatibility. I was delighted to learn that Kursmark, who worked on a Macintosh, would be able to provide me (courtesy of Pagemaker 4.0) with her work on a disk that I would be able to use on my IBM-compatible machine. You'll avoid misunderstandings and protect both parties by signing a simple agreement about the scope and terms of the job before having the designer proceed.

Once you have explained what you need and settled the fee and timetable, you'll probably hear from the designer next when sketches are ready for your approval. Since any design task has innumerable possible solutions, it's reasonable to request the chance to choose among three layouts, roughs or logos. Frank feedback at this stage is essential. Do your best to communicate what you like and don't like about the options. Most experienced designers know how to collaborate in drawing out what works and what doesn't for you and the direction in which you want the design changed. "I don't want you to walk out of my office not liking what I've done," says Kursmark. "Be willing to say what you think." Adds Terri Lonier,

"The best graphic designers have strong egos, but don't be afraid to state your opinion. After all, you are the client." Depending on the complexity of the job, there may be more back and forth until the design is done. Then one of you takes either the camera-ready layout or a computer file on to the printer.

Unless you know you'll never need their services again, don't do any of the things that drive designers nuts. Gail Drinkard, who does desktop publishing in Douglasville, Georgia, rues the clients who say, "I need a letterhead, business card and logo, but I don't know what I want," then suddenly upon seeing her sketches, tell her something very specific (and different from her execution) that they were thinking of. For Christine Reynolds, the big frustration is clients who say they need something immediately, then after the rush tell her that the timing wasn't critical. "The nicer clients are to work with," adds Drinkard, "the more likely I am to toss in little extras for free. Like one client whose first words are always, 'When you have time . . .' When she needs an ad I'd previously done for her resized for another publication, I don't always charge for it." And it should go without saying that freelancers are more eager to work with you when you consistently pay up on time.

Since a good designer creates a spread that accentuates your message, along with a look that's distinctive enough to command attention, don't get too excited about an offer from an advertising medium like the Yellow Pages or a newspaper to design your ad for free. You'll get something that's probably better than you could do yourself but ordinary and not different enough from all the advertising messages around it. Any money you spend on designing your marketing pieces is as vital an investment as the postage necessary to send them out. To make the most of your investment, view the design components as elements that can get reused and incorporated into various other pieces at little or no extra cost. Even if you lack the confidence to modify designs yourself on the computer, you can ask your graphics wizard to keep each creative piece on file for later adaptations.

In any case, when you grow tired of your current look, it's best to update it by transfiguring it rather than starting from scratch. When the pizza place that I patronize, for instance, went from black-and-white takeout menus to much spiffier color ones, the new design incorporated more changes than adding green and red ink. It added squares that help organize the different menu options, and the previous logo of a tilted pizza box saying "My Brother's Place," with "Free Delivery!" and "Pizzas and More!" along the box edges, now had hands gripping the corners of the box and four funky pairs of feet between the box and the ground. This more highly evolved logo was recognizable instantly to loyal customers, yet more appealing. If you truly hate your current look, at least salvage the color or a type style, since a drastic break in visual identity is as jarring to your public as if you were Jerry for thirty years and suddenly showed up as Geraldine.

Working Effectively with the Right Printer

As *Tightwad Gazette* publisher Amy Dacyczyn learned upon launching her newsletter, finding the right printer sometimes involves first suffering through Mr. Wrong. "I called every single printer in my Yellow Pages for a quote—thirty, maybe even fifty printers. One guy quoted a very, very low price, and then a quote came in that was even lower. The lowest guy had lost my paperwork, though, and when I went to visit his shop, it was a hole-in-the-wall that was so tiny you couldn't even turn around. So I went with the second lowest guy. He did a terrible job. There were lots of little specks everywhere, part of the logo was cut off at the top, some things were blurry, others were crooked . . . I didn't want him to run it again and he wouldn't return my money. He said, 'You came to me for price. What did you expect?' " Someone who heard her story recommended the guy with the hole-in-the-wall shop, and the *Tightwad Gazette* has been successfully printed there ever since.

Printing is one of the most variably priced services you'll encounter. Quality, speed and all the intangible factors that contribute to good service vary greatly too. Shop for a printer by asking for recommendations, by visiting the shop to see if it's dirty or clean, frantic or well-organized and by looking at the samples they have chosen to display. To get meaningful price estimates from competing printers, you must already have a relatively specific idea of the quantities, size and type of paper, number of pages and colors you want. So if you're still at the vague stage, you can get your bearings by going in and asking how much it would cost for a hypothetical quantity of one of their samples that you like. "We get calls asking things like 'How much is a letterhead?' " says Michael Macrides, owner of Hercules Press in West Roxbury, Massachusetts. "That's like asking 'How much is a car?' But we're always glad to make suggestions for people who aren't sure what they want." Don't be put off if you can't get instant answers to "How much?" Macrides says that about 60 percent of the nation's quick printers have computerized pricing, but even so, it may take ten or fifteen minutes to plug in the variables and get the results. "By hand, it could take 40 minutes to an hour to come up with an accurate quote," he says. Always ask for prices on several different quantities so you can intelligently balance quantity savings with your probable needs.

Even though pricing may follow formulas, don't be shy about asking for a better deal. Printers who know they are submitting bids on a monthly newsletter may be more willing to offer discounts than if they think it's a one-shot deal. If you're one of the few customers who does not need your printing finished yesterday, ask for a whenever-you-have-time price. "Quotes from printers looking at identical specifications can vary as much as 50 percent even when every shop is well suited to the job," notes printing expert Mark Beach. "And business conditions affecting individual printers influence what they quote on a job from one week to the next. A small shop owner might need business and give you a terrific price.

A month later that same shop might have so much business that the quote on the same job is 50 percent more." Hence if you have a newsletter or direct-mail promotions you'll be printing at regular intervals, try to bargain for one price good through, say, the end of the year.

For a one- or two-color newsletter, brochure, direct mailing or catalog, a so-called "quick printer" should meet your needs, your budget and your timetable well enough. So-called "commercial printers," however, are the ones to turn to for more complicated jobs or huge quantities. "Quick printers are cheaper because they specialize in standard sheet sizes—that's their strength," explains Michael Macrides. "A commercial printer has larger machines, which cost more to operate, but can handle offsize pieces and long runs." When producing a full-color catalog or sales flyers that need to look as slick as the average magazine, you need a commercial printer, and you'll need to schedule much more time than for quick printing. But even at shops that include words like "Instant," "Speedy" and "Quick" in their business name, don't expect the swiftness of a copy shop, warns Gail Drinkard. "Anything that's two-sided will take a minimum of two days, since the ink has to dry totally before the next step. If there's folding, that adds another day. Also, certain colors take longer to dry, and if you rush a job, the ink could smear."

Whether quick or commercial, must your printer be local? I feel most confident that the job will get done well when I can take it in and explain what I need—and if necessary, complain—face-to-face. Also, with someone nearby I don't have to schedule in shipping time in my attempt to meet deadlines. Amy Dacyczyn recommends shopping locally because you have more leverage. You can take a local printer to small claims court—as she did, successfully, with the printer who botched her first newsletter. However, for unusual items such as labels, stickers and color postcards, you may get higher quality and lower prices from a specialized printer whom you deal with by mail and shipping services. Barbara Brabec says that it costs half as much to send her newsletter off for printing in Minnesota as it would to get it printed in her hometown of Naperville, Illinois. For leads on specialized printers, consult magazines for direct marketers (see Chapter 26).

Once you've chosen a printer, deliver your materials together with a dummy layout of how the finished piece should look. Tape sample pages together that should go back to back, fold the piece the way you want it folded, and label parts with written indicators like "top," "bottom," "inside," "outside." The more redundant your instructions, the better the chances that the product comes out exactly the way you had in mind.

Communication with the printer before the job goes onto the press is the key to output you can be proud to distribute. If you've never had a certain kind of piece printed before, ask the printer to look it over before you leave your master copy behind. You might learn that your margins aren't quite big enough to provide gripper space on the press. You might learn that the raised print you've requested for your letterhead will indeed look traditional but could melt in your laser printer. You might learn that one color ink on another color paper doesn't necessarily yield the combination you imagine, since the ink hue changes when it hits colored paper. Ask if you've inadvertently done anything that makes the piece more expensive to print. Perhaps you'd save by eliminating "bleeds"— places where the ink must run to the edge of the paper, forcing the printer to use larger paper that then gets cut. Perhaps you'll discover that recycled paper is not cheaper, as you'd assumed, only more politically correct. When I took the first issue of my newsletter in to the printer, I learned that by requesting that two colors touch on the page, I was necessitating a more complicated and costly printing procedure. I went home and figured out a different way to use the accent color so it wouldn't overlap with or touch the black ink.

When you go to pick up your order, check a sample or two before you leave the counter. If it looks wrong or sloppy to you, calmly explain the problem to the person you've been dealing with. One of three things will happen: They agree that it's their mistake and offer to refund your money or redo the job at no cost to you; they claim that they followed your instructions and that the fault was yours; or, in the vast gray area of misunderstandings and debatable standards, you might be told that they thought you said it should be doublesided, or that their folding machine just can't deliver absolutely, 100-percent-matched edges. "Fussy customers are fine. That's part of the business," says Michael Macrides. "The nightmare is people who have unreasonable expectations." I'm sure I have come across as a fussy customer to some of the mediocre shops I've dealt with, because I believe that black areas on the printed piece should be as black as the original, that folds should be even and that nicely aligned text should not end up cockeyed when printed. If you're really not satisfied, I recommend that you stick to your guns and use all the customer-satisfaction tactics in your repertoire.

CHAPTER 18

Proofreading and Its Pitfalls

Q: How does the most widely known dramatic monologue in the English language begin?

A: "To be or to be . . ."

If that answer didn't look right to you, you're doing better than six professional proofreaders and other personnel responsible for producing a new edition of Shakespeare's plays. "We don't see what's there, but what we expect to be there," explained the volume's editor in a radio interview, when asked how he could have allowed Hamlet's famous soliloquy to be mangled. The company's publishing staff fell victim to the key paradox of proofreading: The more you know how the words go, the more likely you are to unwittingly bless such a world-class blooper as leaving out that crucial "not."

Proofreading slips can produce much more serious problems than a red face. Leave a butchered price or address in your materials and you could end up with angry or lost customers. Let typos by and some clients will question your dedication to quality. In July 1994, the *Wall Street Journal* ran an eight-column-inch story devoted to the irony of a conference on critical and creative thinking sending out a press release containing such errors as a reference to "world renown" researchers "in field of thinking" and our former surgeon general identified as "C. Everett Coop." Could your business withstand that kind of ridicule? Although absolute perfection may remain out of reach, most mortals can come much closer to a flawlessly executed piece than they can to Shakespeare's talent.

First, Get an Attitude

The process of proofreading yields satisfactory results only when you care enough to be thoroughly meticulous. Getting everything right needs to be a number-one concern. Writer Louise Gordon told me that she'd worked at one paper that promoted a restaurant's "overbaked" (instead of "ovenbaked") chicken and had a botched caption poked fun at in *The New Yorker*. At another newspaper, when she pointed out errors that needed to be corrected, people got annoyed, with one woman yelling at her, "It's already been proofed! It's already been proofed!" Getting things right means not only gratefully correcting mistakes someone points out, no matter what the bother, but also paying attention to the slightest twinge of intuition that you may have gotten something wrong.

When in doubt, check. When in a hurry, wait and check again. I've sometimes wondered if the people who staff the telephone reference line at the Boston Public Library know my voice, because when I'm getting something ready to go off to the printer, I may call them three or four times in one day, checking the spelling of words that my dictionary doesn't have or of places and names, such as of our former surgeon general C. Everett Koop. I put things aside for another read-through because I've almost done things like sending off a January press release dated with the wrong year and sending an order form to the printer without my address on it.

Who should have the responsibility of proofreading? Not the typesetter or printer. If the copy you gave them included an error, that error will appear in print, and even if they introduce an error, their liability is limited to providing you with corrected materials. But suppose you already sent out a couple of thousand letters without a phone number or placed the full-page ad with the name of your senior partner spelled wrong? Don't give that responsibility to the designer, either. *Home Office Computing* magazine awarded first prize in a letterhead competition to a designer whose cover letter said she was submitting her "stationary." (It should have been "stationery.") And don't necessarily trust yourself, either. You may not care quite enough. When I lived in a town called "Northampton," I met a dentist who had sent out a practice announcement saying that he was setting out his shingle in "North Hampton." When I pointed this out to him, he shrugged. He seemed to mean not "It's too late to fix it" but "So what?" You may need someone both strict and knowledgeable to save you from such disasters.

Whoever does your proofreading should be able to score 100 percent on the following test. Circle everything that appears to need either correction or checking.

F.O.B., Inc., the world's leading manufacturer of fibbles, is for a limited period or time offering free samples of it's top-of-the line, money-saving product. Instead of having to pour through a stack of   catalogs to find the best price, you can access conveneint fax-on-demand price lists 24 hours a day. FOB offers worldwide same-day shipping from our Cincinati plant.

For your free fobble, call FOB at 911-312-5798 today!

If you did not circle ten items, go back and look again. Here are the problems your proofreading should have caught:

1. Is it "F.O.B." or "FOB"?
2. Is it "fibbles" or "fobbles"?
3. Should be "period *of* time," not "or"
4. Should be "its," not "it's"
5. Missing hyphen in "top-of-the-line"

6. Should be "pore," not "pour"
7. Extra spaces after "stack of" that should be eliminated
8. "Convenient" misspelled
9. It's "Cincinnati"
10. You need to call the phone number to make sure it's correct.

In the last decade, spell-check programs have given many business communicators a false sense of security. Of the ten questionable items above, the typical spell-check program would have caught only two. By all means use your spell-checker to catch typos, but don't rely on it as your sole proof-reading tool.

Ideally, you'll have the most persnickety person you can find proofreading your stuff. But make certain they do it in the right frame of mind. Karen Spiegler, editor of a funny sub-scription newsletter called *Manic Moms*, sent me a sample copy and apologized for a headline that read "Chatting Over a Cyberface [instead of 'Cyberspace'] Fence." "That's the last time I let my husband drink beer and proofread at the same time!" she wrote. If Mr. Finickiness is you and you also wrote the material, try to let it sit overnight and use one of the meth-ods below that help you look at every word and element.

Suppose something wrong slips by you and you've got scads of newsletters or brochures marred by a typo. What then? You've got to weigh the indeterminate but real damage produced by such mistakes against the cost of doing it over. Barbara Winter of Minneapolis once managed to turn a printer's error to her advantage, but that's rare. "At that time, my last name was 'Hinrichs,' " Winter says, "and I made a big deal out of the spelling to the guy printing up my business cards, so he'd get it right. When I ran in to pick up the cards before a big meeting, 'Hinrichs' was spelled correctly but my company name came out as 'The Successful Worman.' I took the cards to the meeting and used the mistake to break the ice with strangers. After I came home, the printer did them over again for free." At the very least, sum up how the lapse got through and change procedures so it won't happen again. Barbara Brabec, editor of *Barbara Brabec's Self-Employment Survival Letter*, says she knows that when she's typing fast, she writes "not" instead of "now," "you" instead of "your" and leaves out apostrophes—so she specifically searches for and fixes those bugaboos.

Proofreading Methods

According to the revered *Chicago Manual of Style*, the most accurate proofreading method is to have someone besides the writer read aloud from the original copy while the writer follows along on the camera-ready copy or proofs supplied by the typesetter. The person who reads aloud should mention each capital letter, punctuation, variation in type style and new paragraph. For those of you who can't follow that time- and personnel-consuming procedure, here's how to do it solo.

You need to check your material in three passes, not necessarily in any specific order. You need to inspect the graphic format; hunt for typos; and check your facts. To inspect for graphic problems, begin by turning your text upside down and examining it for faulty spacing or alignment. If you entered text in a desktop-publishing program, you may not have noticed the places where you pressed the space bar twice—but the reader might. By looking at your photos and illustrations upside down as well, you may be able to detect things like telephone poles growing out of people's heads, suggests Roger Parker. Right side up again, look at things like the patterns of boldface and italics and the typeface of headlines and pull quotes, verifying that you've achieved the consistency you intended. Count up the number of paragraphs and their beginning and ending words, and check them against your original.

To hunt for typos on your own, don't just read the way you

usually do. Either place a straight edge under each line and move it slowly down the page, point your finger word by word as you go along from left to right or read word by word backward. Unless you use one of these methods to help you see what's there, your brain overrides the evidence of your eyes and tells you you've seen what was supposed to be there but wasn't. The larger the words, the harder it is to see what's wrong, so take special care with headlines and display type. Look closely at two-letter words like "of" and "to" in this pass, since they're so easy to mix up.

To check your facts, do another pass in which you read for meaning and circle everything that needs to be confirmed: dates, names, phone and fax numbers, addresses, prices, etc. If you've put together separate pieces of copy, as in a newsletter or a letter with enclosures, now is the time to make sure their information matches. I recently received a sales packet where the letter gave one price and the enclosed brochure another— not the best way to inspire confidence! Run each piece by your own checklist or the one below.

Any time you insert corrections in one spot, look closely again at the entire document. Even a change as tiny as substituting "one" for "on" can make your whole ad longer, with the last line of copy cut off. Or, without one more check, you wouldn't notice that the "one" should have been in italics.

What to Check, in One Handy List

1. Proper names and place names. Never rely on memory alone!
2. Unusual or made-up words, to make sure they're spelled consistently.
3. Facts, whether about your company (founded in 1951) or the outside world (you really do mean the Grand Prix and not the Indy 500).
4. Grammar. See my top eight copy crimes in Chap-

ter 13. See Chapter 26 for information about grammar hotlines that help you with last-minute perplexities like, "Should it be 'she' or 'her'?" Remember that for every mark that opens a quote, there must be a mark that closes the quote.

5. Numbers. This includes prices, street numbers, telephone and fax numbers and ZIP codes. No one is immune from getting these mixed up, even for numbers you know better than the back of your hand.

6. For brochures: Did you include all current contact information? Here as elsewhere, examine headlines extra carefully.

7. For catalogs: When you're updating a previous catalog, verify that you changed any dates, page numbers, available colors, etc. for material carried along from the previous version.

8. For letters: When mail-merging or manually changing one letter for another recipient, have you recustomized everything—the date, the salutation and information internal to the letter?

9. For direct-mail or catalog order forms: Directions for every method of ordering must be accurate and precise, including regular and express shipping fees, sales tax instructions, forms of payment accepted, your guarantee and any expiration date, with all essential information repeated verbatim somewhere off the order form so one piece can generate second orders.

10. For newsletters: The damnedest thing to forget here is to change the date and issue number.

11. For press releases: If the contact phone number isn't right, the whole shebang gets wasted.

12. For ads: Don't settle for less than 100 percent accuracy in your company name, address, phone and the offer on both the ad and any coupon.

CHAPTER 19

Saving Money Without Losing Appeal

"In the 1980s, the thinking was, if you want to be successful, you look successful—wear the success suit, get the fancy office space, give out beautiful business cards. But sometimes people invested so much in overhead they couldn't survive," says Amy Dacyczyn, Maine's and perhaps America's most famous cheapskate. "We've been in business publishing my newsletter, *The Tightwad Gazette*, for four years with no letterhead, and we do a lot of correspondence on ordinary postcards, the kind you buy at the post office. If someone writes me a letter that requires a short answer, I'll usually write a note on the bottom of it and send it back. People expect that of me—they call me 'homespun.' But if I printed some business cards that had the wrong address, I wouldn't scribble in a correction. I'd pay to do it again."

Lowering your printing costs need not compromise your impact. Whether you have a top-of-the-line image or want to outscrimp Amy Dacyczyn, you can save money producing your marketing materials without any noticeable signs of corner-cutting.

Creative Cost Reduction

Here are some ideas different folks have come up with that have made their marketing dollars stretch further.

Multipurpose materials.

Professional speaker Patricia Fripp says she learned thriftiness from her father, who lived by the principle "If you want ten of anything, buy 100 wholesale." She applies his watchword by planning multiple uses for her biggest expenditures, like four-color photos of herself, which she uses in her press kit, as postcards and as cover inserts for her videos. Since she has four different videos, she customizes the covers via stickers that name the title of the enclosed program. The stickers cost a fraction of what four different full-color video covers would. "As a Mom-and-Pop operation doing business with IBM, everything I do has to be IBM-perfect," Fripp adds, "but that doesn't mean I can't economize. I always start by thinking, 'If the world were perfect and money were no object, what would I do?' Then I adapt the ideal situation to the budget I have."

Standard colors.

Many printers have eight or ten colors that cost less than those chosen from their range of hundreds. The same may be true for paper colors. Must you have two shades bluer than teal, or could you make your peace with aquamarine? For a letterhead, the difference in cost might be minute, but for a repeated publication like a newsletter, the savings keep multiplying into the future.

Preprinting and batch printing.

Because two-color printing can get expensive in low quantities, you can save money by designing color #2 to apply only to elements that repeat in every newsletter, like the name banner, masthead and borders. Then you print a year's worth of these shells and, issue by issue, prepare all the changing contents in color #1 (usually black). Similarly, you should get a price break by printing two or three issues of your two-color newsletter at a time, thereby saving the printer the time and therefore expense of changing the ink.

Homemade customized envelopes and mailing labels.

Boston actor Norman George sends out his promotional materials in white envelopes that look like they're imprinted with a large black-and-white theater bill for his one-man show, "Poe Alone." The layout includes an etching of Edgar Allan Poe and two blurbs about George's performance. Upon looking closely, you might notice that his information exists on a separate sheet of something—a mailing label?—stuck onto the white envelope. George told me he achieves this customized look for next to nothing by duplicating his Apropoe Productions stuff at the copy shop, cutting it to size, then affixing it to plain white envelopes with aerosol spray mount. You can get the same money-saving effect in pseudo-shipping labels by making up paper label forms and skipping the gummed backing in favor of clear shipping tape wound around the package on top of the "label."

Standard sizes.

Since envelopes in nonstandard sizes get hugely expensive, feel free to let your creativity go with a differently sized mailing piece so long as the contents fit into a less commonly used but still standard-size envelope, such as 6 by 6 inches or 6 by 9 inches.

Scaling back after your first impression.

"The first piece I send out costs the most," says newsletter publisher and *Homemade Money* author Barbara Brabec. "That makes a general impression, and gets about a 10 percent response. Then I send out something really cheap, as a reminder, which brings in another clump of orders."

Scaling back across the board.

If you've been printing your catalog in two colors, on glossy paper, test whether you lose (or gain!) business in two colors on newsprint or in just black and white. In some businesses, a thrifty, low-key image sells well.

Using store-bought supplies.

Doris Goembel's stationery for her Peacock Hills Business Services looks attractively professional, picking up the "peacock" theme only in a blue-green accent. But for informal correspondence, she uses cards and letter paper with lavish depictions of peacocks, produced by major greeting card companies such as Hallmark. I found her samples stunning. "I special-order them through my local retailer," she told me. "As the greeting card companies change their designs regularly, this helps keep my own 'greetings' from getting stale or overused."

Favors that save on postage.

Before paying the post office to send your promotional pieces, stop and think whether you can get anyone to distribute them for you for free. Jeff Slutsky, a marketing consultant in Gahanna, Ohio, helped a fitness center distribute discount coupons with the newsletter of a noncompeting tennis center by persuading the tennis center manager that his members would perceive the discount as a benefit. The fitness center spent $40 to print the coupons and raked in $1,803 from those who redeemed the coupons. Slutsky calls this strategy "cross-promotion," and it works with discount cards as well as coupons. If you want to try this, remember to present the opportunity to give the other organization's patrons a discount as a favor you're doing them, not a favor they're doing you. I've made a similar deal with seminar and conference promoters to include a sample newsletter or tip sheet of mine in materials distributed to all of their participants.

Piggybacking.

You can also save on postage by tucking flyers, small catalogs or brochures into mailings you're sending out for other purposes. If your marketing piece costs mere pennies, why not include it even when you pay bills or send away for free information? At least half a dozen of the businesses mentioned in this book came to my attention because someone took the chance to do just that.

Downsizing.

If you've been sending out flyers in envelopes, can you substitute postcards? By pruning items in your catalog, can you shorten it from sixteen pages to twelve? By editing more ruthlessly, could you keep your newsletter to two pages instead of sprawling it out over four? Mark Beach, author of *Editing Your Newsletter*, has said that a newsletter should be just "long enough to say what you need to say and short enough to read on the way to the wastebasket." In *Getting It Printed*, Beach says that reducing the size of your catalog just a quarter inch could save you thousands of dollars in paper costs and postage per year.

Invisible reuse.

If you received faxed materials from me, you would have no way of knowing what was on the other side of the paper I sent through the fax machine. So I'll confess here: it's old manuscripts, rough drafts and other people's one-sided stuff I would otherwise toss away. Once *both* sides are full, the paper goes to be recycled. I do the same with laser-printed originals that I'm going to take in to be copied, saying "top side only" when I give my instructions to the clerk. Besides saving me two or three reams of paper every year, this helps me feel virtuous.

Visible reuse.

Get the most out of what you've already done by using elements in other contexts. When you achieve press coverage, blow the clippings up into posters you can hang in your store. Transform a successful flyer into a postcard or an ad. A headline that pulled like crazy in an ad might also work as an opener in a direct-mail letter.

Printing on demand.

Do you use small numbers of your materials steadily over time? Then instead of tying your money up in inventory, switch to a format that you can create as you need it. This might mean a folder with inserts in place of a brochure; a tip sheet designed so that you can duplicate it at the copy shop as orders come in; invoices produced one by one from your laser printer rather than preprinted with your two-color logo.

Remnant and regional advertising.

Some ad agencies specialize in selling space that magazines must fill pronto. Discounts on so-called "remnant" advertising are steep, and Jay Levinson lists such companies in his books (see Chapter 26). You can also save big on ads in national magazines and newspapers by inserting your ad only in their issues for a particular region. You'll reach fewer readers, but you could still say, "As seen in *Newsweek* [or the *Wall Street Journal*]."

Cleaning your lists.

At least once a year, include a checkoff on your order form for people who don't want to remain on your mailing list. Eliminate duplicates and stay away from lists that are a steal to rent because they're out-of-date.

High-class black-and-white.

Without spending money on color, you can upgrade your look by learning techniques that make dramatic use of shades of black. For details, consult *The Gray Book* from Ventana Press (see Chapter 26).

Higher perceived value.

You can increase the apparent value of a catalog, tip sheet or promotional newsletter by placing a price on it even though you distribute it for free. Similarly, I've seen a sales letter called a "booklet" and a brochure or catalog given a title, almost like a book—moves that increase the likelihood that prospects feel you've given them a gift when you are promoting your business.

Knowing what you want.

I know one person who kept changing her mind, even immediately after stuff was printed, about what should go into her brochure. Other people got talked into something that wasn't right for them. In both situations, they failed to get their money's worth from printed materials.

False Economies

As Amy Dacyczyn wisely acknowledges, it's possible to cut back too far. Below are a few ways you might *not* want to save money.

Getting overexcited about price breaks.

Don't pay too much attention to the way higher quantities send cost per unit down. Sure, ordering five thousand may make each piece half-price compared to ordering one thousand, but what kind of bargain is that when you end up with four years' worth of brochures that are outdated by year two?

Using flawed materials.

Again, you save money by using flyers even though they misspell the name of your town (your mistake). But as I've argued elsewhere in the book, this damages your credibility and in this case constitutes poor public relations.

Using predesigned materials in bulk.

A company called Paper Direct and more than half a dozen competitors sell multicolored sets of letterheads and envelopes, business cards, brochures, etc., that you customize with a copier or your laser or inkjet printer (see Chapter 26). If you need respectable stuff in quantities of 100 or 200, this saves you the cost of a designer. But if you plan to use at least 2,000 of any one item, you'll probably save a lot by getting the pieces designed and printed. In addition, if you order one of the more popular designs from Paper Direct, chances are very high someone will recognize the design and conclude you're a tiny operation starting out. That defeats your attempt to look big on a small budget!

Being stingy with prospects or the press.

Suppress any Scrooge tendencies when someone interested in doing business with you or a reporter, editor or producer asks you for your materials. That's exactly the wrong time to economize.

◇

PART V

SOLUTIONS
FOR
PROBLEMS

CHAPTER 20

Articulating What's Special About Your Business

While I was working on this book, a young actress named Nancy Sosnowski wrote to me from Chicago, appealing for help with her cover letters to agents and casting directors. "As you can see, they are quite boring," she said. "I want something that will pop out and make them notice me. I don't want my headshot and résumé to go into the garbage." I couldn't help but agree with her assessment of the letters. Whereas her letter to me was alive, her official letters contained nothing that popped up with personality. For instance:

> Hello:
>
> Enclosed is my photo and résumé for consideration for casting in "Eulogy for a Love Affair."
>
> I am a hardworking and dependable actor. My experience has been mainly with community theater, but I have done on-camera and voice-over work for a local cable company.
>
> Thanks for taking time out of your busy schedule to read this and review my résumé. I can be reached at

_____. I hope we will have the opportunity to meet. Until then, have a wonderful day.

Sincerely,

Nancy Pynes Sosnowski

I couldn't find enough clues in her résumé on how to perk up the cover letter, so I wrote back with ten questions designed to elicit comments that could help attract the directors' attention. One month later she wrote back with answers to less than half of the questions. "I've been having a hard time with this," she confessed. "This may seem strange since most actors are self-centered, but I'm not good at talking about myself and my accomplishments."

If you identify with Sosnowski's difficulty, you and she are not alone. Many who excel at their hobby or profession fall short when it comes to describing how they do it or how their work differs from others'. Don't jump to the conclusion that you're showing some shameful gap in intelligence, because four other factors may account for the difficulty. First, everyone has thousands of competencies they can't put into words. Ever try to teach someone to tie their shoelaces without a hands-on demonstration? The ability to do something and to articulate the process don't automatically parallel each other. Second, when you do your work, you may be too absorbed to be conscious of the steps involved. Engrossed, you work in a kind of spell that precludes observing what you're doing. Third, you may be suffering from a deficit of self-confidence. You can't say what's special about you because you don't believe in yourself. Finally, other people may not share your problem only because they're more conventional—what they do neatly matches society's stock labels and phrases. The more you've invented a career or working method for yourself, the more you may need help figuring out a way to present it verbally.

When you can't easily convey what you do in words, your

marketing materials undoubtedly aren't representing you well. A dangerous state of wordlock may show up in these symptoms:

- You've evolved far past where you were when you last wrote a brochure or company bio, and you keep making excuses about why you're not producing an updated version.

- You feel overwhelmed at the mere idea of putting together your first or new marketing materials.

- You hear or read—and envy—other people's characterization of themselves or their business.

- People don't get it when they read your materials.

- You're relying on in-person forms of marketing but they're no longer bringing in enough business or the kind of clients you want.

- People who get to know your business tell you that it isn't what they expected from your materials.

- Like Nancy Sosnowski, you know your stuff on paper can't hold a candle to what you do.

In my observation, the inability to explain what they do especially plagues pioneering, talented consultants. Caroll Michels adds that most artists have a dreadful time putting anything about their work into words. Whatever your profession, however, you don't have to let the problem eat away at your business success. Your condition has numerous cures.

Cures for the Wordlocked

Ask clients and customers to tell you what you've done for them and how you did it.

Printed evaluation forms can give you useful phrases you can adapt to describe your work, in addition to providing blurb material. One at a time you can also ask people who have benefited from your work for comparisons, descriptions, reminiscences and summaries. Brian Starr and Mark Barnard of Bos'n, Inc. essentially got a client to write their brochure after they'd been operating for some time without one. When a client who'd already bought their training program said he needed something in writing for the people upstairs, Starr asked what he could have said on paper that would have done the job.

Invite a would-be Barbara Walters or Bob Woodward friend to interview you

Some people's tongues become golden when someone else prompts them and listens. Even without a shining performance, you can get the information you need by asking your reporter friend to tell you after your discussion what he or she learned. An entrepreneurial support group can serve the same function, says Barbara Winter, who has spawned "Joyfully Jobless" groups nationally through her seminars and book, *Making a Living Without a Job*. "Ask the group to tell you what your business is as they understand it. You may find that you're projecting the wrong things, or they may give you a better way of saying it."

If friends and associates don't help, a marketing consultant (see Chapter 25) may have the right inquisitiveness and persistence to help you proclaim advantages where you just saw the same blobbety blob-blob as everybody else's. Advertising wizard Robert Pritikin tells a story about trying to uncover some exploitable advantage of Pureta hot dogs by visiting the factory and cross-examining the company president, who insisted that all frankfurters are the same. "Does the whole cow go into the frankfurters?" asked Pritikin, about to give up. Except for some of the scuzzy parts, the president replied. "Do you mean including the New York cuts, the market steaks, the T-bone steaks?" responded Pritikin, who turned an affirmative reply into billboards, radio slogans and print ads carrying a message the president would never have thought of: "Pureta— There's T-bone steak in every frank." Sales went up, up, up, Pritikin recalls.

Interview yourself

Ask yourself the questions a reporter would, then answer them. Even the questions that seem irrelevant can help you dredge up a phrase or an idea that you can develop as a mini-theme. The following should get you started.

- Why should someone buy your product or service rather than someone else's?

- What's your favorite item in your product line, or your favorite service, and why?

- What's the most characteristic praise that comes your way?

- What can you do that other _____ s cannot?

- Have you ever heard people compare your style of service or your product to someone or something else?

- If your mother, spouse or son were boasting about what you do, what would he or she say?

- What's the story about your business that you find yourself repeating most often?

- What do you believe really underlies your success with customers and clients?

- What were some challenges you have overcome in your work, perhaps surprising even yourself?

- If you were retiring and could give one piece of advice

to the person taking over from you, what would that be?

• Is there an image or a feeling that best communicates what you are all about?

• What's the biggest myth about your line of business, and how is it not true about you?

From the questions I asked Nancy Sosnowski, the one she related to the most had to do with overcoming challenges. She polished that into a theme to insert in her cover letters, as in, "I am an actor who will do whatever it takes to deliver a professional performance. Whether that means studying sign language, as I did when playing Annie Sullivan in 'The Miracle Worker' or learning about business, as I did when I played Kate Sullivan in 'Other People's Money,' I relish challenges and always go the extra mile to master a role or skill." Much better than "I am a hardworking and dependable actor," don't you think?

Try teaching what you do to someone else

Your pupil will probably ask the questions that bring what you've been missing out into the open. Instruct your pupil in the "why" as well as the "what." Audiotape or videotape your tutoring session, or your sessions with clients and watch or listen as if to someone else. Reuse your best explanations in your writing, and describe what you see or hear going on, using different levels of detail: a one-sentence or ten-second summary of what happened in the session, a one-paragraph or one-minute review and a one-page or five-minute narration.

Ask someone to observe you at work and present you with an oral or written report

Two clients hired me to do this, knowing that they had trouble being conscious of what they're doing while they're doing it. You too may find the objectivity, fresh observation and different vocabulary of an outsider valuable.

Give yourself permission to convey the enthusiasm and spice in your written materials that you naturally exude when talking or when writing to someone you know. This proved pivotal for Nancy Sosnowski, who found her breakthrough with cover letters after I showed her how to pick up on a theme in the casting ad she was responding to and write to a real person on the other end. For a children's video, she started her response, "Since I am a kid at heart, your casting notice for your children's video caught my eye. I imagine you will need an actor who loves children, is patient, warm and fun. That's me!" To a casting agent who had just moved his office, she wrote, "I hear you've been on the go again, moving into a more spacious and appealing location. I hope the transition went safely and smoothly. Since I have not sent my picture and résumé to you in the past, I am enclosing it now, hoping that it will find you settled and relaxed in your new environment." For a project called "Dear St. Anthony," she wasn't sure if it was a film or video. "Having gone to a Catholic grammar school," she wrote me, "I know that people pray to St. Anthony when they lose things like their keys or wallet. Can I use that somehow?" Yes, I told her. That's exactly the idea!

CHAPTER 21

Collecting Compelling Testimonials

When you brag about yourself, many people look at you askance. But when you include attributed third-party quotes in your marketing materials, your trust quotient soars. "Every client I've ever had is afraid to ask for endorsements," says George Berman. "But when they finally go about it, the client usually gives higher praise than the person expected." Consider the impact of this testimonial, received from an attorney by a title agent Berman worked with, after the agent got up the gumption to ask: "Without _____, I would be out of business."

Having a file of great quotes gives you strong ammunition for brochures, flyers, catalogs, ads, press releases and direct mail. In order to use testimonials to best advantage, however, you need to know not only how to gather them but also how to tell a forceful endorsement from one that fizzles. Let's start there, with a quiz that lets you rate the quotes offered by two prominent businesses.

Evaluate These Endorsements

Imagine that you're mulling over attending a business seminar. You don't want to be bored and you want to learn something that will make you more effective in your work. Which of these quotes, appearing on the brochures of Fred Pryor Seminars and National Seminars Group, would propel you to register? Rate these six, all originally followed by at least a name and job title, either "weak," "stronger" or "incredibly powerful."

1. "National Seminars, Inc. is super! The Powerful Business Writing Seminar has so much to offer."
2. "Many very useful ideas were presented. They will be useful to me at work and home."
3. "Invaluable seminar! This will help a lot!"
4. "This was the most informative and entertaining writing class I've ever attended. I have learned new methods to achieve a better style of business writing."
5. "I feel this seminar will definitely make a difference in the way I communicate with people in every phase of my life."
6. "I have attended several seminars on different subjects (by different companies) and came away from them believing they were a waste of time. This seminar has reaffirmed my faith that they are not a waste of time and money."

Putting myself in the place of a prospective seminar attendee, I found all of them weak, except one. Numbers 1 and 3 convey enthusiasm but nothing about what made the seminar valuable for these people. Number 2 is irredeemably vague, and would have impressed more had it said how the endorser expected to use the ideas. Number 5 says, in effect, "I *feel* the seminar will have results"—not very convincing. Number 6 offers praise so feeble that it almost qualifies as condemnation:

"not a waste" (but not necessarily very valuable, either). Only number 4 seems stronger than the rest, offering three specific points about the seminar that might help erase some doubts about attending. If you rated any of the above as "incredibly powerful," compare these:

7. "The data I obtained has already landed me two nice fat consulting contracts." [from a North Shore Scholars seminar brochure]
8. "After taking your course I was able to convince my boss to go with a new design that ultimately saved the company over $2 million and created a better designed product. Prior to taking this course I would have estimated my chances of success at about 30%. [from Management Resources' brochure]

In numbers 7 and 8, we encounter quantified, actual results instead of just enthusiasm or a projected outcome. Do you agree with me that their persuasiveness could hardly be improved upon? In contrast to numbers 1 through 6, apparently gathered the day of the seminar, numbers 7 and 8 obviously came in some time later—again bolstering these companies' credibility, since that indicates a stronger relationship with participants. Most businesspeople would rather spend money on a seminar that brings benefits afterward than one which merely makes them feel excited and hopeful at the end of the day. I wonder if the national seminar companies tried to get comments from participants later in addition to soliciting feedback at the seminar. They could have called people to find out how they were applying what they'd learned or offered a discount on another seminar for sending in postseminar result-reporting tributes. Your situation is probably more conducive to blurb-gathering than theirs, however. If you have ongoing relationships with clients and customers, gathering praise with the power of examples 7 and 8 requires only a modicum of intelligent effort.

Great Testimonials Can Be Easier to Find

Many people think a testimonial should be a complete letter on the stationery of the person offering praise. A few businesspeople do succeed in collecting these, but I believe that's the cloudy route. You're asking a lot to ask someone to write one of those, or hoping a lot to wish some come in phrased freshly, persuasively and with acceptable grammar. The sunnier route involves looking for pithy quotes and using them where a complete letter would not fit.

Here are five ways to collect compelling nuggets of praise:

1. Unsolicited comments. These might arrive in a thank-you letter, while meeting face-to-face with a customer or during a telephone chat. You must seek permission—preferably in writing—for using these or any other unpublished remarks in your own marketing or you might be liable for, in legal jargon, "misappropriation." Stick written comments in a file, and jot down fleeting praise immediately, asking, "May I quote you on that?"

2. Feedback forms. A book publisher can stick a postage-paid postcard asking for comments into books before they're mailed. A car repair shop could hand out feedback cards along with receipts. A kayak builder could send after-sale letters to buyers asking how satisfied they were with their boat. You get the best quotes when you guide people with germane questions, such as:

- How did your child like our stories?

- What results would you attribute to having used our interpreters?

- Based on your experience, would you recommend our video service to other companies? Why or why not?

- What would you tell other parents who are considering using our scholarship information service?

The best questions come across as if you genuinely want to know how you're doing, and are not just fishing for accolades. As a bonus, they help cement your relationship with happy customers and help you learn from those who offer suggestions and complaints. Use open-ended questions rather than yes-no ones or circle-a-rating scales.

3. Solicited comments. In a more personalized version of method #2, you can call or write regular clients and ask them for something you can quote on a brochure. Make it as easy as possible for them to help you. Flattery helps, as in, "I'd like to feature you as one of my success stories." If someone says, "Go ahead and write something for me to sign," make up something specific, colorful and concise.

4. Writing them for others' signature. If you feel sure this won't backfire with customers you know well, write something and call them up and say, "Would you be willing to say something like this in a press release for my new show?" Offer to adjust the wording so it sounds like them, since you don't want all your quotes to use the same vocabulary and style.

5. Published comments. You don't need permission to cite printed statements from reviews or media coverage. Since people view these as impartial, positive media quotations have phenomenal impact. Even negative mentions benefit you if you say, "As seen in *Newt Breeders' News*."

6. A contest. John Caples, a coffee drinker, once got handed the job of persuading Americans to drink tea at breakfast. He ran an ad offering small cash prizes for the best letters on "Why I drink tea at breakfast." This approach, which brought him dozens of promising ideas, can bring you authentic, believable product endorsements. Caution: It can affect your credibility if you pay, however indirectly, for endorsements.

Finding Them Isn't Enough

Whether unsolicited testimonials pour in or you have to put effort into soliciting them, receiving them represents just the first step in using them well. Next you must examine each endorsement critically to make sure it meets these tests:

- *Is it attributable?* The most convincing quotes include the praiser's name, position and city and state. Anonymous quotes or those from people who won't let you use their name provoke suspicion that you made them up.

- *Is it specific?* General adjectives like "wonderful" or "most beneficial" can't hold a candle to a precise, explicit description of what the product or service did for the praising person.

- *Is it brief?* If a blurb goes on for more than three sentences, you must select the strongest portion and cut the rest. You want nuggets, not blobs of praise.

- *Is it positive?* "Not a waste of time and money" fell down on this count. Repeating backhanded compliments can do you more harm than good.

- *Is it clear?* Often people leave out of blurbs the background that you know and they know but that others need to know too in order to understand a comment. At other times the intended meaning gets lost in muddled phrasing.

When a blurb furnished by an ongoing client or customer falls down on one or more of the above counts, you should figure out what it needs to work persuasively on your behalf and ask your commender for approval of the revised version. Do this diplomatically, as in "Lynne, I'm really grateful for what you wrote about our pet store. Would it be OK if we cut the sentence about the cute puppies and added the fact that you're a city planner in Midtown after your name?"

Here's an example of a testimonial from a brochure for Computer Business Services Incorporated in Sheridan, Indiana, that badly needs editing:

> BEFORE: Prior to learning about CBSI, I was disabled and unemployed with back problems. I now have people helping me and I expect my income to double."   —M.B.

This blurb suffers from four problems: (1) The phrase "now have people helping me" could mean either "now have people taking care of me because of my back problem" or "now have people voluntarily helping me run my business," neither of which attests to the power of the CBSI program. (2) "I expect my income to double" is extremely weak. I've *always* expected my income to double over the previous year, but does that mean it has? (3) Even though "George and Jeanie" say they have this letter from an actual person on file, just "M.B." is flimsy. (4) This quote sits to the right of a color photo of a man and a woman, different from the CBSI owners pictured elsewhere. Is one of them supposed to be "M.B."? The following version would give CBSI a greater boost:

> AFTER: "Prior to working with CBSI, I was disabled and unemployed with back problems. My husband and I now employ three people in a business that grosses $9,600 a month."
> —Marilyn Baxter, Hometown, Kansas

Once you polish each quote, decide how you want to arrange them and use them. Generally the strongest blurbs on a brochure, flyer or ad should catch the reader's eye first and last. A professional designer can sprinkle quotes around on a piece effectively, but it's safest to group testimonials together on one panel, in a separate column or in a box if you're designing something yourself. Those who assemble pieces of paper in a folder should create something called a quote sheet. Terri Lonier, author of *Working Solo*, heads hers with her logo and the line, "Everyone is talking about *Working Solo* and Terri Lonier" (a bit of an exaggeration, by the way). Then there's a quote from Jay Conrad Levinson, author of *Guerrilla Marketing*, followed by four quotes from readers, three from the press and three from radio hosts. Lonier's quote sheet makes an excellent impression, but I recall seeing one years ago that took my breath away. It featured an avalanche of two dozen testimonials crowded together in 8-point type, each linked to a name, a company affiliation and a telephone number. The phone numbers astounded me, since they made the statement merely by their presence, "Not only are we glad to praise this person, we'd be glad to take the time to talk about our experiences further." I imagine few people called, but what a credibility boost came from those numbers!

Be conscious of the collective impact of the quotes you select. If four of your five quotes come from lawyers, readers will conclude you do business primarily with lawyers. Recently I received a fancily designed brochure for a free presentation by someone I'd never heard of named Justin Joseph. The blurb on the front page, from someone named Roy Elkins, immediately put me on my guard: "Justin is to presenting what Joe Montana is to football." Now I know my ignorance of football makes me an untypical American, but this says nothing to me except that perhaps here's a guy who's going to bore me with football metaphors. The brochure included four other quotes, all from men. Several female friends agreed that this pattern of quotes indicated to them a man who is insensitive to his impact on women. If that conclusion misrepresents Justin Joseph, then he'd better make sure his blurbs reflect his values and who he is.

CHAPTER 22

Finding a Creative Twist

As my friends and newsletter subscribers know, I'm one of creativity's all-time biggest fans. Yet I won't try to convince you that you need creative writing in your marketing materials. On the contrary, test after test has shown that straightforward, benefit-oriented or problem-solving copy gets a better response than the average clever, humorous or exotic approach. Examples of advertising campaigns that won creative awards but flunked in marketing pull are legion. So unless you follow my provisos below, I advise you to avoid making your marketing materials cute or sly. Use your creative energy instead to hone a crisp, clear message that will get your target audience to say "Yes! That's exactly what I need."

Gratuitous creativity from bored or uninformed copywriters can even do you harm by damaging your credibility, confusing prospects and sending them to your competitors. Integral creativity, however, offers the taste of a startling new flavor, the enchantment of an unexpected turn in a melody—and an impact aligned to your purpose and message. Used very, very carefully, imaginative ideas enhance your market's urge to buy from you. Here's how to ensure a wise execution of inspired marketing.

Appropriate Creativity: Resonance, Relevance and Surprise

By definition, originality in marketing produces aesthetic, intellectual or emotional surprise. But gratuitous originality functions like irrelevant jokes told as the opening of a speech. You get the laughs, yet afterward people wonder what they had to do with your subject. Or you gain the attention of the wrong people and set them up to expect humor throughout your program. Or you lose the respect of those who believe your subject isn't a laughing matter. As with the jokes, a fresh, unexpected entrance promotes your marketing only when it has pertinence for your audience and reverberates on several levels.

These three advertising headlines and their accompanying graphics exemplify integral creativity:

1. JUST HOW STRONG IS YOUR INFORMATION CHAIN?
   The weak link could be your long distance data network.
   (Across the page, just below the initial question, stretch two sets of thick metal links joined by a paper clip. The ad is from AT&T.)
2. STOP PAYING POSTAGE FOR THESE KINDS OF STAMPS.
   (Surrounding the boxed copy are stamps like "Return to sender," "Insufficient address" and "Incorrect Zip code." From AccuMail, a software program that cleans, corrects and sorts mailing lists.)
3. JUDGE A BOOK BY ITS COVERAGE.
   (The illustration shows a DECpc 425SE notebook computer with a program running on its flipped-up screen. From Digital.)

The first example takes a prevalent metaphor literally with an evocative question and a strong image. At a glance, anyone whose business involved electronic communication would worry about the weakness represented by the paper clip, which the second line makes clear stands for interruptible or corruptible lines for data transmission. The impact here goes much deeper than the unimaginative version of the message, "How secure are your data communication lines?"

In the second example, the prosaic version would be "Stop paying for undeliverable mail"—a message that resounds for anyone who sends high-volume mailings. But by linking the word "postage" with a secondary meaning of the word "stamp," the headline gains an elegant ring that strengthens its relevance for the target market.

The third headline, a takeoff of a conventional saying, puzzled me at first. But as I read on, I discovered that "coverage" referred to Digital's three-year warranty and its promise to repair and return any of its notebook computers within two days. The headline thus makes sense on the level of "Judge our product by its warranty coverage" as well as in the way it turns upside down the saying, "Don't judge a book by its cover."

All three examples rely on wordplay and appeal in a compact way to your intuitive, nonrational sense as well as your intellectual side. And there lies the special satisfaction for readers in a creative approach: rational *and* suggestive communication. Make certain, however, that you are not using an irrelevant gimmick, but an attention-getting technique that shines a brighter spotlight on your offering.

Now compare these three pitches, which catch one's attention but in my judgment flunk the tests of resonance and relevance.

1. LOOKING FOR A NEEDLE IN A HAYSTACK? *(For a technical recruiting company: no illustration, no continuation of the needle/haystack idea in later copy.)* This headline might work in conjunction with an illustrated stack of

résumés, the only justification I can think of for the "haystack" metaphor. Right now "needle" is just as incidental, but it could gain resonance and relevance by meaning some sort of instrument needle. My best suggestion for freshening up this cliché would be: LOOKING FOR A NEEDLE DESIGNER IN A RÉSUMÉ STACK?, which would have special appeal for the intended market of technical companies.

2. WE'VE RAISED SERVICE TO AN ART FORM. *(From the Center for Executive Education at Babson College, accompanied by a color reproduction of* Vase of Flowers *by Claude Monet.)* This perfectly illustrates irrelevant creativity. Since the advertiser is not an art museum but a business conference center, the painting and the phrase "art form" fail to call this message to the attention of the right people. The wordplay creates no special echoes for conference planners, so it represents misdirected effort.

3. SCRATCH & SNIFF! THE SWEET SMELL OF A SUCCESSFUL PRESENTATION. *(For a product called a "film recorder"; the cartoonlike illustration shows a slide wearing sunglasses, a top hat, what appears to be a tux and sneakers.)* I have to wonder what someone was sniffing when they designed this for a postcard deck. Not only can I not understand from the copy what the advertised product is, I cannot think of any connection slides might have with the sense of smell. Hence this ad flops on both the literal and the metaphorical levels.

Your appropriately creative idea might become a central concept of your business rather than a theme for one promotion only. Copy Cop, a chain of copy shops in the Boston area, uses a blue logo of three mustached policemen holding out their palms, above which it says "CALL THE COPS." Their corporate brochure starts off with the headline "Put Boston's Finest to work for you" and features blue as the company color. As someone who is finicky about copy quality, I understand and appreciate the subtle message about quality that comes across in the "cop" metaphor. Similarly, Ann Bloch carries through the theme of her business, Writing Workout, by wearing a headband and sneakers when she trains and explaining her writing instruction under headings called "Warmup," "Target Zones" and "Fat and Flab." She thought up the theme after seeing a group of executives working out at her gym. "Executives wouldn't take a writing course because they thought it would have to be remedial. But when I saw them all exercising, I realized it's not at all remedial to work out. On the contrary, it's how top athletes stay in shape. The philosophy underlying 'Writing Workout' helps me explain why companies need it."

Mark Barnard says he thought up his company name, Bos'n, Inc., after seeing a newspaper photo of two boats, one with its sails down in the middle of a lake, going nowhere, and the other gliding along at full sail. "The person who sits and waits for the wind to come isn't making sales," says Barnard. Not only is "Bos'n" the nautical term for "boatswain," the chief petty officer who steers a ship (with the client company's sales manager the captain), "Bos'n" stands for "Build Opportunity through Sales Navigation." Barnard admits, though, that many people don't grasp the metaphor. "A week might go by without us saying anything about sailing, though navigation is a pretty important concept for us."

Some Recommended Hunting Grounds

The best creativity builds on thorough knowledge of the audience and of your product or service. Given that background, here are a few realms in which superb slogans, headlines and themes can be found:

Drama.
Where is the tragedy or triumph, the cause for despair or

rejoicing in what you sell? If you can find or create a bigger-than-life story that is integral to your product or service, you could see bigger-than-life sales. A wildly successful ad decades ago for the Harvard Classics, a five-foot shelf of great but sometimes abstruse works of literature, philosophy and history, started off with a drawing of an eighteenth-century woman in a carriage and the headline "This is Marie Antoinette riding to her death." Appealing to emotion more than to intellect, the text continued, "Do you know her tragic story? Have you ever read what Burke wrote about the French Revolution—one of the great, fascinating books that have made history?" Since you probably know dramatic persuasion best from television advertising, a good way to proceed might be to think up a gripping scenario that could be enacted on screen, then adapt it for print.

Human interest.

The Harvard Classics ad also relied on the important principle that most people respond more to human predicaments than to abstract dilemmas. Consequently, to hook prospects, hunt for the "people factor" in your service or product. In devising a campaign for a Brooklyn savings bank's new automatic teller machines, marketing consultant Sherman Robbins could have featured the technology. Instead, knowing that the bank's average customer was fifty-five to sixty years old, he used an eighty-one-year-old model to underscore claims that the machines were simple to use. Similarly, instead of featuring its edifying contents in a cerebral pitch, advertising for England's premier literary magazine found the human factor and trumpeted: "Warning: In Britain, more people have *Granta* stolen from their homes than any other magazine."

Turning expectations upside down.

Would you respond to a headline that read, "We're offering countless hours of pain and aggravation for $12.95"? You might if you belonged to the group of puzzle addicts that this full-page ad in the *Atlantic Monthly* targeted for a collection of its cryptic crosswords. The line captures attention because normally people pay to avoid pain and aggravation, yet once you realize what the product is, you understand why paying for trouble makes sense. This strategy worked for the first advertiser who used the approach "Don't buy our product! (Unless . . .)" But that's now clichéd. Find an original paradox by asking if your business gives people something they ordinarily don't want.

Plays on words.
   Here are two examples of wordplay that satisfy my criteria of resonance, relevance and surprise:

- *(Accompanied by a picture of a mountain forest)* We've got 98 billion branches and you've never heard of us? *(For Hanson, a company that produces timber, among other products.)*

- *(With a photo of newspapers bundled for recycling)* Yesterday's newspapers are making headlines all over again. *(For a Hammermill recycled paper made from 100 percent de-inked newspapers and magazines.)*

I can almost hear some readers saying out loud, "Ahhh, I get it!" When these kinds of double meanings succeed, they get prospects to linger over the multilayered message. Notice that in both of these examples, the illustration helps greatly to communicate the pun. To come up with an appropriate play on words, brainstorm lists of key words in your topic area and common sayings involving them. Then wait for inspiration. A software program called Idea Fisher can help in this pursuit, as it presents common cultural references grouped together around more than 100 themes.

Analogies.

Ann Bloch's "Writing Workout" theme consists of an imaginative comparison between a writing workshop and a workout session at a gym. Likewise, a UPS ad puts a pacifier ("Calms children") beside a UPS Guaranteed Air Tracking label ("Calms adults") and then elaborates on the comparison: "Kids can have tantrums over anything. Adults, however, tend to lose their cool when sending important packages. So we suggest using UPS Next Day Air. Only UPS offers guaranteed tracking and guaranteed 10:30 delivery for up to 35% less than other companies charge. And that should pacify just about everyone." To come up with an effective comparison, play the game of "If this were a _____ , [animal, toy, hobby, job, etc.] which one would it be?" A good analogy has several provocative points of comparison.

Helping Inspiration Along

Actually, you don't have to simply wait for inspiration. In Chapter 23 I describe five exercises that can help you generate usable persuasive ideas. There's also the chance that, like Molière's character who'd been speaking prose his whole life without realizing it, you already have the creative nugget you need but have not yet recognized it. To find your buried treasure, ask someone who understands marketing but isn't part of your business to look over your past materials and listen to you talk about your business. Quite possibly, a phrase, a doodle or a concept from a customer's testimonial will prompt the outsider to holler, "That's it!" Before retorting, "*That's* it?" let your friend or consultant spin the idea out a little more.

In work for Data General, adman George Lois says he was entranced by the flat shape and compact size of its AViiON computer. The Data General people casually mentioned that the industry had nicknamed such computers "pizza boxes." "Here was a situation where computer technocrats themselves were describing a high-tech product in human, household language," Lois remembers. "We grabbed this mass, universal image and built our campaign around the pizza box—another example of my almost mystical notion that you don't create big ideas, you discover them as they float by." Lois designed a pizza box for the product, a version of the company logo that incorporated a pizza slice and a two-line selling message on the package:

We fit 117 MIPS of mainframe power in a pizza box!

Call 1-800-DATA GEN (We deliver)

Anyone who had any doubt about the appeal of the pizza metaphor lost it when a columnist elaborated on the metaphor still more in reporting on the ad campaign. In an article headlined "A tasty approach to high tech," the columnist described the innovative box and said, "Inside, it turns out, is a $100,000 computer, without anchovies."

CHAPTER 23

Getting the Writing Done

Although flexibility serves as my watchword for the creative process, I do endorse one absolute rule when it comes to writing marketing materials: Don't leave it till the last minute. Dashing something off to meet a deadline—even if you proofread rigorously—puts you in the position of the Israelites who left Egypt before their bread had risen. The bread they took with them was edible, but flatter and less tasty than you'd want either in a daily staple food or a treat. In Chapters 20, 21, and 22, I presented methods to brainstorm and articulate ideas and collect tributes you can use. Here are additional tips for generating ideas and methods that help you funnel ideas efficiently from your brain onto paper. By making it easier to get started, these techniques help you achieve the substance and flavor of copy that's had the proper time to develop.

How to Kick-Start Your Writing

Most people find it easier to fix up dull, disorganized prose than to conjure the perfect copy out of nowhere. Each of the following five exercises allows you to gather raw material for your ad, release, brochure or letter painlessly in a short amount of time—even a few minutes. This means you can make significant progress while you're sitting grounded in a plane or on hold in customer-service purgatory. One client who learned some of these techniques told me that she'd gotten into the habit of sitting down whenever she turned on the microwave and writing until the timer pinged. "It's amazing," she said, "how much writing you can actually do in three minutes!"

Freewriting

If you're thirty or younger, you may have encountered this simple exercise in a composition class. It has one rule: Start writing and keep writing no matter what until time is up. This means, don't worry about spelling, punctuation, grammar or even making sense. Your one and only goal is to keep the pen going (or the keyboard clicking). When working on your marketing materials, set a timer for five minutes and begin with the phrase, "What I really want to say to potential customers [or clients, or the media] is . . ."

Many people find that freewriting helps disarm the inner critic who tells them things like "That's stupid" or "Everyone knows you can't write." When you just keep writing anyway, you have a chance of producing a very rough version of what you want to say, or at least a useful word here or there. Even when you wander away from your subject, freewriting limbers up your writing muscles and makes it easier to get relevant words onto paper. For those who have trouble concentrating, freewriting brings your distractions to the fore, where you can write them out and then crumple them up and toss them out. If you write on the computer, try a variation on freewriting that I call the "invisible ink" technique: Turn off your monitor. Whatever you type still goes into the machine's memory so that you'll be able to see it when you turn the monitor back on.

But so long as you can't see what you're typing, your inner critic has significantly less to latch on to.

Both freewriting and the next exercise also help with any unanswered question about creating your marketing materials. Your opening phrase could be "The voice I want in my brochure is . . . ," or "What I really want to accomplish with my newsletter is . . . ," or "The advantages I have over the competition are . . ." These exercises may put you in touch with subconscious wisdom about appropriate marketing strategies.

Q & A

As you would probably guess, "Q & A" stands for "Question and Answer," the format of this exercise. To get started you need an open-ended (not yes-or-no) question to which you do not consciously know the answer, such as "What's a good headline for my grand opening flyer?" or "What can I say that would get me into the *Wall Street Journal*?" After setting a timer for eight or ten minutes, you write down your question, then write down the first answer that pops into your mind. Then you allow that answer to suggest a new question, write down the first answer to that that pops into your mind, and keep on going in a chain of questions and answers until time runs out. As with freewriting, you should keep writing quickly rather than stopping to ponder. In a variation that can be fun and surprising, when you're doing this on paper, write the questions with your usual hand, but whenever it's time to write answers, switch the pen to the hand you do not usually use to write.

Some people who have complained that their thoughts keep going around in a circle say that Q & A takes them beyond their previous muddles for the first time. Since almost everyone agrees that freewriting and Q & A "feel different," try both to see which one feels more comfortable and proves fruitful for you.

Word webs

The next exercise helps you come up with persuasive words and phrases to use in the headline or text of a marketing piece. To make a word web, start with a key word or phrase for which you need synonyms, images or neighbors, then write it in the center of a sheet of paper and circle it. Allow yourself to go off on a chain of associations from your initial word or phrase, writing down each word, drawing a line to it from the previous one and circling it. Anytime you run out of associations, go back to your initial word or phrase and start a new chain. Your sheet of paper quickly fills up with what looks like strings of balloons. When you've filled up the page or run out of steam, go back through all the associations and star those that have some potential.

Let's suppose I wanted to write a postcard pitching subscriptions to my newsletter by featuring the current issue on intuition. I produce a word web from the word "intuition" that includes the rather obvious relative "hunch" as well as, through an inexplicable series of mental jumps, something about parking meters expiring. Already I would have two possibilities to either develop or discard: "Why I trust my hunch that you'll like this publication" and "What can help you spot business opportunities and avoid parking tickets?" I could come up with other approaches by making a word web from the word "subscription."

Models

The more analytical, systematic types among you can quickly rough out a draft of a piece using models. Here the "swipe file" I recommended earlier gets put to good use. If you have collected samples of the format you need to create that you like, you can get a quick start by using one or more examples as prototypes. For example, say you want to write copy for a classified ad in a magazine. After scrutinizing the last issue's ads, you can say to yourself, "Let's see, I need four or five words to grab attention, then ten to twelve words to describe the benefit of my product, then as many words as it takes to describe how to order." Or, after looking at the course catalog for which you're supposed to describe your class, you're able to say, "I need one sentence that gets the attention of the right people, three sentences describing what participants will learn, then a come-on invitation to end up with." By using other people's work as a template, you are not copying. You are simply benefiting from their general experience.

Wrong-way driving

If you can't get a sentence down on paper because everything you can think of seems wrong, use that flow of bad ideas to get started. Write down all the wrong ways you can think of to write your piece. Give yourself permission to make them wronger and wronger. Then when you finally run out of gas— if you haven't already felt the approach of a Eureka!—see if there is something salvageable in all the wreckage.

Getting Your Seat onto the Chair to Write

For some of you, getting your pen to stay on the page or your fingers to continue clicking along on the keyboard isn't the problem. You just can't rise above the morass of all your other to-dos and make writing a priority. Procrastination stalls you. In that case, here's a shelfful of remedies to try, the untraditional ones first.

Confront fears that may be stopping you.
Do you find writing a drag because you can't imagine doing it well? Might you be afraid of too much fame and fortune? Could you be holding off having to deal with the post office because that's something new for you? To pinpoint fears, write

this phrase down and complete it ten times with whatever comes to mind: "I can't write because I'm afraid of . . ." As with some of the exercises above, when you grant yourself permission to write down any nonsense that occurs to you, some of what you write down usually hits the spot. Once you've identified a fear or two, argue with each one like this:

> Fear: I'm afraid I won't be able to come up with anything original.
> Backtalk: So what if it's the oldest pitch in the book but gets them lining up outside the store?

Creatively make the writing task more pleasurable.

You might be shirking the writing because you feel it's a dreadfully unpleasant way to spend your energy. If so, think about whether you can combine the writing with something you love to do. Perhaps you could write while listening to your favorite CD's, or hike off with a notebook to your special spot in the woods. Could you turn it into some sort of a contest, if that's what revs you up, or pretend you're writing your bio because the *New York Times* already asked you for it?

Do a small piece at a time.

If your newsletter or brochure feels overwhelming, break it up into a dozen or more minitasks. Today you only have to call people who may know a designer; tomorrow you can brainstorm a list of possible articles; the day after you can write the letter to readers. This usually works when you make each minitask small enough that it feels doable.

Enlist a friend's help.

Tell a friend you're trying to get this bit of writing done, and ask her to come and sit with you while you write, call you up once a week to ask how it's going, collect samples for you during her weekly rounds or tell you she knows for certain you can do it—whatever will help keep you on track.

Make your procrastination more noticeable.

If you've been letting yourself forget to get around to doing this, make it easier to remember. Write it down as item number one in your appointment book, slip reminders in your in-box, leave a message for yourself on your voice mail. Nag yourself until you're sick and tired of not having done it.

Promise yourself rewards.

When you can't remove the torture from a task, by setting up pleasures you will indulge in after you finish, you can still make doing it more palatable. Studies have shown that rewards work best when they're distributed throughout a longish task rather than held off for the end, so for optimal results, combine this method with the little-bit-at-a-time system. For me, that would mean for each page that I completed, allowing myself to watch movies during the daytime, eat a box of cookies or talk to my best friend long distance.

Hire someone to do it for you.

Would it be simpler and more satisfying to have someone else write the damned thing already? Then turn to Chapter 25, where I offer guidelines for hiring and working effectively with a consultant or writer.

CHAPTER 24

Fitting into Available Space

I received a dramatic lesson when I turned in an assigned article to *Ms.* magazine in 1987. "We like your piece," the editor called to tell me, "and I know we said two thousand words, but we've decided the article has to fit on two facing pages. Your manuscript is a page and a half too long. But don't panic—I think we can slice out from page 6 through the middle of page 7. Is that OK with you?" Reluctantly, I agreed that the topic there wasn't central to my theme, and together we came up with a way to stitch together smoothly the before- and after-cut paragraphs. But the editor called again two days later with more bad news. "We've set the article in type and it's seventeen lines too long. There isn't any other chunk of content we can cut, so we have to figure out 17 places to drop a line." Separately, then conferring over the phone again, we managed to find seventeen places where extra words, unnecessary elaborations and nonessential examples had been lurking. I realized that no matter how tightly I thought I'd written, it would usually still be possible to unobtrusively trim something here and there.

Until I launched my newsletter, I only knew about the too-long dilemma. But in my newsletter, I occasionally confronted one column that would only match up with the others if it were a line or two longer. I was relieved to learn that some of the cutting techniques could be reversed. In fact, whether you're struggling with copy that overflows the final brochure panel or leaves it too bare, you don't have to follow the example of Procrustes, son of the sea god Poseidon, who used violence to make sure that his bed fit his guests. Those who were too short had their legs stretched to the length of the frame; those who were too tall had their feet lopped off. The art of copyfitting helps you stay kind to your material and fit your message into a fixed space without any trace of chopping or stretching visible to the outsider.

Graphic Techniques for Copyfitting

When you're working on a one-time piece such as an ad, a brochure or even a press release, you have considerable latitude in fiddling around with graphic elements to fit in everything you want to include. Some of these adjustments would disrupt the consistent look of a newsletter or a catalog, though, so take care using them in just one portion of a longer piece. So long as the result passes aesthetic inspection, consider changing the following elements:

- *Type size.* Increasing or decreasing the size of the type 1 point shouldn't make a big difference in readability.

- *Leading.* Changing the amount of space between the lines gives you much more flexibility than with simple single- or double-spacing. When I lay out a press release, which I always keep to one page, I single space it and then keep adding leading until the text fills the page.

- *Margins.* By widening or narrowing the text a hair on each side, you might be able to drop or add a couple of lines. Only trial and error will tell you, because the effect depends on the specific combination of words in a passage and whether the margins allow a word or syllable to fit on a line or force it to the next one.

- *Typeface.* As I mentioned in Chapter 16, some typefaces, like Times Roman, use space economically, while others pudge along. If you've chosen a typeface for its look, but your text just won't fit, see if you can find a similar but more spartan face. Also, be aware that the bold and italic versions of most typefaces each take up a different amount of space than the regular roman version.

- *White space.* If you're struggling to make chunks of text match up, try liberating them from the rigidity of regular rectangles. Maybe allowing one column to descend much lower than the others could create an attractive, informal look. Leaving extra white space below the shorter columns is the vertical equivalent of ragged right margins.

Alignment. Justified copy (with even right-hand margins) uses less space than unjustified copy.

- *Hyphenation.* Whether manual or automatic, hyphenation allows you to fit more words on many lines. But since no perfect word-division program exists, proofread for word breaks. If you're fiddling around with manual hyphenation, always check for some hy-phens you may have unintentionally left behind (like that one).

- *Boxing.* Any element that's too short will look bigger and take up more space if you surround it with a box. A box may also give you a legitimate excuse for placing a chunk of text in bold or italics.

- *Size of your marketing piece.* When nothing enables everything to fit, consider buying a larger ad or using legal-size instead of regular paper for your flyer.

In a newsletter, you'd be wise to design in some flexibility via graphic elements that can grow, shrink or disappear as the length of your copy demands. These include optional cartoons, illustrations and photos, subheads, pull quotes—extracts from your article featured in large type—and kickers—supplements or introductions to headlines, usually placed above them in underscored small type.

Always double-check your entire text after making any of the above changes. Sometimes copyfitting produces unsightly by-products, like a column that starts with a few words that end a paragraph (an "orphan"), a column that ends with the first line of a new paragraph (a "widow") or a subhead separated from the text that should follow it.

Verbal Techniques for Copyfitting

Before I explain how to trim or stretch your copy, why not take a simple test? Go back to the first paragraph under "Graphic Techniques for Copyfitting" (page 291—starting with "When you're working . . .") and see if you can make enough inconspicuous changes to shorten that paragraph one line.

Do that before reading further.

Now here's my snipped but not harmed version. We could safely cut all the words in bold in the paragraph below, with the words in italics added for coherence.

When **you're** working on **a one-time piece such as** an ad, **a** brochure or **even a** press release, **you have considerable latitude in** fiddling around with graphic elements *helps you* **to** fit in everything **you want to include.** Some **of these** adjustments **would** disrupt the consistent look of a newsletter or **a** catalog, though, so take care *there* **using them in just one portion of a longer piece.** So long as the result passes aesthetic*ally* **inspection**, consider changing the*se* **following** elements:

These changes actually shorten the text by three lines. If I changed "So long as " to "If," I'd tighten it up even further, but I think that would change the meaning. We could also shorten "consider" to "try." Here's the trimmed version:

> When working on an ad, brochure or press release, fiddling around with graphic elements helps you fit in everything. Some adjustments disrupt the consistent look of a newsletter or catalog, though, so take care there. So long as the result passes aesthetically, try changing these elements:

After reading the following suggestions for shortening or swelling copy, you may want to practice with a marketing piece you consider pretty well written. The more experience you have at this, the less pain and stress you'll feel next time you have to change the size of a block of text.

Search for large sections of unnecessary or omitted material

Can you make do with three testimonials instead of four? Do you have leftovers of an old product to describe in that blank half-page of your catalog? Scrutinize your brochure for selling points that don't matter much to your primary audience, or your sales letter for doubts you neglected to address. Pay special attention to whether your opening grabs the reader from the first few words or not until the second paragraph, which you should probably then make the first.

Eliminate or add redundant information

If you've provided two examples, one will probably get your point across. Or, an additional example might fill up two more lines without giving the impression of "padding." Instead of repeating long nouns, can you maintain clarity while substituting pronouns—or vice versa? Can you get away with an unexplained "EPA" instead of "Environmental Protection

Agency"—or use the official agency name where you've used the acronym? Look for points that may come across well without you saying so. In the test passage above, I didn't need the word "piece" as well as "ad, brochure, or press release," except to carry along the idea of "one-time," but I think the mention of a newsletter or catalog in the next sentence implicitly conveyed my intended contrast.

Tinker with transitions

Annunciatory or topic sentences may needlessly take up space at the beginning of a paragraph. For a bridge sentence that makes a link with the preceding paragraph, substitute a transitional word or phrase, such as "accordingly," "on the other hand" or "also." For example, from the middle of a consultant's bio:

BEFORE: Before joining Empire State Service Bureau, Ms. Mansfield held several other communications positions. She worked as an editor for a New York state agency and as a proposal writer for a corporate marketing firm.

AFTER: Ms. Mansfield's background in communications also includes editorial work for a New York state agency and proposal writing for a corporate marketing firm.

Contrarily, you can often expand a transitional phrase into a whole sentence.

BEFORE: Also, Knox-a-Lot keeps the skin on your knuckles smooth and young-looking.

AFTER: And Knox-a-Lot has another attractive advantage. It keeps the skin on your knuckles smooth and young-looking.

Check out adjectives, adverbs and qualifiers

Often modifiers prove optional—you can take them out or add them without affecting the essence of your message. Although this means that usually you should blue-pencil them out anyway, in a pinch you can add a "virtually" or "usually" to extend a paragraph one more line. Qualifiers and hedge words, by the way, are expressions that reduce the force of other words or soften your commitment to what you're saying, such as "really," "just," "very," "somewhat" and "rather."

Focus on the "little words"

Sometimes a lot of microchanges add up to a sufficient modification of length. Pay attention to these minutiae:

- *Articles.* If you look back at our test passage above, you'll see a few places where I was able to cut tiny words like "a," "an" and "the." Since this sometimes creates a telegraphic style, make sure you won't jar the reader with one isolated change. You can also sometimes sprinkle in extra articles with impunity.

- *Verbs.* Can you get away with incomplete sentences? With an informal tone, the answer may be "yes." For example, in an ad for a catering service:

  BEFORE: Our chefs came to us from the world's finest restaurants and culinary schools. They are inventive, responsive and refined.

  AFTER: Our chefs? From the world's finest restaurants and culinary schools—inventive, responsive, refined.

  On the other hand, sentence fragments will take up more space when you plop in the verbs.

- *Synonyms.* Just changing a long word to a short one or vice versa can solve a length problem in a caption or blurb. In our test passage, for "consider," I substituted "try." If I really had to tighten up the text another line, I could have inserted "changes" for "adjustment" and "artistically" for "aesthetically."

Use bullets instead of sentences in paragraphs

You can learn a lot by studying the space-saving techniques of *USA Today*. Our national newspaper has made it its mission to communicate in a condensed, compact style. One key device for fulfilling that calling is the colon, a punctuation mark that they use idiosyncratically. Rather than introduce a list as I have throughout this book with "For example:" or "Here are a few ideas:" *USA Today* places the colon immediately after the point the bullets illustrate. For instance, in an article on a boom in the commodities market, "Investors have been flocking to commodity markets:" introduces three signs of the phenomenon. Later in the same article, "Also affecting trading:" sets up a list of two reasons for the rise in interest. This technique would work well in many newsletters.

Minimize space gaps by advance planning

If your designer has already decided which typeface will be used where in your piece, he or she should be able to give you the approximate number of words that fit in each space. Then you can keep an eye on length as you write through the word-count function in your word-processing program. If you act as your own designer, you can do the same yourself by calculating a translation factor: approximately how many characters or words correspond to a certain number of lines or inches for a given typeface, leading and column width. According to desktop design expert Roger Parker, such planning prevents design sins caused by "shoehorning" previously written text into existing space.

CHAPTER 25

Finding Writing and Marketing Help

While I've presented step-by-step instructions that I believe virtually any businessperson could profitably follow to create marketing materials, you may lack the time, energy or confidence necessary to get the writing right. You may need the objectivity of someone not beset with your day-to-day clutter of problems and opportunities. Also, there may be times when the job is too big, the stakes too high to risk not seeking out expert guidance. But who to call?

Lots of different kinds of specialists are available to help you conceptualize and execute your persuasion on paper. No one can help you well, however, until you know the level of advice and implementation that meets your needs. To make sure you get the most on-target assistance, it's also vital to understand the strengths and weaknesses of each neighborhood in which you might shop.

Aisles in the Help Supermarket

Advertising agencies

If you have a large advertising budget, using an ad agency can be a terrific deal. You pay them only for production expenses, and they get the bulk of their compensation from the 15 percent commission of the very same media fees you would be paying if you placed the ads yourself. At little cost to you, these specialists develop a concept, execute it in the form of ads and place them with appropriate media. What could be more convenient?

Be forewarned, however, that according to insiders, most ad agencies have little expertise in or enthusiasm for marketing methods besides advertising, such as direct mail. The commission structure may also influence them to be overenthusiastic about your need to advertise when spending a lot of money there is not your best option.

Public relations firms

Fueled by monthly retainers and expenses from their clients, PR firms take charge of the entire process of getting you profitably into the public eye. They develop a press kit for you, issue news releases, work the phones to get you onto radio and TV and steer you through the dangers of an image crisis if, say, your director of product development gets arrested for stealing from kids. If you can afford their fees and need their full range of services, this choice may make sense for you. But if you have time, energy and nerve, it's not difficult to get media coverage on your own. See Chapter 8 and the resources in Chapter 26.

With both PR firms and ad agencies, you'll get the best service if you match your size to theirs. In other words, if you practice solo, deliver your account to a PR or advertising person on his or her own rather than to a multinational megainstitution.

Literary agents

You may be under the impression that literary agents help you get published, but this is broader than the truth. In today's publishing world, literary agents represent you primarily on book deals, and primarily with the two or three dozen major publishing companies. Agents help you find the best publisher for your book and negotiate the best contract possible. Because they work on commission only, they are generally not interested in representing your magazine articles or newspaper columns, or books for smaller (and lower-paying) publishers. Thus when breaking into print with articles and columns, you're on your own. Look up names, addresses and specialties of literary agents in *Literary Marketplace*, which virtually every library has, or in an annual guide from Writer's Digest Books called *Guide to Literary Agents*.

Marketers

These folks, going by such titles as "marketing consultant," "communications consultant" or "marketing communications consultant," help you plan marketing strategy and execute almost anything from a press campaign to a newsletter. If they truly know what they're doing, they have a wider view than most others in the help supermarket. Therefore you'll get the most benefit from their work when you feel at sea without a compass in regard to your marketing. Since education, certification and training have no bearing whatsoever on competence here, you'll have to go by reputation, references and gut instincts in judging whether someone claiming to be able to help you actually can. In this category, you'll pay either hourly or project fees.

If your marketer specializes in your industry or profession, you'll spend less time and perhaps therefore money getting him or her up to speed on the problems, opportunities and market conditions your business is facing. Look for such experts in both the editorial pages and the ads of magazines and newsletters serving your field. Other marketers specialize in a particular marketing format, such as direct mail or newsletters. Look for their ads in the *Metropolis Business News*, or whatever its counterpart is called in your local area.

Writers

People who compose the text of brochures, sales letters, newsletters and other so-called "collateral material" may bill themselves as "copywriters" or just "writers." The more experience they have, the more marketing savvy they tend to have, too. However, you probably want to shop in this aisle when you already know that you want to try a direct-mail campaign, say, rather than an advertising blitz. Many proficient copywriters advertise in the classifieds of trade publications such as *Adweek* and *Advertising Age*. One task many can perform I haven't mentioned yet in this book: They can ghost-write articles and columns that appear in publications under your byline. If their rates appear steep, remember that they aren't merely churning out a certain number of words; they are putting in the creative effort necessary to get the results you desire. Expect to pay per-project or, less commonly, hourly fees.

Editors

Here I mean freelance editors and editorial service companies that take your draft of a marketing piece and revise, rewrite and polish it for you. Although I have done editing for businesses for several years, I haven't noticed many competitors offering such services for the business market, compared with the popularity of the full-service approach for businesses or editorial services for aspiring authors. Usually editors either charge by the hour or by the page. If you're pretty confident you've come up with a good marketing approach but need help smoothing out the rough edges, this is an option to consider.

Coaches

Also a fairly rare breed, these helpers may go under the name of "consultant," but they play a very different role from those under Marketers above. Rather than plan and execute your marketing in consultation with you, they teach you how to do it yourself, and provide guidance and feedback throughout the process. Since you'll be the one sweating over your first draft and stuffing envelopes, you pay much less than for the full-service options. You'll also use the coach's time more effectively as you absorb his or her instruction and guidance. This is my very favorite role to play because I love both the problem-solving involved and the cheering when my clients succeed.

Questions to Think About When Selecting Helpers

To avoid paying for assistance that you feel uncomfortable putting to use, make sure that you're in tune philosophically and personally with the helper you choose. If you're a refined, Mercedes-level professional, you might not get along well with helpers from the "abrasiveness sells" school of marketing. On the other hand, if you're up for bold, irreverent moves, you won't like the advice of someone who advocates tasteful, time-tested marketing methods. Here are some other factors to consider.

Do they have a vested interest in turning you in one direction rather than another?
You may decide you'd rather trust your work to a free-lancer than someone who makes money from convincing you to spend your marketing budget here rather than there. For instance, when the Yellow Pages sales representative tells you you should advertise in six categories, not three, how can you judge if that's sound advice or mostly a way to reach the

monthly sales quota? Less obviously, Kathy Murtagh advises against using the services of former Yellow Pages reps who call themselves "consultants" and offer to cut your Yellow Pages bills. "They get paid a percentage of the money they save you, and their sole purpose is screwing the Yellow Pages company, not helping your business. Even if you shouldn't cut your listings, they'll urge you to, since that will make them money," Murtagh says.

Is the individual you'll be working with a good listener?

I believe this characteristic may do better than any other to predict how well the marketing pieces someone creates for you match your objectives. Run the other way from anyone who knows exactly what you need before hearing about your goals, capabilities and competitive situation. On the other hand, if you clam up when your helper asks to hear what you've already done and hope to accomplish, any misdirected final results may partly be your fault.

Can you work together effectively at a distance or must you meet with them at their office or yours?

It's important to separate the issue of whether *you* feel most comfortable talking over a task with a consultant face-to-face from whether the consultant actually needs an in-person meeting to get the job done well. Some copywriters and consultants dislike making time for meetings, knowing they can get the information they need more efficiently by simply getting a collection of your previous sales materials and filling in the gaps through asking questions by phone. If you're skeptical that remote-control consulting and writing can really work, ask for a few references of previous clients and get their testimony on the subject.

Do their ethics match yours?

I eliminated two marketing newsletters from my recommended list in Chapter 26 because the author/publisher praised a deceptive sales strategy—lying—as "innovative marketing." I do not subscribe to the doctrine that all's fair in marketing and war. Similarly, I was shocked to see another high-priced consultant recommend decorating ads with an irrelevant photo of a "gorgeous bikini-clad girl." In 1994! This is another area in which you simply must see eye-to-eye with someone trying to advise you or implement marketing for you.

Do they guarantee results?

A very ticklish question, this one. In the field of public relations, most firms will tell you that it's unethical for them to guarantee that your investment will actually produce media coverage. Yet a few renegade firms do in effect guarantee results by having you pay per placement, with different fees for mere mentions than for feature stories. Similarly, I've seen ads from direct-mail copywriters who say that if they fail to beat the pulling power of your current direct-mail piece you need pay them nothing. Other copywriters or marketing consultants take part of their fee in royalties—a percentage of the profits produced by their work, as long as you keep using it. By motivating your helper to work harder for results, such fee structures resemble guarantees. I have to warn you, however, that just bringing up the subject of guarantees can make some members of the advice profession upset. When I broached the subject in the PR and Marketing Forum (PRSIG) on CompuServe, I triggered heated and at times acrimonious debate that raged on for weeks.

Are their services confidential?

Usually it doesn't matter much if people know you used any kind of marketing help for your business. However, you do not want to have given a consultant inside information on your competitive situation and have him or her use that privileged intelligence to help another client. If this concerns you, ask what assurances your helper candidate can give you that this won't happen. Many established firms have policies that protect regular clients on this score.

A final word on working together effectively with your marketing partner: Don't hand over *total* responsibility for your ads, brochures or publicity campaign. You're still the one to establish goals and evaluate whether or not any given approach still makes sense for your business. But don't step on their toes, either, or try to take over the part of the process you've delegated. Strike a balance between those two extremes, and then enjoy the fruits of marketing materials that pull in business.

PART VI

◇

RESOURCES

CHAPTER 26

Guide to Resources

1. Recommended Books

Unless otherwise noted, all books are currently available in paperback.

On Marketing

Brabec, Barbara, *Homemade Money* (Cincinnati, OH: Betterway, 1994). Encyclopedic orientation for the newly or not-yet-profitably self-employed, from legal issues of doing business at home through marketing and publicity tactics, pricing and computerizing your business.

Considine, Ray, and Raphel, Murray, *The Great Brain Robbery* (Atlantic City, NJ: Raphel Publishing, 1987). An energetic assemblage of profitable promotional antics, from retail and direct-mail specialists. Hardcover.

Edwards, Paul and Sarah, and Douglas, Laura Clampitt, *Getting Business to Come to You* (Los Angeles: Jeremy P. Tarcher, 1991). A comprehensive manual on spreading the word about yourself and producing promotional materials, for people inclined to find marketing a chore.

Kremer, John, *1001 Ways to Market Your Books* (Fairfield, IA: Open Horizons, 1993). Even for a business far afield from publishing, you'll find oodles of creative marketing tactics here, from contests to product inserts to promotional events.

Levinson, Jay Conrad, *Guerrilla Marketing Excellence: The Fifty Golden Rules for Small-Business Success* (Boston: Houghton Mifflin, 1993). From the master of low-cost marketing, this distillation of principles of effective marketing offers uncommon wisdom.

Michels, Caroll, *How to Survive and Prosper as an Artist*, 3rd edition (New York: Henry Holt, 1992). How to create art without succumbing to the lousy-marketing, starving-artist syndrome.

Ott, Richard, *Creating Demand: Powerful Tips and Tactics for Marketing Your Product or Service* (Burr Ridge, IL: Irwin, 1992). Based on the psychology of attention and decision making, shows how to stimulate sales through wording, strategy and design.

Putman, Anthony O., *Marketing Your Services* (New York: Wiley, 1990). Commonsense, workable approaches for professionals who loathe marketing.

Ross, Marilyn and Tom, *Big Ideas for Small Service Businesses* (Buena Vista, CO: Communication Creativity, 1994). If you sell services and want to try telemarketing, word of mouth and other techniques not involving print, this book shows how to get "Madison Avenue results on a Main Street budget."

On Letter Writing

Gnam, René, *Direct Mail Workshop* (Englewood Cliffs, NJ: Prentice-Hall, 1989). One thousand thirteen specific tips for producing more effective direct-mail pieces. A highly readable collection you'll mark up and refer back to.

Hodgson, Richard S., *The Greatest Direct Mail Sales Letters of All Time* (Chicago: Dartnell, 1986). A treasure trove of classic and somewhat dated sales letters from large companies, with commentary and complete texts, in a high-priced three-ring binder. Worth studying.

Kennedy, Daniel S., *The Ultimate Sales Letter* (Holbrook, MA: Bob Adams, 1990). Step-by-step guidance for writing a direct-mail letter, with lots of useful examples.

On Advertising

Caples, John, *Tested Advertising Methods* (Englewood Cliffs, NJ: Prentice-Hall, 1974). I adore the analytical wit of this book and its vintage reproductions of pre-1960s ads. Caples's commentary and instruction remain relevant today.

Floyd, Elaine, and Wilson, Lee, *Advertising from the Desktop* (Chapel Hill, NC: Ventana, 1994). A must-buy if you'd like to produce visually appealing, profit-generating ads through desktop publishing. Includes tools and techniques for producing black-and-white or color ads, brochures, signs and more.

Levinson, Jay Conrad, *Guerrilla Advertising* (Boston: Houghton Mifflin, 1994). Ponder Levinson's advice carefully before investing scarce dollars in advertising. As usual, he offers wry, hard-bitten counsel on getting the most profitable bang for your bucks.

Lewis, Herschell Gordon, *Big Profits from Small Budget Advertising* (Chicago: Dartnell, 1992). A learn-advertising-on-your-own course in a three-ring binder. Test your advertising acumen with Lewis's twenty-five examples of good and bad ads and thought-provoking exercises (with possible solutions) for each chapter.

On Newsletters

Bivens, Thomas H., *Fundamentals of Successful Newsletters* (Lincoln, IL: NTC, 1992). Takes you through the process of producing a newsletter, from strategizing on goals to collecting and writing content to printing and sending it out.

Floyd, Elaine, *Marketing with Newsletters* (St. Louis: EF Communications, 1991). The only book I know of devoted to promotional (nonsubscription) newsletters. Extremely valuable tips on naming the newsletter, choosing promotional content, saving time and money and staying on your marketing track.

On Publicity

Parinello, Al, *On the Air: How to Get on Radio and TV Talk Shows and What to Do When You Get There* (Hawthorne, NJ: Career Press, 1991). Delightful guide to doing your best on radio and TV talk shows. Most valuable features: translations of studio hand signals, data on the top 100 broadcast markets, list of professions producers are wary of for guests and contact information for top TV and radio talk shows.

Yudkin, Marcia, *Six Steps to Free Publicity* (New York: Plume, 1994). According to Alan Weiss, author of *Million-Dollar Consulting*, "Marcia Yudkin provides pragmatic help to any professional, entrepreneur or business owner who seeks to gain the public eye." According to Terri Lonier, author of *Working Solo*, "This books shows how to spend creativity instead of cash to generate high-impact marketing results."

On Printing and Design

Beach, Mark, *Getting It Printed* (Cincinnati, OH: North Light, 1993). Comprehensive and comprehensible introduction to printing technologies, terminology and procedures. Explains the different ways of creating color and much more than you probably imagined there was to learn about paper.

Gosney, Michael, *The Gray Book: Designing in Black and White on Your Computer* (Chapel Hill, NC: Ventana, 1993). How to create a classy look for your printed materials without the expense of color.

Parker, Roger C., *Looking Good in Print: A Guide to Basic Design for Desktop Publishing* (Chapel Hill, NC: Ventana, 1990). To avoid visual gaffes in your newsletters, ads and brochures, refer to this elegant primer on good and bad design. Guidelines galore, along with fascinating before-and-after makeovers.

Williams, Robin, *The Non-Designer's Design Book* (Berkeley, CA: Peachpit, 1994). A witty, illuminating survey of basic design principles. Encourages daring with her #1 guideline: Don't be a wimp.

On Better Writing

Associated Press Stylebook and Libel Manual (Reading, MA: Addison-Wesley, 1992). Alphabetical directory to standardized spelling, usage, punctuation, etc., with special chapters on avoiding libel, respecting copyright and using the Freedom of Information Act.

Bly, Robert W., *The Copywriter's Handbook* (New York: Henry Holt, 1985). If you enjoy copywriting enough to want to do it for others, this book contains several chapters on breaking into the business.

Judd, Karen, *Copyediting: A Practical Guide* (Menlo Park, CA: Crisp Publications, 1991). Provides a thorough grounding in the art of making any manuscript or marketing piece correct and consistent. Includes test-yourself exercises (and answers).

Lant, Jeffrey, *Cash Copy: How to Offer Your Products and*

Services So Your Prospects Buy Them . . . Now (Cambridge, MA: JLA Publications, 1992). If you can take the relentless pounding of Lant's hectoring voice, you'll find a good deal of sound copywriting advice in here.

Lauchman, Richard, *Plain Style: Techniques for Simple, Concise, Emphatic Business Writing* (New York: Amacom, 1993). Pungent instruction in clear business communication.

Lewis, Herschell Gordon, *Herschell Gordon Lewis on the Art of Writing Copy* (Englewood Cliffs, NJ: Prentice-Hall, 1988). Full of hairsplitting delights, such as the connotations of sounds in made-up words, the persuasiveness of questions versus statements and the many permutations of guarantees.

Strunk, William, Jr., and White, E. B., *The Elements of Style* (New York: Macmillan, 1979). This slim, timeless volume has tutored millions in lean, concise writing. Go thou and learn likewise!

Venolia, Jan, *Rewrite Right: How to Revise Your Way to Better Writing* (Berkeley, CA: Ten Speed Press, 1987). Highly recommended handbook for editing your own copy. Advice on cutting out jargon, clichés and sexist language, and on putting in the commas, apostrophes and capital letters that readers expect.

On Getting Published

Applebaum, Judith, *How to Get Happily Published* (New York: HarperCollins, 1992). Excellent overview of book publishing options and procedures.

Yudkin, Marcia, *Freelance Writing for Magazines and Newspapers* (New York: Harper & Row, 1988). A clear, focused guide to writing, revising and placing articles and columns. Contains sample query and cover letters to magazines.

On Creativity

Norins, Hanley, *The Young & Rubicam Traveling Creative Workshop* (New York: Prentice-Hall, 1990). A collection of ideas and checklists from the internal training program of one of the world's leading ad agencies. Assumes you have a large team and a hefty budget.

Mattimore, Bryan, *99% Inspiration: Tips, Tales and Techniques for Liberating Your Business Creativity* (New York: Amacom, 1994). Anecdotes and exercises that foster creativity, particularly in groups.

On Respecting Relevant Laws and Regulations

Federal Trade Commission, *A Business Guide to the Federal Trade Commission's Mail Order Rule*. You can obtain this and other helpful guides to FTC regulations by calling (202) 326-2222 or writing to Public Reference, Room 130, Federal Trade Commission, Washington, DC 20580.

Kemp, Erwin J., *Mail Order Legal Guide* (Grants Pass, OR: Oasis Press, 1993). Contains the actual text of national and state regulations affecting mail order advertising and sales. Much less readable but more complete than Meyerowitz, below.

Meyerowitz, Steven A., *An Ounce of Prevention: Marketing, Sales & Advertising Law for Non-Lawyers* (Detroit: Visible Ink, 1994). Highly recommended compendium of cases and principles of laws governing advertising, marketing and customer relations, capably explained for the layperson.

United States Postal Service, *Designing Business Letter Mail*. Publication 25. If you plan to design bulk mailings, presorted or barcoded mail or business reply postcards, you need this readable manual of regulations, available from your local Postal Business Center.

II. Newsletters

I recommend all of the following subscription newsletters, most of which focus on do-it-yourself marketing. Unlike books, which you can read once, enjoy and forget, newsletters provide fresh reminders, information and inspiration when they show up in your mailbox four, six or twelve times per year. Send a self-addressed stamped envelope to the listed address for current subscription information.

The Accidental Entrepreneur (Dixie Darr, editor), 3421 Alcott St., Denver, CO 80211. Bimonthly.

The Art of Self-Promotion (Ilise Benun, editor), P.O. Box 23, Hoboken, NJ 07030. Quarterly.

Barbara Brabec's Self-Employment Survival Letter (Barbara Brabec, editor), P.O. Box 2137, Naperville, IL 60567. Bimonthly.

The Creative Glow: How to Be More Original, Inspired & Productive in Your Work (Marcia Yudkin, editor), P.O. Box 1310, Boston, MA 02117. Bimonthly.

Cyberpower Alert! (Wally Bock, editor), 1441 Franklin St., Oakland, CA 94612; E-mail: 71260.3150@compuserve.com. Monthly, available electronically only.

Guerrilla Marketing Newsletter (Jay Conrad Levinson, editor), P.O. Box 1336, Mill Valley, CA 94942. Bimonthly.

Newsletter News & Resources (Elaine Floyd, editor), EF Communications, 6614 Pernod Ave., St. Louis, MO 63139. Quarterly.

Winning Ways (Barbara Winter, editor), P.O. Box 39412, Minneapolis, MN 55439. Bimonthly.

Working Solo Newsletter (Terri Lonier, editor), Portico Press, P.O. Box 190, New Paltz, NY 12561. Quarterly.

III. Magazines

My selection of magazines that help you polish the skills discussed in this book.

Direct Marketing, 224 Seventh St., Garden City, NY 11530. Articles and columns on better sales letters; critiques of big mailers' sales pieces.

Entrepreneur, 2392 Morse Ave., Irvine, CA 92619. Amidst wide-ranging articles on starting up and running a business, a monthly makeover column on marketing materials.

Flash, Riddle Pond Rd., West Topsham, VT 05086. How to use your laser printer for effective desktop publishing.

Home Office Computing, 740 Broadway, New York, NY 10003. Despite the title, contains almost as much on marketing as on computers.

Target Marketing, 401 North Broad Street., Philadelphia, PA 19108. No-nonsense articles on direct-mail marketing.

Writer's Digest, 1507 Dana Ave., Cincinnati, OH 45207. Articles on how to get published and make money from your writing.

IV. Useful Reference Works

I've listed those that are most likely to be available in your local library.

Bacon's: Newspaper/Magazine Directory; Radio/TV/Cable Directory. Annual lists of media contacts, in several volumes.

Directories in Print. A great source of information about reference works where you should plant free listings about your business.

Gale Directory of Publications and Broadcast Media. Another

list of weekly and daily newspapers, magazines and radio and
TV stations.

Standard Rate and Date Service. A multivolume source of information on rates and availability of various advertising vehicles, including newspapers, magazines, direct-mail lists and
more.

Writer's Market. Lists thousands of consumer and trade magazines that accept submissions from freelancers—and pay for
articles.

V. Other Resources

Custom Crossword Creations, 17 Emerson Way, Sudbury, MA
01776. For a very reasonable price, Herb Hill will create a customized crossword puzzle using your clues.

Deluxe Business Systems, P.O. Box 64495, St. Paul, MN
56164. Source for custom-printed Post-it brand notes.

Grammar Hotline Directory, c/o Donna Reiss, Tidewater
Community College Writing Center, 1700 College Crescent,
Virginia Beach, VA 23456, free with SASE.

Paper Direct, 205 Chubb Ave., Lyndhurst, NJ 07071; 800-A-
PAPERS. The granddaddy supplier of predesigned letterheads
and brochures. Also call for the catalogs of these competitors:
BeaverPrints: 800-9-BEAVER; Paper Access: 800-PAPER-
01; Premier Papers: 800-843-0414.

Turn Your Computer Into a Money Machine. NSMI, 2574 N.
University Drive, Suite 201, Fort Lauderdale, FL 33322. An
"electronic book," available in IBM and Macintosh versions,
covering the fundamentals of electronic marketing. Mention
my name for a discount from creator Sheila Danzig.

CHAPTER 27

Getting in Touch

I'd be glad to do my best to put you in touch with any individual or company mentioned in this book. To receive the address of anyone I interviewed, just send me a self-addressed stamped envelope and the name of the person or firm you'd like to contact.

I'd love to receive samples of the improved materials you were able to create after reading *Persuading on Paper*. Send them along with a personal note and you may find yourself mentioned in my next book!

If you need coaching on how to get the word out to your audience, or feedback on specific pieces, I offer those services by mail, by fax, by E-mail, and, to a limited extent, in person. Here's how to reach me:

Marcia Yudkin
Creative Ways
P.O. Box 1310
Boston, MA 02117
(617) 266-1613 or (800) 898-3546—(800) 8YU-DKIN
Fax: (617) 871-1728
E-mail to yudkin@world.std.com

INDEX